Flutter Projects

A practical, project-based guide to building real-world cross-platform mobile applications and games

Simone Alessandria

BIRMINGHAM - MUMBAI

Flutter Projects

Copyright © 2020 Packt Publishing

Commissioning Editor: Amarabha Banerjee
Acquisition Editor: Karan Gupta
Content Development Editor: Divya Vijayan
Senior Editor: Mohammed Yusuf Imaratwale
Technical Editor: Shubham Sharma
Copy Editor: Safis Editing
Project Coordinator: Kinjal Bari
Proofreader: Safis Editing
Indexer: Tejal Daruwale Soni
Production Designer: Joshua Misquitta

First published: April 2020

Production reference: 1070420

Published by Packt Publishing Ltd.
Livery Place
35 Livery Street
Birmingham
B3 2PB, UK.

ISBN 978-1-83864-777-3

www.packt.com

For my beloved wife, Giusy, who makes my life worth living every day, and for the developer who struggles when learning a new language: you have all my sympathy. I've been there and will be there again, hopefully.

- Simone Alessandria

Packt.com

Subscribe to our online digital library for full access to over 7,000 books and videos, as well as industry leading tools to help you plan your personal development and advance your career. For more information, please visit our website.

Why subscribe?

- Spend less time learning and more time coding with practical eBooks and Videos from over 4,000 industry professionals

- Improve your learning with Skill Plans built especially for you

- Get a free eBook or video every month

- Fully searchable for easy access to vital information

- Copy and paste, print, and bookmark content

Did you know that Packt offers eBook versions of every book published, with PDF and ePub files available? You can upgrade to the eBook version at www.packt.com and as a print book customer, you are entitled to a discount on the eBook copy. Get in touch with us at customercare@packtpub.com for more details.

At www.packt.com, you can also read a collection of free technical articles, sign up for a range of free newsletters, and receive exclusive discounts and offers on Packt books and eBooks.

Contributors

About the author

Simone Alessandria wrote his first program when he was 12: it was a text-based fantasy game for the Commodore 64. A few years later, he is now a trainer (MCT), author, speaker, passionate software architect, and always a proud coder. He has published several courses on Dart and Flutter on Pluralsight. His mission is to help developers achieve more through training and mentoring.

About the reviewers

Rohan Bethune is a professional software architect and developer with over 20 years in the industry. He has in-depth, hands-on experience crafting intuitive software solutions ranging from writing complex high-performance blotters and trading applications for leading investment banks to creating immersive cloud-based mobile solutions. Currently, he is the chief architect and founder of Rozella Software, where he is creating an education portal for Rozella.iStudy, a Flutter-built app that allows anyone to study and learn practically anything through its intelligent content creation engine and series of fun quizzes, reports, and test graphs.

Tom Alabaster has been a production-level Flutter developer for over a year, architecting projects of all different levels from small single-user applications to a large-scale project registered as a medical device. He's given talks and run workshops, as well as having written several plugins and packages for others to use. Having followed Flutter for a while, he's been carefully developing an ideal clean architecture for Flutter apps in order to help demonstrate Flutter's scalability and performance for real-world large-scale production use.

Packt is searching for authors like you

If you're interested in becoming an author for Packt, please visit authors.packtpub.com and apply today. We have worked with thousands of developers and tech professionals, just like you, to help them share their insight with the global tech community. You can make a general application, apply for a specific hot topic that we are recruiting an author for, or submit your own idea.

Table of Contents

Preface

The fastest way to learn programming, in any language or framework is… programming. That's exactly the purpose of this book: helping you **learn Flutter by doing**.

Flutter is a developer-friendly, open source toolkit created by Google that you can use to create applications for Android and iOS mobile devices, and now also for the web and desktop.

There are eleven projects in this book, covering the main concepts useful to develop real-world apps with Flutter. In each project, you'll learn and **immediately use** some of the features that make Flutter so successful: widgets, state management, asynchronous programming, using web services, persisting data, animations, creating full-stack applications with Firebase, and even developing responsive apps that work with different form factors, including the web.

Each project builds an app from scratch. You can choose to follow the flow of the book or skip to any project if you feel confident with the concepts introduced in earlier chapters.

Flutter uses **Dart** as a programming language. In the first chapter, you'll see an introduction to Dart, giving you the necessary knowledge to be productive and create your first Flutter app.

In later chapters, you'll see Flutter projects that go beyond basic examples. You'll get the opportunity to play with code and **get hands-on experience building apps**. While you progress through this book, you'll see that some of the concepts introduced in earlier chapters are used again, in different ways, on later projects, so that you get deeper knowledge on several topics.

Who this book is for

This book is for developers. You should be familiar with any object-oriented programming language: if you understand variables, functions, classes, and objects, this book is for you.

The programming language used in Flutter is **Dart.** If you've never seen Dart before, don't worry: basic knowledge of languages like Java, C#, Kotlin, Swift, or JavaScript will be enough to follow along with the projects in this book. Dart is an extremely intuitive language for developers, with a smooth learning curve.

This book is not a Dart course, but throughout the book, and in particular in Chapter 1, *Hello Flutter*, you'll get all you need to get started with Dart as well.

To sum it up, if you have some knowledge of any object-oriented programming language, and want to start building great mobile or web apps with Flutter, this book is for you!

What this book covers

Chapter 1, *Hello Flutter!*, is an introductory chapter, where you'll build "Hello Flutter," an app that shows the presentation screen of a fictitious travel agent. The project will focus on how to create a very basic app with Dart and Flutter and give you the foundation necessary for the rest of the book.

Chapter 2, *Miles or Kilometers? Using Stateful Widgets*, shows how to build a Measures Conversion App. The main goal of this chapter is to introduce **State** into a Flutter app, to make it interactive. In this project, you will use TextFields, DropDownButtons, and the setState() method to update the state of a stateful widget.

Chapter 3, *My Time – Listening to a Stream of Data*, shows a more advanced way of dealing with state: listening to streams of data. In this project, you will create a productivity timer, with an animation based on streams. This chapter will introduce asynchronous programming in Flutter and several core concepts, such as navigation, using libraries, and storing data.

Chapter 4, *Pong Game – 2D Animations and Gestures*, is about making a simple two-dimension animated game, where a ball will move across the screen, and the player will need to prevent the ball from "falling" out of the screen. The main topics of this chapter include using animations, detecting gestures with the Gesture Detector, and generating random numbers.

Chapter 5, *Let's Go to the Movies – Getting Data from the Web*, deals with the creation of an app that shows a list of movies taken from a web service. The main topics include using ListViews, parsing JSON data, connecting to remote services through the HTTP protocol, and building GET requests to perform searches on the API. Asynchronous programming in Dart is used throughout the chapter.

Chapter 6, *Store That Data - Using Sq(F)Lite to Store Data in a Local Database*, shows how to create a shopping list that will be built in this project. The main concepts in this project include using SQLite in Flutter; creating model classes; performing **Create**, **Read**, **Update**, and **Delete (CRUD)** actions; and using the *singleton* model.

Chapter 7, *Firing Up the App – Integrating Firebase into a Flutter App*, shows how to create a full-stack application, designing both the frontend UI and the backend in record time, leveraging Firebase.

Chapter 8, *The Treasure Mapp – Integrating Maps and Using Your Device Camera*, builds an app that allows users to mark places on a map and add some data and a picture over it. Pictures will be created by using the camera. This project covers two important features of mobile programming: geolocation and using a device's camera.

Chapter 9, *Let's Play Dice: Knockout – Creating an Animation with Flare*, focuses on a project where you'll build a dice game in Flutter, using Flare, an online tool that makes it easy to create beautiful animations and include them directly in Flutter.

Chapter 10, *ToDo App – Leveraging the BLoC Pattern and Sembast*, shows how to leverage the BLoC (Business Logic Component) pattern to manage app state. You'll also see how to use the Simple Embedded Application Store database to store data in your device.

Chapter 11, *Building a Flutter Web App*, shows how to build a Flutter app that runs on a browser and how to create responsive user interfaces.

To get the most out of this book

Some experience in at least one object-oriented programming language is strongly recommended.

I suggest playing with the code while you type it: try asking yourself if you could write a project in a different way. This will make the concepts much clearer and easier to reuse in your future projects. Answering the questions at the end of each project will also help you get a different perspective on the app you built in the chapter.

In this book, we use the Flutter version 1.12.13 and Dart version 2.7.2. In order to follow along with the code, you will need a Windows PC, Mac, Linux, or Chrome OS machine connected to the web, with the permissions to install new software. An Android or iOS device is suggested but not necessary as there are simulators/emulators that can run on your machine. All software used in this book is open source or free to use.

If you are using the digital version of this book, we advise you to type the code yourself or access the code via the GitHub repository (link available in the next section). Doing so will help you avoid any potential errors related to the copy/pasting of code.

If you like this book or want to share your ideas about it **please write a review** on your favorite platform. This will help us make this book better, and you'll also earn the author's and reviewers' everlasting gratitude.

Download the example code files

You can download the example code files for this book from your account at www.packt.com. If you purchased this book elsewhere, you can visit www.packtpub.com/support and register to have the files emailed directly to you.

You can download the code files by following these steps:

1. Log in or register at www.packt.com.
2. Select the **Support** tab.
3. Click on **Code Downloads**.
4. Enter the name of the book in the **Search** box and follow the onscreen instructions.

Once the file is downloaded, please make sure that you unzip or extract the folder using the latest version of:

- WinRAR/7-Zip for Windows
- Zipeg/iZip/UnRarX for Mac
- 7-Zip/PeaZip for Linux

The code bundle for the book is also hosted on GitHub at https://github.com/PacktPublishing/Flutter-Projects. In case there's an update to the code, it will be updated on the existing GitHub repository.

We also have other code bundles from our rich catalog of books and videos available at https://github.com/PacktPublishing/. Check them out!

Conventions used

There are a number of text conventions used throughout this book.

CodeInText: Indicates code words in text, database table names, folder names, filenames, file extensions, pathnames, dummy URLs, user input, and Twitter handles. Here is an example: "In the main.dart file, remove the example code."

A block of code is set as follows:

```
void main() {
 var name = "Dart";
 print ("Hello $name!");
}
```

When we wish to draw your attention to a particular part of a code block, the relevant lines or items are set in bold:

```
return Stack(
    children: <Widget>[
        Positioned(
            child: Ball(),
            top: posY,
            left: posX,
),
```

Any command-line input or output is written as follows:

```
cd hello_world
flutter run
```

Bold: Indicates a new term, an important word, or words that you see onscreen. For example, words in menus or dialog boxes appear in the text like this. Here is an example: "From the Android Studio **File** menu, select **Open...**."

Warnings or important notes appear like this.

Tips and tricks appear like this.

Get in touch

Feedback from our readers is always welcome.

General feedback: If you have questions about any aspect of this book, mention the book title in the subject of your message and email us at customercare@packtpub.com.

Errata: Although we have taken every care to ensure the accuracy of our content, mistakes do happen. If you have found a mistake in this book, we would be grateful if you would report this to us. Please visit www.packtpub.com/support/errata, selecting your book, clicking on the Errata Submission Form link, and entering the details.

Piracy: If you come across any illegal copies of our works in any form on the Internet, we would be grateful if you would provide us with the location address or website name. Please contact us at copyright@packt.com with a link to the material.

If you are interested in becoming an author: If there is a topic that you have expertise in and you are interested in either writing or contributing to a book, please visit authors.packtpub.com.

Reviews

Please leave a review. Once you have read and used this book, why not leave a review on the site that you purchased it from? Potential readers can then see and use your unbiased opinion to make purchase decisions, we at Packt can understand what you think about our products, and our authors can see your feedback on their book. Thank you!

For more information about Packt, please visit packt.com.

Hello Flutter! 1

Welcome to this adventure learning Flutter!

The approach that we'll be following during this book is *learn by doing*. In each chapter of the book, you'll create a project from scratch, and in each project you'll learn something new and build an app that you'll be able to use immediately on your Android or iOS device.

The first project that most developers encounter while learning a new language or framework is a *Hello World* app, and this book is no exception. This Hello World project assumes that you have no knowledge whatsoever of Flutter or Dart. If you have already created apps with Flutter before, you can probably skip this chapter and go straight to the next one. By the end of this chapter, you'll be able to build the presentation screen of the **Hello World Travel** company, as shown here:

In order to create the app, you'll have to complete several steps. We will go through them in this chapter, one by one:

- Understanding the Dart language basics
- Creating your first Flutter app:
    - Using some basic widgets: `Scaffold`, `AppBar`, `RaisedButton`, and `Text`
    - Downloading an image and showing it to the user
    - Responding to a button click and showing a dialog

So during this project, you'll learn all this and more.

This project should take no longer than 2 hours to complete. You should probably add 2 more hours to complete the setup process described in the appendix if you haven't completed it yet, but this estimate may vary a lot, depending on your system.

Technical requirements

In order to start your Flutter adventure, you will need a few tools:

- A PC with a recent Windows version, or a Mac with a recent version of the macOS or Linux operating system. You can also use a Chrome OS machine, with a few tweaks. Currently, the only way to build apps that target iOS devices is using a Mac, unless you use a third-party service. Of course, you can write your code on any operating system, but the `.ipa` file, which is the iOS installation file, can only be created from a Mac.
- A GitHub account.
- An Android/iOS setup. You'll need to set up your Android and iOS environments to build apps.
- The Flutter SDK. It's free, light, and open source.
- Physical device/emulator/simulator. In order to try your code, you will need an Android or iOS device. Alternatively, you can also install an Android emulator or iOS simulator.
- Your favorite editor. The supported editors at this time are:
    - Android Studio/IntelliJ IDEA
    - Visual Studio Code

Actually, you could use any other text editor, combined with the Flutter CLI, but using the supported editors will make your life much easier as you get code completion, debugging support, and several other advantages.

The detailed steps for setting up your environment to build Flutter Projects are given in the Appendix section.

You can find the code files of this chapter on GitHub at `https://github.com/ PacktPublishing/Google-Flutter-Projects`.

Let's get started with some basic Dart concepts!

Understanding the Dart language basics

When you write Flutter apps, you use Dart, a programming language that was developed by Google. It's relatively new; the first version of Dart was released on November 14, 2013, and version 2.0 was released in August 2018.

It's now also an official ECMA standard. It's open source, object oriented, strongly typed, class defined, and uses a C-style syntax… which is to say, it's like many other modern programming languages, including Java or C#, and to some extent, even JavaScript.

So, you might be wondering (and you are not alone): why another language? I'm sure there isn't a unique answer to that question, but there are some features worth mentioning here that make Dart noteworthy, even without considering Flutter:

- It's easy to learn: If you have some knowledge of Java, C#, or JavaScript, Dart will be extremely easy to learn, as you'll see in the next few pages.
- It's aimed at productivity: Its syntax is exceptionally concise and easy to read and debug.
- It can transpile to JavaScript, in order to maximize compatibility with web development.
- It has a general purpose: You can use it for client-side, server-side, and mobile development.
- As an added bonus, Google is deeply involved in this project and has some big plans for Dart, including a new operating system, called Google Fuchsia.

As the approach of this book is extremely practical, this is all the theory you'll get. Let's see Dart in action, with a few code examples, which will make it easier to build your first Flutter project later in this chapter.

The goal of this section is to give you a jump-start on using Dart, so that when you write your first Flutter app, you'll be able to focus on Flutter and not too much on Dart itself. This is certainly not a comprehensive guide, but hopefully just enough to get you started.

Hello Dart

For the examples in this section, we'll be using DartPad. It's an online tool that lets you play with Dart code from any browser, without having to install anything on your system. You can reach it at `https://dartpad.dartlang.org/`.

In this Hello Dart example, you'll see how to use DartPad, write the simplest Dart app, declare variables, and concatenate strings. Let's look at the steps for how we can go about it:

1. When you open the tool for the first time, you should see something very close to the following image. On the left, you have your code, and when you click on the **RUN** button, you'll see the result of your code on the right:

2. For our first example, let's delete the default code and write the following:

```
void main() {
  String name = "Dart";
  print ("Hello $name!");
}
```

If you run this code, you should see **Hello Dart!** on the right of your screen:

3. The `main()` function is the starting point of every Dart application. This function is required, and you'll also find it in every Flutter app. Everything begins with the `main()` function.

4. The `String name = "Dart";` line is a variable declaration; with this instruction, you are declaring a variable called `name`, of type `String`, whose value is `"Dart"`. You can use single (') or double (") quotation marks to contain strings, as follows:

```
String name = 'Dart';
```

The result would be identical:

5. The `print ("Hello $name!");` line calls the `print` method, passing a string. The interesting part here is that instead of doing a concatenation, by using the $ sign, you are inserting a variable into the string without closing it nor using the + concatenation operator. So, this is exactly like writing the following code:

```
print ("Hello " + name + "!");
```

There's also a generic variable declaration, in which you don't specify any type; you could write the same code like this:

```
void main() {
 var name = "Dart";
 print ("Hello $name!");
}
```

6. In this case, you might think that name is a dynamic variable, but this is not the case. Let's try to change the variable type and see what happens:

```
void main() {
 var name = "Dart";
 name = 42;
 print ("Hello $name!");
}
```

If you try running this code, you'll receive a compilation error as follows:

```
Error: A value of type 'int' can't be assigned to a variable of
type 'String'. name = 42;  Error: Compilation failed.
```

Actually, you can declare a dynamic type as follows, although I believe you should avoid it in most cases:

```
void main() {
 dynamic name = "Dart";
 name = 42;
 print ("Hello $name!");
}
```

If you try this code, you'll see **Hello 42** in the console.

So the name variable, which was a string when we first declared it, has now become an integer. And as we are talking about numbers, let's delve into those next.

Area calculator

In this example, you'll see the use of numbers, functions, and parameters in Dart.

There are two types of numbers in Dart:

- int: Contains integer values no larger than 64 bits
- double: Contains 64 -bit, double-precision floating-point numbers

You also have the num type: both int and double are num.

Consider the following example:

```
void main() {
  double result = calculateArea(12, 5);
  print ('The result is ' + result.toString());
}
```

In this code, we are declaring a variable called result, of a type called double, which will take the return value of a function called calculateArea, which we'll need to define later. We are passing two numbers—12 and 5—to the function.

After the function returns its value, we will show the result, after converting it to a string.

Let's write the function:

```
double calculateArea(double width, double height) {
  double area = width * height;
  return area;
}
```

Since Dart 2.1, the int literals are automatically converted to doubles; for example, you can write: double value = 2;. This is instead of having to write: double value = 2.0;.

In this case, the width and height parameters are required. You can also add optional parameters to functions, by including them in square brackets. Let's insert an optional parameter to the calculateArea() function, so that the function can also calculate the area of a triangle:

```
double calculateArea(double width, double height, [bool isTriangle]) {
  double area;
  if (isTriangle) {
  area = width * height / 2;
  }
  else {
  area = width * height;
  }
  return area;
}
```

Now, from the `main()` method, we can call this function twice, with or without the optional parameter:

```
void main() {
  double result = calculateArea(12,5,false);
  print ('The result for a rectangle is ' + result.toString());
  result = calculateArea(12,5,true);
  print ('The result for a triangle is ' + result.toString());
}
```

The full function with the expected result is shown here:

At this time, function overloading is not supported in Dart.

 Overloading is a feature of some OOP languages, such as Java and C#, which allows a class to have more than one method with the same name, provided that their argument lists are different in number or type. For example, you could have a method called `calculateArea (double side)` to calculate the area of a square, and another method called `calculateArea (double width, double height)` to calculate the area of a rectangle. This is currently not supported in Dart.

For loops and strings

Dart supports the same loops as many other C-influenced languages: the `for`, `while`, and `do while` loops. In this example, you'll see a `for` loop, which you'll use to reverse a string.

Strings can be included in single quotes ('`Dart`') or double quotes ("`Dart`"). The escape character is \. So, for instance, you could write the following:

```
String myString = 'Throw your \'Dart\'';
```

And the `myString` variable would contain `Throw your 'Dart'`. For our example, let's begin with the `main()` method:

```
void main() {
    String myString = 'Throw your Dart';
    String result = reverse(myString);
    print (result);
}
```

Nothing major to note here. We are just setting a string and calling a `reverse` method, which will reverse the string, to print the result.

So let's write the `reverse()` method next:

```
String reverse(String old) {
    int length = old.length;
    String res = '';
    for (int i = length-1; i>=0; i--) {
        res += old.substring(i,i + 1);
    }
    return res;
}
```

Strings are actually objects, so they have properties, for example, `length`. The `length` property of a string, quite predictably, contains the number of characters of the string itself.

Each character in a string has a position, beginning at 0. In the `for` loop, first, we declare an `i` variable and set it to an initial value of the length of the string, minus one. The next two steps are setting the condition (or exit criteria) and the increment. The loop will keep repeating until `i` is equal to, or bigger than, 0, and at each repetition, it will decrease the value of `i` by one.

What this means is that starting at the end of the string, we will loop until we reach the beginning of the string.

The `+=` operator is a concatenation. This is a shortened syntax for `res = res + old.substring(i,i + 1);`.

The `substring()` method returns part of a string, starting at the position specified at the first parameter, included, and ending at the position specified at the second parameter. So, for example, the following code would print **Wo**:

```
String text = "Hello World";
String subText = text.substring(5,8);
print (subText);
```

There's actually another way that we could extract a single character from a string, instead of using the `substring()` method: using the position of the character itself in the string.For example, instead of writing this:

```
res += old.substring(i,i + 1);
```

We could also write the following code:

```
res += old[i];
```

The end result of the full code that we have written is shown here:

You'll never need to write a code like this in a real-world application. You can achieve the same result just by writing this:

```
String result = myString.split('').reversed.join();
```

Next, you'll see two features that we will use extensively throughout the book: the arrow syntax and the ternary operator.

The Arrow syntax and the ternary operator

The arrow syntax is a concise and elegant way to return values in a function.

Take, for instance, the following function. It takes an integer as an argument (`value`), and if `value` is zero, it returns `false`, otherwise, it returns `true`. So every number that you pass, except zero, will return `true`:

```
bool convertToBoolLong(int value) {
  if (value == 1) {
   return false;
  }
  else {
   return true;
  }
}
```

With the `=>` notation and the ternary operator, you can write the same function in a single line of code, as follows:

```
bool convertToBool(int value) => (value == 0) ? false : true;
```

Chances are you'll probably see this kind of syntax quite often in Dart and Flutter.

The `=>` arrow operator is a shortcut that allows you to simplify writing a method, particularly when it has a single `return` statement. Here, you can see an example of what the arrow syntax does:

```
String sayHello(String name) {
    return "Hello " + name;
}

String sayHello(String name) => "Hello " + name;
```

In short, you could say that with the arrow syntax, you can omit the curly braces and the `return` statement, and instead write everything in a single line.

The ternary operator is a concise way to write an `if` statement. Consider the following code:

```
if (value == 0) {
    i = false;
}
else {
    i = true;
}


i = (value == 0) ? false : true;
```

With the ternary operator, you can omit the `if` statement, the curly braces, and the `else` statement. In the optional parentheses, you put the Boolean control expression, `value == 0`.

Together, the arrow syntax and the ternary operator are a powerful and elegant combination.

While loops, lists, and generics

One of the first features that you generally meet when you learn a new language are arrays. In Dart, you use `List` objects when you want to define a collection.

Consider the following code:

```
void main() {
 String mySongs = sing();
 print (mySongs);
}

String sing() {
 var songs = List<String>();
 var songString = '';
 songs.add('We will Rock You');
 songs.add('One');
 songs.add('Sultans of Swing');
 int i=0;
 while (i < songs.length) {
 songString += '${songs[i]} - ';
 i++;
 }

 return songString;
}
```

In the `main()` method, we are calling the `sing()` method and printing its result. The `sing()` method defines a list of strings:

```
var songs = List<String>();
```

A list can contain several types of objects. You could have a list of integers, Booleans, or even user-defined objects. You can also avoid specifying the kind of object that is contained in a list by just writing the following:

```
var songs = List();
```

The `<String>` after `List` is the **generic** syntax. The use of generics enforces a restriction on the type of values that can be contained in the collection, creating a type-safe collection.

Lists implement several methods. You use the `add()` method to insert a new object into the collection:

```
songs.add('We will Rock You');
```

The new object is added to the end of the list. You could reach exactly the same result by writing the following code:

```
var songs = ['We will Rock You', 'One', 'Sultans of Swing'];
```

The `songs` variable would still be a list of strings. If you tried to add a different data type, such as `songs.add(24)`, you would get an error. This is because an integer cannot be inserted into a list of strings, and type safety is enforced by default.

The `while` statement contains the condition that needs to be true for the loop to continue:

```
while (i < songs.length) {
```

When the condition (`i < songs.length`) becomes false, the code in the loop won't execute anymore.

As you've already seen before, the `+=` operator is a concatenation of strings. The `$` character allows you to insert expressions into quotes:

```
songString += '${songs[i]} - ';
```

Here is the end result of the full code:

As you can see, the three wonderful songs are concatenated, and after each song, you've added a – sign.

Now, let's see a few interesting features that you can leverage while using lists in Dart.

foreach()

The `for` and `while` loops can be generally used for any type of loop, but lists also have some specific methods that help you write elegant and readable code.

The `foreach` method of a list lets you run a function on each element in the array. So, you could delete the `while` loop and use the following code instead, in order to achieve the same result:

```
songs.forEach((song) => songString += song + " - ");
```

The `foreach` method takes a function as a parameter. This function may be anonymous. This anonymous function takes an argument (`song` in this case), of the same data type as the list itself. So, as the `songs` list is a list of strings, `song` will be a string as well.

You've seen the `=>` arrow syntax in the previous topic. In this case, instead of returning a value, we are setting the value of a variable, and this is totally acceptable as well.

map()

The `map()` method transforms each element in a list and returns the result of the transformation in a new list. Let's see this method in action by editing our code:

```
void main() {
  String mySongs = sing();
  print (mySongs);
}

String sing() {
  var songs = List<String>();
  songs.add('We will Rock You');
  songs.add('One');
  songs.add('Sultans of Swing');
  var capitalSongs = songs.map((song)=> song.toUpperCase());
  return capitalSongs.toString();
}
```

The result of this code is that the songs are now printed in uppercase, but the interesting part of the code is the following line:

```
var capitalSongs = songs.map((song)=> song.toUpperCase());
```

Here, you can see the `map()` method of a list in action. For each element of the list, in this case a `song`, the element is transformed into `song.toUpperCase()`, and the end result is passed to a new variable, called `capitalSongs`. The `toString()` method transforms a list into a string. The result that you'll see printed on the screen is as follows:

```
(WE WILL ROCK YOU, ONE, SULTANS OF SWING)
```

where()

The last method that I'd like to introduce in this short overview is the `where()` method. Let's change the `sing()` function, using the `where` method as shown in the following example:

```
String sing() {
  var songs = List<String>();
  songs.add('We will Rock You');
  songs.add('One');
  songs.add('Sultans of Swing');
  var wSongs = songs.where((song)=>song.contains('w'));
  return wSongs.toString();
}
```

The `where()` method only returns the elements that satisfy the `song.contains('w')` test expression. This test will only return the songs that contain the "w". So, the end result that you'll see printed on the screen is as follows:

```
(We will Rock You, Sultans of Swing)
```

There are several other methods that can help you sort and transform lists, and find elements inside lists. We'll certainly use some of them throughout this book, but for now, you can leverage the `foreach()`, `map()`, and `where()` methods to start using lists in your Dart and Flutter code.

Classes and objects

Dart is an object-oriented programming language, and objects and classes are important parts of what you'll be creating in Dart and Flutter. If you are not familiar with OOP concepts, I suggest reading an excellent article at the following address: https://medium. freecodecamp.org/object-oriented-programming-concepts-21bb035f7260.

Here, we'll have a quick overview of creating classes and objects in Dart. Let's begin by creating a `Person` class with two fields, `name` and `surname`:

```
class Person {
  String name;
  String surname;
}
```

You can create instances of the `Person` class from the `main` method, and set the `name` and `surname` as follows:

```
main() {
  Person clark = Person();
  clark.name = 'Clark';
  clark.surname = 'Kent';
  print ('${clark.name} ${clark.surname}');

}
```

There are a couple of interesting features in this code that are worth noting. Name and surname are both accessible from outside the class, but in Dart, there are no identifiers such as **Private** or **Public**. So, each property of a class is considered public unless its name begins with an underscore character (_). In this case, it becomes inaccessible from outside its library (or file).

In the `Person clark = Person();` line, you are creating an instance of a `Person()` class, and the resulting object is contained in the `clark` variable. In Dart, you don't need to explicitly specify the new keyword, as it is implied. So writing `Person clark = new Person();` would be exactly the same.

You'll find the omission of the `new` keyword extremely common with Dart developers, especially when developing in the Flutter framework.

Using getters and setters

Getters and setters are the methods that are used to protect data in your classes: a **getter** method returns a property value of an instance of the class, while a **setter** sets or updates its value. In this way, you can check values before reading (getters) or writing (setters) them in your classes.

You specify getters and setters by adding the `get` and `set` keywords before the field name. The getter returns a value of the type that you specify, and the setter returns `void`:

```
main() {
  Person clark = Person();
  clark.name = 'Clark';
  clark.surname = 'Kent';
  clark.age = 30;
  print ('${clark.name} ${clark.surname} ${clark.age}');

}
class Person {
```

```
String name, surname;
int _age;

void set age(int years) {
  if (years > 0 && years < 120) {
    _age = years;
  }
  else {
    _age = 0;
  }
}

int get age {
  return _age;
}
}
```

In this example, we protect our data in the setter by making sure that the years are a number between 0 and 120; the getter just returns _age without any update.

Constructors

Classes can have constructors. A constructor is a special method that is automatically called when an object of a class is created. It can be used to set initial values for properties of the class. For instance, let's change our code to use a constructor to build a Person instance:

```
main() {
  Person clark = Person('Clark', 'Kent');
  print ('${clark.name} ${clark.surname}');

}
class Person {
  String name, surname;
  Person(String name, String surname) {
    this.name = name;
    this.surname = surname;
  }
}
```

`Person(name, surname)` is a constructor method that requires two parameters: `name` and `surname`. You are required to pass both parameters when you create a new instance of the class. For example, if you try to create a `Person` instance, without passing two strings, you receive an error. You can make positional parameters optional by enclosing them in square brackets:

```
Person([String name, String surname]) {
```

Now, what if you want to add a second constructor that takes no parameters? You could try to add the second constructor as follows:

```
Person();
```

However, you would get an error: **"The default constructor is already defined."** That's because, in Dart, you can have only one *unnamed* constructor, but you can have any number of *named* constructors. In our example, we could add the following code:

```
Person.empty() {
```

This would create a second named constructor. In the following screenshot, you can see an example of a class with an unnamed constructor, `Person()`, and a named constructor, `person.empty()`:

In this case, the difference between the two is that when you call the default (unnamed) constructor, you also need to pass the two required parameters, name and surname, while the named constructor allows you to create an empty object and then set the name and surname later in your code.

 Just to reiterate, you can have only one default unnamed constructor in Dart, but you can have as many named constructors as you need.

This keyword

The task of assigning a constructor argument to an object variable is something that we probably do very often, and Dart makes it extremely easy with the this shortcut. For example, here is the code for writing the Person constructor, which we used previously:

```
Person(String name, String surname) {
  this.name = name;
  this.surname = surname;
}
```

However, you could also just write the following code:

```
Person(this.name, this.surname) {}
```

With classes and objects, you have all the Dart tools that you need to get started with your first Flutter project. There are many other features and topics in Dart that you'll see throughout this book, but we'll cover them when they are needed for our projects. So, let's build your first Flutter project, the "Hello World Travel" company app!

Creating your first Flutter app

A Flutter application is made of **widgets**, and widgets are the description of a part of the user interface. Every user interaction, and everything that the user sees when navigating your app, is made of widgets. The app itself is a widget!

That's why when you begin using Flutter, one of the concepts that you'll hear most often is that "in Flutter almost everything is a Widget." This is mostly true.

You use Dart to write widgets. If you have some experience in mobile or web programming, then you may find this a bit unsettling. Most of the other mobile frameworks use some form of XML or HTML to describe the user interface, and a full programming language for business logic. In Flutter, you use Dart to describe both—the user interface, as well as the business logic of your app.

The app we'll build in this chapter is a single-screen app, with some text, a picture, and a button that, when clicked, gives the user a message. So, even if the app is extremely simple, you'll get to see many features of Flutter, including the use of widgets, styling text, downloading images from the web, and the creation of alerts.

Running your first Hello World app

For this first project, we'll be using the Flutter CLI to create the app. So, to get started, let's make sure everything's ready in your system:

1. Open your terminal window and type `flutter doctor`.

   You should see a few messages, such as in the following screenshot (this is from a Windows machine that was set up for Android):

   If you see some errors here, please make sure that an emulator/simulator is currently loaded, or that a physical device is correctly connected. If that doesn't solve your issues, please review the installation steps in the appendix.

2. Then, type the `flutter create` CLI command in order to create a new app:

```
flutter create hello_world
```

`flutter create` creates a new project, called `hello_world`. The rule for naming projects is `lowercase_with_underscores`. The `flutter create` command should have created a new folder, called `hello_world`, which contains all the default project's files that are required for the execution of your app.

3. To see the result of this step, from your terminal, type the following code:

```
cd hello_world
flutter run
```

After a few seconds, you should see the Flutter default app, similar to the following screenshot:

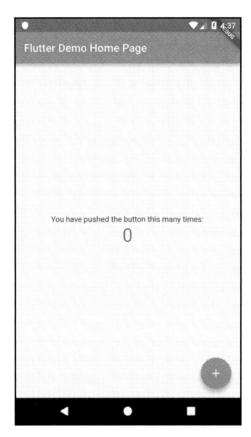

Now, we need to change this project so that it serves our Hello World Travel agent. In order to do this, continue with the following steps:

1. Let's stop the project by typing, *Ctrl + C* on your terminal, and then *Y*.
2. Next, open your editor. For this chapter, we'll use Android Studio.
3. From the Android Studio **File** menu, select **Open...**, then navigate to the project folder and click the **OK** button:

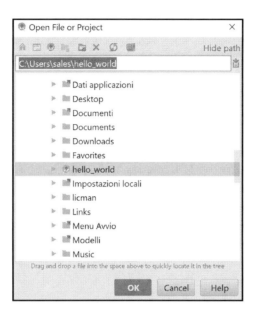

This will open the Flutter project in the IDE.

4. In the editor, you should see a file called `main.dart`, which contains the code of the default app. Let's delete all the content of the `main.dart` file, and type the following code:

```dart
import 'package:flutter/material.dart';

void main() => runApp(MyApp());

class MyApp extends StatelessWidget {
  @override
  Widget build(BuildContext context) {
    return Center(
        child: Text('Hello World Travel',
        textDirection: TextDirection.ltr,),
    );
```

```
    }
  }
```

You can try out this code by pressing the **Run** button on the Android Studio toolbar, or by using the *Shift + F10* keyboard shortcut. You should see that the app now looks like the following screenshot:

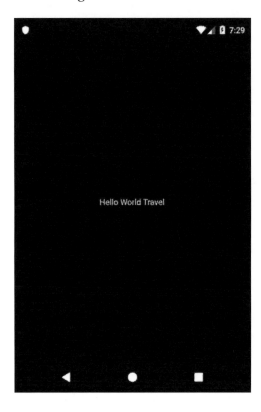

Let's see the code that we have written, line by line:

```
import 'package:flutter/material.dart';
```

In the first line, we import the `material.dart` package. A package is a library that contains reusable code. The `material.dart` package is a container of widgets, and in particular, *material* widgets that implement Material Design. Material Design is a visual design language that was developed by Google.

Next, we create a method, called `main`:

```
void main() => runApp(MyApp());
```

As you've seen in the Dart examples, this is the entry point of any Dart app, and this is the same for Flutter apps.

For the `main()` method, we use the arrow syntax to call `runApp()`. The `runApp()` method *inflates* a widget and attaches it to the screen. To put it simply, the `runapp()` method will show the widgets that you have placed inside the app on the screen.

Flutter's widgets aren't views themselves, so they don't draw anything: they are simply a **description of the user interface**. This description gets "inflated" into an actual view when the objects are built.

The following line states that `MyApp` is a class that extends `StatelessWidget`:

```
class MyApp extends StatelessWidget {
```

In Flutter, there are two kinds of widgets: **stateless** and **stateful**. You use stateless widgets when you do not need to change the widget after its creation. In this case, the text in the screen (**"Hello World Travel"**) will never change during the app lifecycle, so a stateless widget is enough for this app. On the other hand, you'll use stateful widgets when their content (or state) needs to change.

In Flutter, the **widget tree** is the way that you organize widgets in an app.

While HTML pages have the **DOM**, or **Document Object Model**, Flutter calls the **hierarchical list of widgets that makes the UI** a "widget tree."

The `build()` method in the following line of code is automatically called by the Flutter framework when a widget is inserted into the widget tree:

```
Widget build(BuildContext context) {
```

In our example, the widget tree is made of only two widgets: the `Center` widget and the `Text` widget. The `build()` method returns a widget.

`Center` is a *positional widget* that centers its content on the screen:

```
return Center(
```

So, whatever you put inside a `Center` widget will be centered horizontally and vertically.

`child` is a property that allows you to nest widgets inside other widgets. `Text` is a widget to show text:

```
child: Text('Hello World Travel',
        textDirection: TextDirection.ltr,),
```

Note that in this case, you also need to specify a `textDirection` instruction. `ltr` means left to right. So, you are using the `child` property of the `Center` widget, to put a `Text` widget in the center of the screen. By default, the background color of the screen is black.

This is probably not the most beautiful app that you've ever seen, but we'll keep working on it, and, most importantly, congratulations! You have written your first Hello World app!

Using MaterialApp and Scaffold

A black screen with small white text doesn't really look like a real app. We'll try to fix that by taking the following steps:

1. Let's introduce the `MaterialApp` widget, which is the container that you'll use when creating *Material Design* apps. Material Design is a design language that Google developed in 2014, based on "materials," such as ink or paper, with an implementation that was even more advanced than physical materials. Flutter fully supports Material Design.

If you are interested in learning more about Material Design, have a look at the material.io (`https://material.io/`) website. It's full of examples and ideas that you can use for the web, mobile, and of course, your next wonderful app in Flutter!

2. For most of your apps, you'll probably wrap your content in a `MaterialApp` widget. This also allows you to give a title to your app. So let's change our code like this:

```
import 'package:flutter/material.dart';

void main() => runApp(MyApp());

class MyApp extends StatelessWidget {
  @override
  Widget build(BuildContext context) {
    return MaterialApp(
        title: "Hello World Travel Title",
        home: Center(
          child: Text('Hello World Travel')
        ));
  }
}
```

3. Instead of returning a `Center` widget, we are now returning `MaterialApp`, which has two properties: `title` and `home`. `Home` is what the user will actually see on the screen of the app. You may notice that when you use `MaterialApp`, you don't need to specify the text direction, as the text direction is chosen based on the device's locale information.

 Currently, languages that use the right-to-left text direction are Arabic, Farsi, Hebrew, Pashto, and Urdu. All other languages use left to right.

4. If you run the app, you'll see that a couple of things changed in it. If you are using Android, you will now see the app title if you scroll through your apps, and the font size has changed:

5. It looks even worse than before. Let's quickly add a Scaffold widget. A Scaffold widget represents a screen in a MaterialApp widget, as it may contain several Material Design layout widgets, including AppBar, a bottom navigation bar, floating action buttons, and the body of the screen. We'll use those widgets extensively throughout the book.
6. A Scaffold widget allows you to add an application bar to your app. In the appBar property, we'll place an AppBar widget, which will contain the text that you want to show in the application bar.

7. Let's set the text to be added to the Hello World Travel App, as shown in the following code block:

```
class MyApp extends StatelessWidget {
  @override
  Widget build(BuildContext context) {
    return MaterialApp(
        title: "Hello World Travel Title",
      home: Scaffold(
          appBar: AppBar(title: Text("Hello World Travel App")),
          body: Center(
            child: Text('Hello World Travel')
      )));
  }
}
```

The `Scaffold` widget has two properties that we used: `appBar`, which contains an application bar, and `body`, which contains the main content of the screen.

So, our app now definitely looks more like an app, even though it only contains a small amount of text:

Let's now add a few more widgets to make our app more interesting.

Formatting Text and Using Columns

Our customer, Hello World Travel, loves blue and purple, and so we need to change the colors of our app, as well as the formatting of our text. Let's change the MyApp class code as shown here:

```
class MyApp extends StatelessWidget {
  @override
  Widget build(BuildContext context) {
    return MaterialApp(
        title: "Hello World Travel Title",
        home: Scaffold(
          appBar: AppBar(
            title: Text("Hello World Travel App"),
            backgroundColor: Colors.deepPurple,),
          body: Center(
            child: Text(
              'Hello World Travel',
              style: TextStyle(
                  fontSize: 26,
                  fontWeight: FontWeight.bold,
                  color: Colors.blue[800]),)
    )));
  }
}
```

We've added a couple of features to the app. First, we added a background color for the AppBar as shown here:

```
backgroundColor: Colors.deepPurple,
```

The Colors class contains several colors that we can use out of the box, including deepPurple, which we used there. In the color, you can also choose a shade, which is generally a number from 100 to 900, in increments of 100, plus the color 50. The higher the number, the darker the color. For example, for the text, we chose a color of blue[800], which is rather dark:

```
style: TextStyle(   fontSize: 26,
                    fontWeight: FontWeight.bold,
                    color: Colors.blue[800]),)
```

In the `Text` widget, we used the `style` property to add a `TextStyle` class, and there we chose a bigger `fontSize`, a bold `fontweight`, and of course, `color`.

Our app is definitely getting better, but we aren't finished yet. We now need to add a second piece of text below the first one. The problem right now is that the `Center` widget only takes one child, so we cannot add a second `Text` widget there. The solution is choosing a container widget that allows more than one child, and as we want to place our widgets on the screen, one below the other, we can use a `Column` container widget. A `Column` has the `children` property, instead of `child`, which takes an array of widgets. So let's change the body of the `Scaffold` widget, like this:

```
body: Center(
    child: Column(children: [
  Text(
    'Hello World Travel',
    style: TextStyle(
        fontSize: 26,
        fontWeight: FontWeight.bold,
        color: Colors.blue[800])),
  ),
  Text(
    'Discover the World',
    style: TextStyle(
        fontSize: 20,
        color: Colors.deepPurpleAccent),
  )
]))
```

Now, the `Center` widget still contains a single `child`, but its `child` is a `Column` widget that now contains two `Text` widgets, 'Hello World Travel' and 'Discover the World.'

Showing images and using buttons

Let's now add an `Image` widget under the two texts, as follows:

```
Image.network(
'https://images.freeimages.com/images/large-previews/eaa/the-beach-1464354.
jpg',
  height: 350,
),
```

Image is a widget that has a `network()` constructor, which automatically downloads an image from a URL with a single line of code. The image is taken from FREEIMAGES (`https://www.freeimages.com/`), which contains a stock of free photos for personal and commercial use.

The `height` property of an image specifies its height, depending on the pixel density of the screen. By default, the width will be resized proportionally.

In Flutter, when we speak of **pixels,** we are actually speaking of *logical* pixels, and not *physical* pixels.

Physical pixels are the actual number of pixels that a device has. But, there are several form factors, and the resolution of a screen may vary substantially.

For example, the Sony Xperia E4 has a screen size of 5", and a resolution of 960 * 540 pixels. The Xperia X has the same screen size of 5", but a resolution of 1920 * 1080. So, if you wanted to draw a square of 540 pixels per side, it would be much smaller on the second device. That's why there's the need for logical pixels. Each device has a multiplier, so that when you use logical pixels, you don't have to worry too much about the resolution of a screen.

Let's also put a button under the image:

```
RaisedButton(
    child: Text('Contact Us'),
    onPressed: () => true,),
```

`RaisedButton` shows a button that a user can press (or click). Inside `Raisedbutton`, we have placed `Text` as the widget child, and in the `onPressed` property, we have created an anonymous `()` function with an arrow operator, and in the function, we are just returning `true`. This is only temporary. When the user presses the button, we want to show a message, and we'll do that later.

Next, you can see the code of the `MyApp` class so far, and the result on an Android emulator:

We have almost reached the end result that we wanted to achieve, but there are a couple of things that we need to fix. We should add some space between the widgets, and show a message when the user selects the `Contact Us` button. Let's begin with the message.

Showing an AlertDialog box

`AlertDialogs` are widgets that you use to give feedback or to ask for some information from your user. It is a small window that stays on top of the current screen, and only covers part of the user interface. Some use cases include asking for confirmation before deleting an item (**Are you sure?**), or giving some information to the user (**Order completed!**). In our code, we'll show our user the contact information of the Hello World Travel company.

Showing an `AlertDialog` widget requires a few steps:

1. Calling the `showDialog()` method
2. Setting `context`
3. Setting `builder`
4. Returning the `AlertDialog` property
5. Setting the `AlertDialog` properties

Let's write a new method, called `contactUs`, at the end of the `MyApp` class:

```
void contactUs(BuildContext context) {
  showDialog(
    context: context,
    builder: (BuildContext context) {
      return AlertDialog(
        title: Text('Contact Us'),
        content: Text('Mail us at hello@world.com'),
        actions: <Widget>[
          FlatButton(
            child: Text('Close'),
            onPressed: () => Navigator.of(context).pop(),
          )
        ],
      );
    },
  );
}
```

We are creating a `contactUs` method, that takes a `context` parameter. We then call the `showDialog()` function, which is required in order to show a message to the user. The `showDialog` function has a few properties that we need to set. The first one is `context`, which is basically where the dialog should be shown. This is passed to our method through the `context` parameter.

Next, we need to set the `builder` property. This requires a function, so we need to create a function that accepts a single argument of the `BuildContext` type, and returns a widget—in our example, `AlertDialog`, as shown here:

```
builder: (BuildContext context) {
    return AlertDialog(
```

An `AlertDialog` widget has several properties that set the behavior of the message that you show to the user. The three properties that we are using in this example are `title`, `content`, and `actions`. In the following screenshot, you can see the result of using those properties:

You can see the **Contact Us** title, the **Mail us at hello@world.com** content, and the actions—the **Close** button. In the `actions`, when you have more than one choice, you can place more than one button.

In the following excerpt of the code, the `pop()` method of the `Navigator` class will close `AlertDialog`. We'll talk more about screens and navigation in Flutter in the other projects in this book:

```
return AlertDialog(
        title: Text('Contact Us'),
        content: Text('Mail us at hello@world.com'),
        actions: <Widget>[
          FlatButton(
            child: Text('Close'),
            onPressed: () => Navigator.of(context).pop(),
          )
        ],
```

Our `AlertDialog` is not showing yet. We need to make a couple of changes before you can use it. The first change is that we need to call the `contactUs` function that we have just created. We'll do that in the `onPressed` property of the `RaisedButton` widget:

```
onPressed: () => contactUs(context),
```

The second change that we need to perform is enclosing the `Center` widget in the body of the `Scaffold` widget in a `Builder` widget. This allows us to take the context of the Scaffold so that we can pass it to the `showDialog` method, as shown here:

```
body: Builder(builder: (context)=>Center(
```

For your reference, here is the final code that we have written so far:

```
import 'package:flutter/material.dart';

void main() => runApp(MyApp());

class MyApp extends StatelessWidget {
  @override
  Widget build(BuildContext context) {
    return MaterialApp(
        title: "Hello World Travel Title",
        home: Scaffold(
            appBar: AppBar(
              title: Text("Hello World Travel App"),
              backgroundColor: Colors.deepPurple,
            ),
            body: Builder(builder: (context)=>Center(
                child: Column(children: [
              Text(
                'Hello World Travel',
                style: TextStyle(
```

```
                        fontSize: 26,
                        fontWeight: FontWeight.bold,
                        color: Colors.blue[800]),
                ),
                Text(
                  'Discover the World',
                  style: TextStyle(fontSize: 20, color:
                  Colors.deepPurpleAccent),
                ),
                Image.network('https://images.freeimages.com/
                  images/large-previews/eaa/the-beach-1464354.jpg',
                  height: 350,
                ),
                RaisedButton(
                  child: Text('Contact Us'),
                  onPressed: () => contactUs(context),
                ),
            ]))))));
  }

  void contactUs(BuildContext context) {
    showDialog(
      context: context,
      builder: (BuildContext context) {
        return AlertDialog(
          title: Text('Contact Us'),
          content: Text('Mail us at hello@world.com'),
          actions: <Widget>[
            FlatButton(
              child: Text('Close'),
              onPressed: () => Navigator.of(context).pop(),
            )
          ],
        );
      },
    );
  }
}
```

Note that, should you get lost when writing your code while following any project in this book, you can always check the final version of the app at the GitHub repository. In particular, the project for this chapter is available at `https://github.com/ PacktPublishing/Google-Flutter-Projects`.

In the next section, let's see how to use padding to add some space to our app.

Using padding

All the functions of our app are there, but everything seems too crowded on our screen. Let's add some space between the widgets. Generally speaking, you can create space between elements through padding and margin properties. In Flutter, some widgets have a padding and a margin property to deal with the space. Padding is the space between the content and the border of a widget (which may also not be visible), and the margin is the space outside the border, as shown in the following diagram:

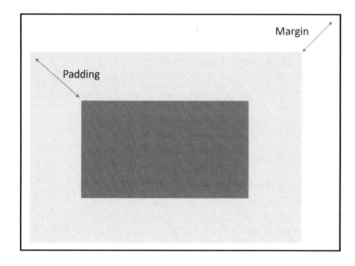

Flutter also has a widget that has been specifically created to deal with space: the Padding widget. In order to specify the distance (also called the *offset*), you use the EdgeInsets class. This class specifies offsets, for the margin or the padding, from left, top, right, and bottom. There are several named constructors for the EdgeInsets class.

The Edgeinsets.all constructor creates an offset on all four sides of a box: top, right, bottom, and left. In the next example, it creates an offset of 24 logical pixels on all sides of a box:

```
EdgeInsets.all(24)
```

In order to choose the side, or sides, for the offset, you can use the only() constructor. In the following example, you see on the screen, for instance, that you are creating a margin of 80 pixels on the right of a widget:

```
EdgeInsets.only(right:80)
```

The `EdgeInsets.symmetric(vertical: 48.5)` constructor allows you to create symmetrical vertical and horizontal offsets. All the constructors take double values as parameters:

```
EdgeInsets.symmetric(vertical:48.5)
```

So, in our code, let's add some spacing now:

1. Let's enclose `Center` itself into a `Padding` widget, giving it an `EdgeInsets.all` class with 20 logical pixels on each side:

```
body: Builder(
    builder: (context) => Padding(
        padding: EdgeInsets.all(20),
        child: Center(
            child: Column(children: [
```

2. Then, we'll repeat the same process for the two `Text` widgets—`Image` and `RaisedButton`. Let's begin by giving a 10-pixel padding to the `'Hello World Travel'` text:

```
Padding(
    padding: EdgeInsets.all(10),
    child: Text(
      'Hello World Travel',
```

3. Next, let's add the padding to the `'Discover the world'` text:

```
Padding(
    padding: EdgeInsets.all(5),
    child: Text(
      'Discover the World',
```

4. Next, we add padding to the `Image` widget:

```
Padding(
    padding: EdgeInsets.all(15),
    child: Image.network(
```

5. Finally, we add padding to the button:

```
Padding(
    padding: EdgeInsets.all(15),
    child: RaisedButton(
```

If you try the app right now, depending on your device, everything might look okay, but we still have a problem. Let's see what it is in the next section.

Using SingleChildScrollView

Now that we added some space into the screen, we might run into a problem. Try to rotate your device so that you have horizontal view. You should see something like the following screenshot:

We have an error: **Bottom overflowed by 250 pixels**. This happens because the size of the UI is bigger than the size of the screen.

 Always check your app in every orientation when developing for mobile.

There's an easy solution for this. We need to enclose everything in
`SingleChildScrollView`:

```
builder: (context) => SingleChildScrollView(
    child: Padding(
```

`SingleChildScrollView` is a widget that scrolls and has a single child, in our example, `Padding`. This is especially useful when your widget might take more space than the available space on the screen and you want to enable scrolling for the overflowing content.

If you try this now, you'll see that everything is working perfectly, and the user can scroll up and down if needed.

You have completed your first project in this book! Congratulations, you are well on your way to becoming a Flutter developer.

Summary

In this first chapter, we've covered several of the basics that you'll build upon on your journey learning Flutter. The content covered here included how to use the Flutter CLI and how to test your installation with the `flutter doctor` command. You also saw how to try your apps on an emulator (Android) or a simulator (iOS).

We introduced Dart and its syntax: using the DartPad online tool, we looked at some of the Dart syntax, including variables, loops, using strings, the arrow syntax, lists, generics, and the `Map()` method.

We've touched upon the basics of object-oriented programming with classes and objects, including constructors, properties, and methods. Finally, we introduced Flutter and created our first Hello World app. We saw that almost every piece of UI in Flutter is a widget, and we introduced several basic widgets, including `Center`, `Text`, `MaterialApp` and `Scaffold`, `Column`, `RaisedButton`, and `Image`.

We modified the style of our app using the widgets' properties, such as choosing colors and sizing fonts. We also saw how to deal with the space on the screen with padding, and how to respond to events such as the click of a button.

Finally, we used an `AlertDialog` widget in order to give feedback to the user.

The topics introduced in this chapter will be the foundation of your progress in Flutter, and the skills that you have acquired here will allow you to follow along with the remaining projects of this book, and will be invaluable when developing your own apps.

In the next chapter, we'll introduce the concept of state, which will allow you to create interactive apps with Flutter.

Questions

At the end of each project, you'll find a few questions to help you remember and review the content that has been covered in the chapter, and this first chapter makes no exception. Please try to answer the following questions, and if in doubt, have a look at the content in the chapter itself, you'll find all the answers there!

1. What is a widget?
2. What is the starting point of a Dart and Flutter app?
3. How many named constructors can you have in a Dart/Flutter class?
4. Can you name three `EdgeInsets` constructors?

5. How can you style the text in a `Text` widget?
6. What is the purpose of the `flutter doctor` command?
7. What widget would you use to contain several other widgets, one below the other?
8. What is the "arrow syntax"?
9. Which widget can you use to create space between widgets?
10. How can you show an image to the user?

Further reading

- In technology, things change very fast, so the information provided for the installation of Flutter may have changed when you read this book. For the up-to-date process for installing Flutter on a Windows, Mac, or Linux machine, have a look at the following link: `https://flutter.dev/docs/get-started/install`.

- Chrome OS is not officially supported at the time of writing this book, but there are several blog articles and guides that show the process of successfully installing the Flutter SDK on Chrome OS. To install Flutter on a Pixelbook that is running, for example, Chrome OS have a look at this link: `https://proandroiddev.com/flutter-development-on-a-pixelbook-dde984a3fc1e`.

- Material Design is a fascinating topic. For a full description of the design patterns, rules, and tools visit the comprehensive Material Design website at `https://material.io/`.

- With this book, I truly hope to transfer to you some of the passion for the Flutter technology that I have. I often find inspiration and great ideas at the Flutter community website on Medium. You can find it at `https://medium.com/flutter-community`.

2
Miles or Kilometers? Using Stateful Widgets

The world is a strange place. Most of us are aware that when you travel to other countries, you may find different languages, culture, and food, but you would expect that at least numbers and measures would stay the same wherever you go, right? Well, this is not so.

Measures such as distance, speed, weight, volume, and temperature change based on where you live. Actually, there are two main measurement systems in use today: the imperial system, which is used mainly in the United States; and the metric system, which is used in most of the other countries.

In this chapter, you'll bring some order to this confusing world: you will build a measures conversion app, in which distance and weight measures will be converted from imperial to metric, and vice versa.

We'll cover the following aspects in this chapter:

- Project overview
- Understanding state and stateful widgets
- Creating the measure converter project

Technical requirements

Should you get lost in the construction of the app, you'll find the completed app code at the end of this chapter, or on the book's GitHub repository at `https://github.com/PacktPublishing/Google-Flutter-Projects`.

To follow along the code examples in this book, you should have the following software installed on your Windows, Mac, Linux, or Chrome OS device:

- The Flutter SDK.
- When developing for Android, you'll need: the Android SDK – easily installed by Android Studio.
- When developing for iOS, you'll need: macOS and Xcode.
- An emulator (Android), a simulator (iOS), or a connected iOS or Android device enabled for debugging.
- An editor: Visual Studio Code, Android Studio, or IntelliJ IDEA are recommended. All should have the Flutter/Dart extensions installed.

You'll find an installation guide in the *Appendix* of this book.

The necessary time to build the app in this chapter should be approximately 2.5 hours.

Project overview

The measures conversion app will allow your users to select a measure – metric or imperial – and convert it to another measure. For example, they'll be able to convert a distance in miles to a distance in kilometers, or a weight in kilograms to a weight in pounds. So, next time you travel to a country with a different system, you'll be able to easily understand the speed of your car (and maybe avoid a fine), or the weight of the food you can buy at the market, and along the way, you'll build on your Flutter skills.

By the end of this chapter, you'll know how to leverage State using widgets such as TextFields to interact with users and make your apps interactive.

While doing so, you'll encounter several fundamental concepts in Flutter, and in particular, the following:

- You'll see what State is in Flutter, start using *stateful widgets,* and understand when you should use *stateless* or *stateful* widgets.
- You'll see how and when to update the *State* in your app.
- You'll also see how to handle events, such as onChanged and OnSubmitted in a TextField.

- You'll see how to use the most common user input widget—TextField.
- Another very important widget that you'll use for this project is DropDownButton. It's a drop-down list where you decide the choices that your users have. And those choices are called DropDownItems in Flutter.
- You'll see how to start separating the logic of your app from the **User Interface (UI)**, and you'll gain a few tips on how to build the structure of your app.

 While stateful widgets are the most basic way to deal with State in an app, there are other, more efficient ways to deal with State in Flutter. Some of those will be shown in the upcoming projects.

The following is the final layout of the project that you'll build in this chapter:

As you can see, this is a rather standard form with Material Design widgets, which should be very easy to compile for your users. You can use it as a starting point for any form that you use in your future apps.

Understanding state and stateful widgets

The widgets that we've seen so far are stateless widgets, meaning that once created they are immutable, and they do not keep any state information. When you interact with your users, you expect things to change. For example, if you want to convert a measure from one system to another, the result must change, based on some user input.

The most basic way to deal with changes in Flutter is using State.

State is information that can be used when a widget is built and can change during the lifetime of a widget.

An important part of this definition is that state is **information that can change**, and the most obvious takeaway of this concept is that when you want to add interactivity to your app, you can use State. But, if you read this definition thoroughly, it also means that **it's not the widget itself that will change, it's the State of a widget that will change**, and when it does, the widget will be rebuilt. When a widget has a State, it's called a stateful widget. And in Flutter, stateful widgets are immutable. It's only the State itself that changes.

 Each time the State changes, the widget gets rebuilt.

Let's have a look at the main differences between a stateless widget, which we've used so far, and a stateful widget. Of course, the most obvious difference is explained by the name itself, the State: State/*less* and State/*ful*.

But there is a different implementation as well. In order to see it in detail, we'll create a new app and see it in practice.

Creating the measure converter project

We will now create a new app that we'll use throughout this chapter to build a fully functioning measure converter:

1. From your favorite editor, create a new app. Name the new app Unit Converter.

2. In the main.dart file, remove the example code and write the code given as follows:

```
import 'package:flutter/material.dart';

void main() => runApp(MyApp());

class MyApp extends StatelessWidget {
@override
  Widget build(BuildContext context) {
    return MaterialApp(
      title: 'Measures Converter',
      home: Scaffold(
      appBar: AppBar(
          title: Text('Measures Converter'),
      ),
      body: Center(
          child: Text('Measures Converter'),
      ),),
  );}
}
```

As you may have noticed, the preceding code makes use of a Stateless widget:

```
class MyApp extends StatelessWidget {
```

A Stateless widget is a **class** that extends a StatelessWidget. Extending a StatelessWidget class requires overriding a build() method.

In the build() method, you describe the widget returned by the method:

```
@override
Widget build(BuildContext context) {
```

The build() method that takes a *context* and returns a *widget*:

```
return MaterialApp(...)
```

So to summarize, in order to have a stateless widget you need to do the following:

1. Create a class that extends `StatelessWidget`.
2. Override the `build()` method.
3. Return a widget.

Once built, a Stateless widget never changes.

Using stateful widgets

Let's now transform the `MyApp` class into a stateful widget, so that you can see the different implementations of the class:

```
class MyApp extends StatefulWidget {
```

You can see immediately that you get two errors. If you hover over the `MyApp` class, the error that you see is "**Missing concrete implementation of StatefulWidget.createState**," and if you hover over the `build` method you see "**The method doesn't override an inherited method**."

What these errors are trying to tell us is the following:

1. A stateful widget requires a `createState()` method.
2. In a stateful widget, there is no `build()` method to override.

Let's fix both these issues using the following steps:

1. Add the necessary `createState()` method, which will return `MyAppState`, which we'll create shortly. In the `MyApp` class, just under its definition, write the following code:

   ```
   @override
   MyAppState createState() => MyAppState();
   ```

2. Create a new class called `MyAppState`, that extends the State, and in particular, the State of `MyApp`:

   ```
   class MyAppState extends State<MyApp> {}
   ```

3. In order to solve the second error ("**Missing concrete implementation of State.build**"), cut the `build()` method that is now in the `MyApp` class, and paste it into the `MyAppState` class. The revised code should look like this:

```
import 'package:flutter/material.dart';

void main() => runApp(MyApp());

class MyApp extends StatefulWidget {
  @override
  MyAppState createState() => MyAppState();
}

class MyAppState extends State<MyApp> {
  @override
  Widget build(BuildContext context) {
    return MaterialApp(
      title: 'Measures Converter',
      home: Scaffold(
        appBar: AppBar(
          title: Text('Measures Converter'),
        ),
        body: Center(
          child: Text('Measures Converter'),
        ),
      ),
    );
  }
}
```

To sum it up, from a *syntax* perspective, the difference between a Stateless widget and a stateful widget is that the former overrides a `build()` method and returns a widget, whereas a stateful widget overrides a `createState()` method, which returns a State. The `State` class overrides a `build()` method, returning a widget.

From a functional point of view, in the code that we have written, there is no difference whatsoever between the two, as in both cases the app looks and behaves exactly in the same way. So, let's add a feature that **requires** a stateful widget, and could not be achieved with a Stateless Widget.

Here, you can see the app layout so far:

Next, let's see how to read the user input from `TextField`.

Reading user input from TextField

In the `State` class, let's add a member called _numberFrom. As shown in the following code, this is a value that will change based on user input:

```
double _numberFrom;
```

Then, in the body of the `build()` method, let's delete the text widget, and add `TextField` instead:

```
body: Center(
    child: TextField(),
),
```

You generally use `TextField` when you want to take some input from your users.

As you can see, there's now `TextField` in the center of your app, and you can write into it by clicking over the line and typing something:

Right now, `TextField` does nothing, so the first thing we need to do is *read* the value that the user inputs into it.

While there are different ways to read from `TextField`, for this project, we'll respond to each change in the content of `TextField` through the `onChanged` method, and then we'll update the State.

In order to update the State, you need to call the `setState()` method.

 The `setState()` method tells the framework that the state of an object has changed, and that the UI needs to be updated.

Inside the `setState()` method, you change the class members that you need to update (in our case, `_numberFrom`):

```
child: TextField(
    onChanged: (text) {
       var rv = double.tryParse(text);
       if (rv != null) {
          setState(() {
             _numberFrom = rv;
          });
       }
    },
 ),
```

In the preceding code, each time the value of `TextField` changes (`onChanged`), we check whether the value that was typed is a number (`tryParse`). If it's a number, we change the value of the `_numberForm` member: in this way, we have actually updated the State. In other words, when you call the `setState()` method to update a class member, you are also updating the State of the class.

We are not giving any feedback to the user, so unless we use the debugging tools of our editor, we cannot actually check whether this update actually happened. In order to solve that, let's add a `Text` widget that will show the content of the `TextEdit` widget, and then wrap the two widgets into a `Column` widget:

```
body: Center(
    child: Column(
       children: [
          TextField(
             onChanged: (text) {
                var rv = double.tryParse(text);
                if (rv != null) {
                   setState(() {
                      _numberFrom = rv;
```

```
                });
            }
        },
    ),Text((_numberFrom == null) ? '' : _numberFrom.toString())
        ],
    ),
),
```

Before trying the app, let's add another method to the `MyAppState` class:

```
@override
void initState() {
_numberFrom = 0;
super.initState();
}
```

The `initState()` method is called once for each `State` object when the State is built. This is where you generally put the initial values that you might need when you build your classes. In this case, we are setting the _numberFrom initial value. Also note, that you should always call `super.initState()` at the end of the `initState()` method.

Now, if you write a number in the `TextField`, you'll see the same number in the `Text` widget, as well. In this apparently simple example, many things are happening at once:

- You are setting an initial State of the app through the _numberForm class member in the `InitState()` method.
- The widget is drawn on screen.
- You are responding to a `TextField` event: the `onChanged` event, which is called every time the content of the `TextField` changes.
- You are changing the State by calling the `setState()` method, and there you change the value of _numberForm.
- The widget is redrawn with the new State, which contains the number that you write in `TextField`, so the `Text` widget, which reads _numberForm, contains the modified value of the State.

Here is a diagram that highlights the steps described previously: with a few variations, you'll notice a similar pattern whenever you use stateful widgets in your apps:

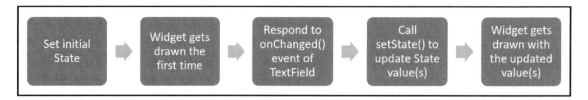

To sum it up, calling `setState()`, does the following:

- Notifies the framework that the internal state of this object has changed
- Calls the `build()` method and redraws its children with the updated `State` object

Now you have the ability to create an app that responds to the user input and changes the UI based on a changing State, which in Flutter is the most basic way to create interactive apps.

Next, we need to complete the UI of our app, and in order to do that, we need another widget: `DropDownButton`. Let's create this in the following section.

Creating a DropdownButton widget

`DropdownButton` is a widget that lets users select a value from a list of items. `DropdownButton` shows the currently selected item, as well as a small triangle that opens a list for selecting another item.

Here are the steps that are required to add `DropdownButton` to your apps:

1. Create an instance of `DropdownButton`, specifying the type of data that will be included in the list.
2. Add an `items` property that will contain the list of items that will be shown to the user.

3. The `items` property requires a list of `DropdownMenuItem` widgets. Therefore, you need to map each value that you want to show into `DropdownMenuItem`.

4. Respond to the user actions by specifying an event; typically, for `DropdownButton`, you will call a function in the `onChanged` property.

As an example, the following code creates a `DropdownButton` widget that shows a list of fruits (that are good for your health):

```
var fruits = ['Orange', 'Apple', 'Strawberry', 'Banana'];

DropdownButton<String>(
    items: fruits.map((String value) {
        return DropdownMenuItem<String>(
          value: value,
          child: Text(value),);
        }).toList(),
        onChanged: (String newValue) {}
),
```

`DropDownButton` is a generic, as it's built as `DropDownButton<T>`, where the generic type, `T`, is the type of item in your `DropDownButton` widget (in this case, *T* is a string).

 Dart supports **generics** or **generic types**. For example, a list can contain several types: `List<int>` is a list of integers, `List<String>` is a list of strings, and `List<dynamic>` is a list of objects of any type. Using generics helps to ensure type safety: in the example of the list, for instance, you cannot add a number to `List<String>`.

The `map()` method iterates through all the values of the array, and performs a function on each value of the list. The function inside the `map()` method returns a `DropDownMenuItem` widget, which, in the previous example, has a `value` property and a `child` property. The child is what the user will see, in this case, a `Text` widget. The `value` is what you'll use to retrieve the selected item on the list.

The `map()` method returns an iterable, which is a collection of values that can be accessed sequentially.

Over that, you call the `toList()` method, which creates a list that contains the elements that should be returned. This is required by the items property.

In our app, we need two DropdownButton widgets, one for the starting unit, and one for the converted unit:

1. Let's create a *list* of *strings* that will contain all the measures that we want to deal with. At the beginning of the State class, let's add the following code:

```
final List<String> _measures = [
    'meters',
    'kilometers',
    'grams',
    'kilograms',
    'feet',
    'miles',
    'pounds (lbs)',
    'ounces',
];
```

2. Next, we'll create a DropDownButton widget, which will read the values of the list, and place it at the top of the *column*, above the TextField:

```
DropdownButton(
  items: _measures.map((String value) {
  return DropdownMenuItem<String>(value: value, child:
Text(value),);
  }).toList(),
  onChanged: (_) {},
),
```

If you try out the app now, you'll see that at the top of the screen there's a small triangle. When you click on it, the list of measures is shown, and you can click on any of them to select one. At this time, when you select a value, DropdownButton still remains empty. This is because we need to implement the function inside the onChanged member of DropDownButton.

The following screenshot shows how `DropdownButton` contains a list of items:

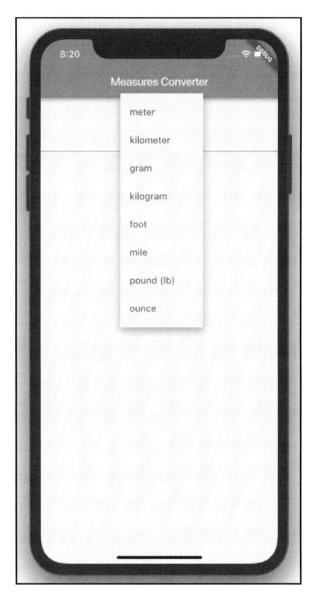

In the next section, we will learn how to respond to the user input when they change the value in `DropDownButton`.

Updating a DropdownButton widget

Let's modify the onChanged property using the following steps:

1. Create a new string called _startMeasure at the top of the MyAppState class. It will contain the selected value from DropdownButton:

   ```
   String _startMeasure;
   ```

2. Instead of the underscore, call the parameter that is passed to the function, value.

3. Inside the function, call the setState() method to update _startMeasure with the new value that's passed. Here is the resulting code:

   ```
   onChanged: (value) {
     setState(() {
         _startMeasure = value;
       });
   }
   ```

4. The last step of this task is reading the selected value so that DropdownButton reads it when the app starts and every time it changes. Let's add the following line to DropDownButton:

   ```
   value: _startMeasure,
   ```

   Now, if you try the app, when you select a value from the list, the value shows up in DropdownButton, which is exactly the behavior that you would expect from it.

In the next section, we'll complete the UI for this screen.

Completing the UI of the app

Let's now complete the UI of our app. The final result is shown in the following screenshot:

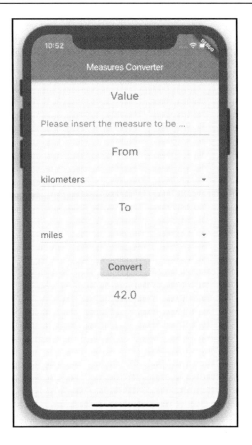

We actually need to show eight widgets on screen:

- `Text` containing **Value**
- `TextField` for the start value
- `Text` containing **From**
- A `DropdownButton` widget for the start measure
- Another `Text` containing **To**
- A `DropdownButton` widget for the measure of the conversion
- `RaisedButton` to call the method that will convert the value.
- `Text` for the result of the conversion

Each element of the `Column` should also be spaced and styled.

Let's begin by creating two `TextStyle` widgets. The advantage of this approach is that we can use them several times without needing to specify the styling details for each widget:

1. At the top of the `build()` method, let's first create a `TextStyle` widget, which we'll use for `TextFields`, `DropDownButtons`, and `Button`. We'll call it `inputStyle`:

```
final TextStyle inputStyle = TextStyle(
    fontSize: 20,
    color: Colors.blue[900],
);
```

2. Then, let's create a second `TextStyle` widget, which we'll use for the `Text` widgets in the column. We'll call it `labelStyle`:

```
final TextStyle labelStyle = TextStyle(
    fontSize: 24,
    color: Colors.grey[700],
);
```

3. We also want `Column` to take some distance from the horizontal device borders. So, instead of returning a `Center` widget, we can return `Container`, which takes a `padding` of 20 logical pixels. `EdgeInsets.symmetric` allows you to specify a value for the horizontal or vertical padding:

```
body: Container(
    padding: EdgeInsets.symmetric(horizontal: 20),
    child: Column(
```

4. And speaking of spacing, we want to create some space between the widgets in the column. A simple way of achieving this is using the **Spacer** widget: `Spacer` creates an empty space that can be used to set spacing between widgets in a flexible container, such as the `Column` in our interface. A `Spacer` widget has a `flex` property, whose default value is 1, which determines how much space we want to use. For instance, if you have two `Spacer` widgets, one with a `flex` property of 1, and another with a `flex` property of 2, the second will take double the space of the first. At the top of the `Column` let's add an initial `Spacer` widget:

```
child: Column(
    children: [
        Spacer(),
```

5. Under the `Spacer` widget, add the first text in the `Column` containing the `'Value'` string. We'll also apply `labelStyle` to this widget, and under `Text` we will place another `Spacer`:

```
Text(
    'Value',
    style: labelStyle,
),
Spacer(),
```

6. Under the `Text` that contains `'Value'` and its `Spacer`, we need to place the `TextField` that we previously created, to allow the user to input the number that they want to convert. Let's edit `TextField` so that it takes the `inputStyle` `TextStyle`. We'll also set the `decoration` property of the `TextField`.

 The `decoration` property of a `TextField` takes an `InputDecoration` object. `InputDecoration` allows you to specify the border, labels, icons, and styles that will be used to decorate a text field.

7. `hintText` is a piece of text that is shown when `TextField` is empty, to suggest which kind of input is expected from the user. In this case, add `"Please insert the measure to be converted"` as a `hintText` prompt for our `TextField`:

```
TextField(
    style: inputStyle,
    decoration: InputDecoration(
       hintText: "Please insert the measure to be converted",
    ),
    onChanged: (text) {
       var rv = double.tryParse(text);
       if (rv != null) {
          setState(() {
             _numberFrom = rv;
          });
       }
    },
),
```

8. Under `TextField`, place another `Spacer()`, then a `Text` with `'From'` and the `labelStyle` style:

```
Spacer(),
  Text(
    'From',
    style: labelStyle,
  ),
```

9. Under the `'From'` `Text`, place the `DropDownButton` widget, whose value is `_startMeasure`, which you wrote in the previous section:

```
DropdownButton(
    isExpanded: true,
    items: _measures.map((String value) {
        return DropdownMenuItem<String>(
            value: value,
            child: Text(value),
        );
    }).toList(),
    onChanged: (value) {
        setState(() {
            _startMeasure = value;
        });
    },
    value: _startMeasure,
),
```

10. Next, add another `Text` for the second dropdown: in this case, the `Text` will contain `'To'`, and the style will be `labelStyle`, as before:

```
Spacer(),
Text(
    'To',
    style: labelStyle,
),
```

11. Under the `'To'` `Text` we need to place the second `DropdownButton` widget, and this requires another class member: the first `DropdownButton` widget used `_startMeasure` for its value; this new one will use `_convertedMeasure`. **At the top of the** `MyAppState` **class,** add the following declaration:

```
String  _convertedMeasure;
```

12. Now, we are ready to add the second `DropDownButton` widget: this will contain the same measures list as the previous one. The only difference here is that it will reference the `_convertedMeasure` variable. As usual, don't forget to add a `Spacer()` before the widget:

```
Spacer(),
DropdownButton(
    isExpanded: true,
    style: inputStyle,
    items: _measures.map((String value) {
        return DropdownMenuItem<String>(
            value: value,
            child: Text(
                value,
                style: inputStyle,
            ),
        );
    }).toList(),
    onChanged: (value) {
        setState(() {
            _convertedMeasure = value;
        });
    },
    value: _convertedMeasure,
),
```

13. Next, add the button that will apply the conversion: it will be a `RaisedButton` with a `Text` of `'Convert'`, and the style of `inputStyle`. At this time, the `onPressed` event will do nothing, as we don't have the logic of the app ready yet. Before and after the button we'll place a `Spacer`, but this time, we will also set its `flex` property to 2. This way, the space between the button and the other widgets on screen will be twice the amount of the other spacers:

```
Spacer(flex: 2,),
    RaisedButton(
        child: Text('Convert', style: inputStyle),
        onPressed: () => true,
    ),
    Spacer(flex: 2,),
```

14. Finally, we'll add the `Text` for the result of the conversion. For now, let's just leave the `_numberFrom` value as `Text`; we'll change that in the next section. At the end of the result, we'll add the largest `Spacer` of this screen, with a `flex` value of `8`, in order to leave some space at the end of the screen:

```
Text((_numberFrom == null) ? '' : _numberFrom.toString(),
    style: labelStyle),
Spacer(flex: 8,),
```

15. There's one very last step that we need to perform before we complete the UI. On some devices, the UI that we have designed may be bigger than the available screen when the keyboard appears on screen. This may cause an error in your app. In order to solve this issue, there's a simple solution, which I recommend that you always use when designing your layouts with Flutter. You should put the `Column` widget into a scrollable widget, in this case, `SingleChileScrollView`. What this will do is make the widgets on the screen scroll if they take more space than is available on screen. So just enclose `Column` into a `SingleChildScrollView` widget like in the following example:

```
body: Container(
    padding: EdgeInsets.symmetric(horizontal: 20),
    child: SingleChildScrollView(
        child: Column(
            ...
        ),
    ),
```

If you try the app now, you should see the final look of the app, but other than for choosing values from the `DropdownButton` widgets, and adding some text to `TextField`, the screen doesn't do anything useful. Let's add the logic of the app next.

Adding the business logic

You have completed the layout of the app, but right now the app is missing the part that converts the values that are based on the user input.

Generally speaking, it's always a good idea to separate the logic of your apps from the UI, and there are great patterns in Flutter that help you achieve this result. You'll use some of those, such as `ScopedModel` and **Business Logic Components (BLoCs)**, in the following projects, but for now, we can just add the conversion functions into our class.

There are certainly several ways to write the code to perform the conversion between measures for this app. The approach that I find easiest is seeing the formulas that we need to apply as a two-dimensional array of values, also called a *matrix*. This matrix contains all the possible combinations of choices that the user can perform.

A diagram of this approach is shown here:

MEASURES	0 - Meters	1 - Kilometers	2 - Grams	3 - Kilograms	4 - Feet	5 - Miles	6 - Pounds	7 - Ounces
0 – Meters	1	0.0001	0	0	3.28084	0.00062	0	0
1 – Kilometers	1000	1	0	0	3280.84	0.62137	0	0
2 – Grams	0	0	1	0.0001	0	0	0.0022	0.03527
3 – Kilograms	0	0	1000	1	0	0	2.20462	35.274
4 – Feet	0.3048	0.0003	0	0	1	0.00019	0	0
5 – Miles	1609.34	1.60934	0	0	5280	1	0	0
6 – Pounds	0	0	453.592	0.45359	0	0	1	16
7 – Ounces	0	0	28.3495	0.02835	0	0	0.0625	1

So, for example, when you want to convert 100 kilometers into miles, you multiply 100 by the number that you find in the array (in this case, **0.621371**). It's a bit like playing Battleships. When the conversion is not possible, the multiplier is 0, so any impossible conversion returns 0.

As you might recall from Chapter 1, *Hello Flutter!*, in Dart we use List in order to create arrays. In this case, it's a two-dimensional array or matrix, and therefore we'll create an object that contains List's. Let's look at the steps:

1. We'll need to convert the Strings of the measure units into numbers. At the top of the MyAppState class, add the following code, using Map:

```
final Map<String, int> _measuresMap = {
  'meters' : 0,
  'kilometers' : 1,
  'grams' : 2,
  'kilograms' : 3,
  'feet' : 4,
  'miles' : 5,
```

```
    'pounds (lbs)' : 6,
    'ounces' : 7,
};
```

2. Maps allow you to insert key–value pairs, where the first element is the key, and the second is the value. When you need to retrieve a value from `Map`, you can use the following syntax:

```
myValue = measures['miles'];
```

The `myValue` variable will have a value of 5.

3. Next, we'll create a list that contains all of the multipliers that were shown in the previous diagram:

```
final dynamic _formulas = {
'0':[1,0.001,0,0,3.28084,0.000621371,0,0],
'1':[1000,1,0,0,3280.84,0.621371,0,0],
'2':[0,0,1,0.0001,0,0,0.00220462,0.035274],
'3':[0,0,1000,1,0,0,2.20462,35.274],
'4':[0.3048,0.0003048,0,0,1,0.000189394,0,0],
'5':[1609.34, 1.60934,0,0,5280,1,0,0],
'6':[0,0,453.592,0.453592,0,0,1,16],
'7':[0,0,28.3495,0.0283495,3.28084,0,0.0625, 1],
};
```

If you don't want to type this code, I've created a `Gist` file that contains the `Conversion` class. You'll find the full file at `https://gist.github.com/simoales/66af9a23235abcb537621e5bf9540bc6`.

4. Now that we have created a matrix that contains all of the possible combinations of conversion formulas, we only need to write the method that will convert the values using the formulas and the measures `Map`. Add the following code at the bottom of the `MyAppState` class:

```
void convert(double value, String from, String to) {
  int nFrom = _measuresMap[from];
  int nTo = _measuresMap[to];
  var multiplier = _formulas[nFrom.toString()][nTo];
  var result = value * multiplier;
}
```

The `convert()` method takes three parameters:

- The number that will be converted (*double value*)
- The unit of measure in which this value is currently expressed, as a `String` (*String from*)
- The unit of measure unit in which the value will be converted, also a `String` (*String to*)

For example, if you want to convert 10 meters into feet, 10 is the number, meters is the unit in which the value is currently expressed, and feet is the unit to which the number will be converted.

Let's see in detail how the `convert()` method has worked so far:

1. Inside the `convert()` method, you find the number associated with the `from` the measure:

   ```
   int nFrom = measures[from];
   ```

2. Then, you do the same with the `to` measure:

   ```
   int nTo = measures[to];
   ```

3. Next, you create a `multiplier` value that takes the correct conversion formula from the `formulas` matrix:

   ```
   var multiplier = formulas[nFrom.toString()][nTo];
   ```

4. Finally, you calculate the result of the conversion:

   ```
   double result = value * multiplier;
   ```

In this case, if the conversion is not possible, for example, when the user tries to convert a weight measure into a distance measure, this function does not raise any error.

Next, we need to show the result of the conversion to the user:

1. Declare a `String` variable at the top of the `MyAppState` class:

   ```
   String _resultMessage;
   ```

2. In the `convert()` method, after calculating the result, populate the `_resultMessage` String, and call the `setState()` method to notify the framework that an update to the UI is needed:

```
if (result == 0) {
    _resultMessage = 'This conversion cannot be performed';
  }
  else {
    _resultMessage = '${_numberFrom.toString()} $_startMeasure are
${result.toString()} $_convertedMeasure';
  }
  setState(() {
    _resultMessage = _resultMessage;
  });
```

3. Finally, we need to call the `convert()` method when the user taps on the **Convert** button. Before calling the method, we'll check that every value has been set to prevent potential errors. Edit `RaisedButton`, as shown here:

```
RaisedButton(
    child: Text('Convert', style: inputStyle),
    onPressed: () {
        if (_startMeasure.isEmpty || _convertedMeasure.isEmpty ||
_numberFrom==0) {
            return;
        }
        else {
            convert(_numberFrom, _startMeasure, _convertedMeasure);
        }
    },
),
```

4. In order to show the result, let's also update the `Text` widget, so that it shows the string that contains the message to the user:

```
Text((_resultMessage == null) ? '' : _resultMessage,
    style: labelStyle),
```

Congratulations, the app is now complete! If you try it out now, you should see a screen like the one shown here:

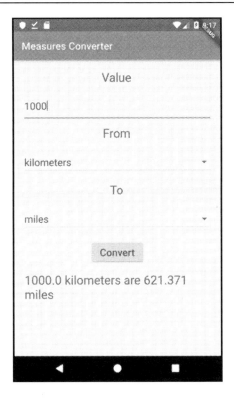

As you can see in the preceding screenshot, when we select two compatible measures, you should get the correct result on the screen.

Summary

In the project that you've built in this chapter, you've seen how to create interactive apps using State.

You've created a Stateless widget and transformed it into a stateful widget. In doing so, you've seen the different implementations between the two, and you've learned that in Flutter, widgets are immutable. It's the State that changes.

You have used two very important widgets, which help you to interact with the users: TextField and DropdownButton.

For TextField, you've used one of the possible ways to respond to the user input, which is using the onChanged() event, and from there, you called the setState() method, which updates the inner State of a widget.

You've seen how to add a `DropdownButton` widget to your apps, and also how to set the `items` property that will contain a list of `DropdownMenuItem` widgets to show to the user, and again, how to use the `onChanged` property to respond to the user input.

In other projects in this book, you'll see other, more efficient ways to deal with State in Flutter. In the next chapter, in particular, you'll see how to leverage streams of data in your apps in order to build a timer app.

Questions

At the end of each project, you'll find a few questions to help you remember and review the contents that have been covered in the chapter, and this chapter is no exception. Please try to answer the following questions, and when in doubt, have a look at the content in the chapter itself: you'll find all the answers there!

1. When should you use stateful widgets in your apps?
2. Which method updates the `State` of your class?
3. Which widget would you use to allow your user to select an option from a dropdown list?
4. Which widget would you use to allow your user to type some text?
5. Which event can you use when you want to react to some user input?
6. What happens when your widgets take more space than what's available on the screen? How do you solve this issue?
7. How can you get the width of the screen?
8. What is `Map` in Flutter?
9. How can you style your text?
10. How can you separate the logic of your apps from the UI?

Further reading

As Flutter is rapidly gaining momentum, you'll find a lot of articles and documents on the topics that we've touched in this project.

For padding, `EdgeInsets`, the box model, and layouts in general, the Flutter official documentation has a fantastic article to get you started at: `https://flutter.dev/docs/development/ui/layout`.

For `TextFields` **have a look at:** `https://flutter.dev/docs/cookbook/forms/text-input`.

For use cases of `DropdownButton` widgets, again the official documentation has a nice page at: `https://docs.flutter.io/flutter/material/DropdownButton-class.html`.

3

My Time - Listening to a Stream of Data

As you are reading this book, you are probably at war. It's a war with battles that happen daily and has an impact on the quality of your life. It's the war against distractions.

Right now, you may be tempted to check your email or have a look at social media, to listen to the people talking nearby or grab that snack waiting for you in the room nearby, or to have a quick look at your smartphone.

Well, please don't!

There are several studies showing that, if you want to be successful in your activities, you need to practice deep work. Deep work is in a state of concentration that allows you to maximize your cognitive capabilities. You can use deep work when you study a book such as this, when you learn a new language, or when you write an app—in short, whenever you need to perform work that creates value or improves your skills.

The definition of deep work comes from the bestselling book "Deep Work: Rules for Focused Success in a Distracted World," by Cal Newport.

There is a simple solution, and we will address that in the app that we'll be building in this chapter: you need to plan work and break time, and you have to stick to that plan. In this chapter, you'll build an app that will help you set the time intervals that work for you, and measure your work and break time. In fact, you'll be building a productivity app containing a countdown that tells you your remaining working or break time, with an animation on the screen. On a second screen, you'll also be able to set the duration of your work time, short break, and long breaks, and save them on your device.

By the end of this chapter, you'll know how to use Stream and `StreamBuilder`, add simple navigation to your apps, integrate external libraries in your Flutter projects, and use SharedPreferences to persist data.

It will be a good exercise in learning several important Flutter features that we haven't touched on so far, such as the following:

- Building a layout leveraging an external library
- Listening to data streams and using asynchronous programming
- Navigating from one screen to another in your app
- Using shared preferences to persist data in your device
- Using a GridView and choosing the right colors for your app

Following this project should take approximately 3 hours.

Technical requirements

You'll find the completed app code on the book's GitHub repository at `https://github.com/PacktPublishing/Google-Flutter-Projects`.

To follow along with the code examples in this book, you should have the following software installed on your Windows, Mac, Linux, or Chrome OS device:

- The Flutter software development kit (SDK).
- When developing for Android: the Android SDK, easily installed by Android Studio.
- When developing for iOS: macOS and Xcode.
- An emulator (Android), simulator (iOS), or a connected iOS or Android device enabled for debugging.
- An editor: **Visual Studio Code** (**VS Code**), Android Studio, or IntelliJ IDEA are recommended. All should have the Flutter/Dart extensions installed.

Building the timer home page layout

In the following screenshot, you can see the layout we will be building in this first part. In order to make it easier to understand what we need to do for this layout, I've added borders that show how the widgets will be placed on the screen:

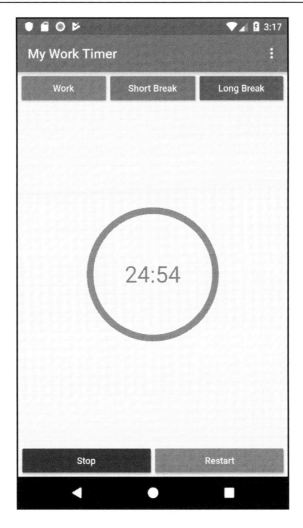

I believe the easiest way to build this layout is by using a combination of Column and Row widgets. The main container widget in this screen will be a column that will divide the space into three parts, as follows:

1. The three buttons at the top: **Work**, **Short Break**, and **Long Break**
2. The timer in the middle
3. The two buttons at the bottom: **Stop** and **Restart**

We will now create a new app that we'll use throughout this chapter to build the productivity timer, as follows:

1. From your favorite editor, create a new app.
2. Name the new app `productivity_timer`.
3. In the `main.dart` file, remove the example code.
4. Type the following code (If you want to save some time typing, I've created a gist on GitHub. It's a generic start for a basic Flutter app, which you can reuse whenever you start a new project. The link is `http://bit.ly/basic_flutter`.):

```dart
import 'package:flutter/material.dart';
void main() => runApp(MyApp());

class MyApp extends StatelessWidget {
@override
    Widget build(BuildContext context) {
        return MaterialApp(
            title: 'My Work Timer',
            theme: ThemeData(
        primarySwatch: Colors.blueGrey,
    ),
            home: Scaffold(
            appBar: AppBar(
                title: Text('My Work Timer'),
            ),
            body: Center(
                child: Text('My work Timer'),
            ),),
        );}
}
```

This code creates a basic `Scaffold`, which is the base layout for most of our screens, and puts a title in the `AppBar`—My Work Timer—and a Text at the center of the body (again, My Work Timer). The result should be similar to the following screenshot:

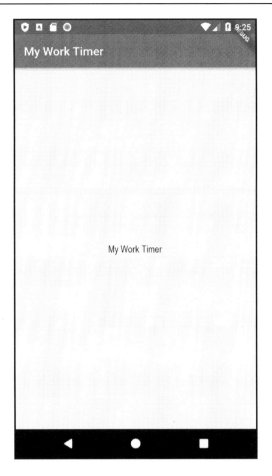

5. Next, instead of just returning a Text, let's create a class for the layout of the screen at the bottom of the `main.dart` file. Let's call it `TimerHomePage()`. If you are using VS Code, Android Studio, or IntelliJ IDEA, you can also use the `stless` shortcut to make the framework write part of your code. After the end of the `MyApp` class, just type `stless`.

6. As for the class name, let's choose `TimerHomePage`. The final result should be as follows:

```
class TimerHomePage extends StatelessWidget {
@override
Widget build(BuildContext context) {
 return Container();
 }
}
```

7. In the `build()` method, instead of returning a Container, we'll move the `Scaffold` from the `MyApp` class: in the `appBar`, we'll show the title of the app and in the body a Center widget containing a Column. Add the following code in the `TimerHomePage` class:

```
@override
  Widget build(BuildContext context) {
    return Scaffold(
      appBar: AppBar(
        title: Text('My work timer'),
      ),
      body: Center(
        child: Column(),),
    ); }
}
```

8. We can simplify the code on the `build()` method of the `MyApp` class by calling the new class we've just created, like this:

```
home: TimerHomePage(),
```

If you try the app right now, you should still see an empty screen, with the My Work Timer app bar title, just as before.

Now, we are ready to start placing the widgets on the screen. As we need to build five button widgets that will have very similar features, it might be a good idea to create a new class for those, in order to keep the rest of the code cleaner and save a bit of typing.

So, let's create a new file in the lib folder of the app, called `widgets.dart`, as follows:

1. Here, we'll create a new stateless widget called `ProductivityButton`. This will expose four fields: a `color`, a `text`, a `size`, and a `Callback` method, with a constructor that sets the values. The code for the widget is as follows:

```
import 'package:flutter/material.dart';
class ProductivityButton extends StatelessWidget {
  final Color color;
  final String text;
  final double size;
  final VoidCallback onPressed;

  ProductivityButton({@required this.color, @required this.text,
@required this.onPressed, @required this.size});
  @override
  Widget build(BuildContext context) {
    return MaterialButton(
```

```
        child:Text(
          this.text,
          style: TextStyle(color: Colors.white)),
        onPressed: this.onPressed,
        color: this.color,
        minWidth: this.size,
      );    }
  }
```

You may have noticed that the parameters are included in curly brackets ({ }) and have a @required annotation. This is because we are using named parameters here. The purpose of using named parameters is that when you call the function and pass values, you also specify the name of the parameter you are setting. For example, when creating an instance of ProductivityButton, you can use the syntax ProductivityButton(color: Colors.blueAccent, text: 'Hello World', onPressed: doSomething, size: 150). As named parameters are referenced by name, they can be used in any order.

Named parameters are optional, but you can annotate them with the @required annotation to indicate that the parameter is mandatory.

Now that we have created a generic button widget, we need to place a few instances of the button on the screen.

The top buttons should be placed on a single row at the top of the screen. They should take all the available horizontal space, save for some space for the margins, and they should vary their width based on the size and orientation of the screen.

2. Create a temporary empty method to have a method to pass to the buttons. We'll remove it later on. Add the following code at the bottom of the MyApp class:

```
void emptyMethod() {}
```

3. At the top of the MyApp class, let's declare a constant for the default padding we want to use in our screen, as follows:

```
final double defaultPadding = 5.0;
```

4. Now, let's place the top buttons on the screen: we'll need to use a Row widget here, and include it as the first element of the Column widget. In Flutter, it's actually possible to include Row widgets into Column widgets, and the opposite is also true.

We want the buttons to take all the available horizontal space. To achieve that, we'll use an Expanded widget that takes all the available space of a Column (or a Row) after placing the fixed elements. Each button will have a leading and trailing Padding, to create some space between the elements. Write the code to add the first three buttons to the screen, as follows:

```
body: Column(children: [
  Row(
    children: [
      Padding(padding: EdgeInsets.all(defaultPadding),),
      Expanded(child: ProductivityButton(color: Color(0xff009688),
        text: "Work", onPressed: emptyMethod)),
      Padding(padding: EdgeInsets.all(defaultPadding),),
      Expanded(child: ProductivityButton(color: Color(0xff607D8B),
        text: "Short Break", onPressed: emptyMethod)),
      Padding(padding: EdgeInsets.all(defaultPadding),),
      Expanded(child: ProductivityButton(color: Color(0xff455A64),
        text: "Long Break", onPressed: emptyMethod)),
      Padding(padding: EdgeInsets.all(defaultPadding),),
    ],
  ),
])
```

5. Try the app. The result of the preceding code should be similar to the following screenshot:

6. The timer should be placed in the middle of the screen and take all the remaining space after placing the top and bottom rows, which have a fixed size. For now, we'll just use a "Hello" Text as a placeholder, under the Column widget. Note that, in this case, Expanded is used in a column instead of the row, so it takes all the vertical available space, as illustrated in the following code snippet:

```
Expanded(child: Text("Hello")),
```

7. We'll then place the remaining two buttons, Stop and Restart, at the bottom of the screen, and they will also take all the horizontal space, except for some padding between them and the border of the screen, as illustrated in the following code block:

```
Row(children: [
    Padding(padding: EdgeInsets.all(defaultPadding),),
    Expanded(child: ProductivityButton(color: Color(0xff212121),
text: 'Stop', onPressed: emptyMethod)),
```

```
    Padding(padding: EdgeInsets.all(defaultPadding),),
    Expanded(child: ProductivityButton(color: Color(0xff009688),
text: 'Restart', onPressed: emptyMethod)),
    Padding(padding: EdgeInsets.all(defaultPadding),),
  ],)
```

8. The final result should look like the following screenshot:

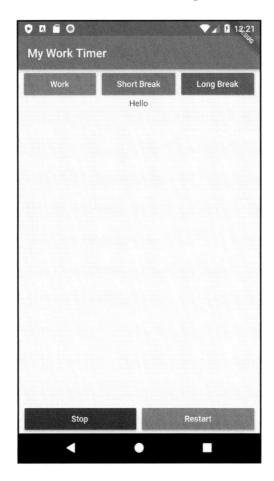

Now, you might wonder: where do these colors come from?

Personally, I'm not a designer, and it's sometimes difficult for me to choose the right colors for my apps, so I need a tool to guide me with the choice. There are several excellent tools that generate colors, but the one I use consistently—and, therefore, my suggestion for you, at least at the beginning—is the materialpalette.com website.

This tool allows you to choose two main colors for your layout, and it will automatically create for you the best combination of the two, giving the color codes you can use in your layouts. You can use it for any **User Interface** (UI) or website design.

For example, for the colors of the app we are building now, the colors are a combination of **BLUE GREY** and **TEAL**, as shown in the following screenshot:

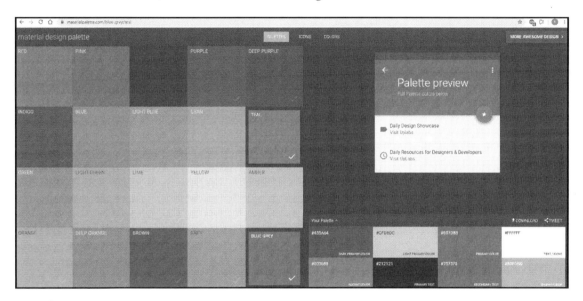

Now, we have completed the layout for the buttons of our app, but we still need to put the main content at the center of the screen, which is the timer itself. Let's add it to our layout next.

Installing the percent_indicator Package in your app

We need to place the Timer in the center of the screen, where the "Hello" Text is now showing. For this timer, we'll use the `CircularPercentIndicator` widget, which is included in the `percent_indicator` package, that you can get at `https://pub.dartlang.org/packages/percent_indicator`. This is a nice widget that makes it very easy to create circular and linear percent indicators in your apps.

In Flutter, packages are reusable bits of code generally developed by the community that you can include in your projects. Using packages, you can quickly build an app without having to develop everything from scratch.

The main site where you can look for packages is `https://pub.dev/flutter`.

We'll now use a procedure that is valid to install any package in your Flutter apps, as follows:

1. In order to use the `CircularPercentIndicator` package, from the `https://pub.dev/flutter` website, let's look for `percent_indicator`. The first result should be the package we need, which is the **percent_indicator** library, as shown in the following screenshot:

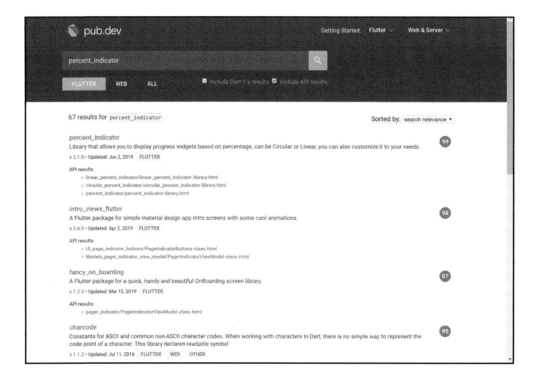

2. Click on the `library` link. The package page shows information and examples on how to install and use the package. In particular, for any package, we need to add the dependency in the `pubspec.yaml` configuration file.

3. Copy the dependency from the *Getting Started* section. At the time this book is written, it is `percent_indicator: "^2.1.1+1"`, but it might have changed when you read this.

4. Open the `pubspec.yaml` file in the root folder of your app. Every Flutter project has a file named `pubspec.yaml`, written in the YAML language. This is where you specify the required dependencies in your Flutter project.

5. Find the dependencies section and add the `percent_indicator` dependency under the Flutter SDK, as shown in the following code snippet:

```
dependencies:
  flutter:
    sdk: flutter
  percent_indicator: ^2.1.1+1
```

The `percent_indicator` dependency MUST be indented like the flutter dependency, as shown in the preceding code, as YAML files use indentation to represent relationships between layers.

6. Next, back in the `main.dart` file, let's add the `percent_indicator` import, as follows:

```
import 'package:percent_indicator/percent_indicator.dart';
```

7. Then, in the column, let's delete the "hello" text, and, in its place, let's use a `CircularPercentIndicator`. We'll include it in an `Expanded` widget so that it takes all the available vertical space in the column. The code is shown under bullet point 9.

8. A `CircularPercentIndicator` requires a `radius` property that represents the size of the circle, in logical pixels. We could certainly choose an arbitrary size, such as 200, but a better approach might be choosing a relative size that depends on the available space on the screen.

   In this case, we can use a `LayoutBuilder`. A `LayoutBuilder` provides the parent widget's constraints, so that you can find out how much space you have for your widgets.

9. In the body of the `Scaffold`, instead of returning a `Column`, let's return a `LayoutBuilder` in its builder method; we'll find the available width by calling the `maxWidth` property of the `BoxContraints` instance that was passed to the method and put it into an `availableWidth` constant, like this:

```
body: LayoutBuilder(builder: (BuildContext context, BoxConstraints
constraints) {
    final double availableWidth = constraints.maxWidth;
    return Column(children: [
```

10. Inside the `Column` widget, under the first row containing the Work and Break buttons, let's add a `CircularPercentIndicator`. The radius of the circle will be half of the `availableWidth`, and the `lineWidth` will be 10. If you like a thicker border, you can also try another value, such as 15, or even 20. The code is shown in the following snippet:

```
Expanded(
  child: CircularPercentIndicator(
  radius: availableWidth / 2,
  lineWidth: 10.0,
  percent: 1,
  center: Text("30:00",
  style: Theme.of(context).textTheme.display1),
  progressColor: Color(0xff009688),
  , ),
```

The layout of the main screen of our app is now ready. Now, we need to add the logic to make the timer actually count the time. This is what we're doing next.

Using a stream and asynchronous programming in Flutter

Until now in this book, you've seen two kinds of widgets: Stateless and Stateful. The State is what allows you to use data that can change over the lifetime of the widget. And, while this works perfectly in several cases, there are other ways to change data in your app, and one of those is using Streams.

Streams provide an asynchronous sequence of data.

The key concept here is that streams are asynchronous. This is a very powerful concept in programming. Asynchronous programming allows a piece of code to run separately from the main line of execution. That means that the execution of several tasks can run at the same time, instead of running sequentially.

Dart is a single-threaded programming language and uses Isolates to process multiple tasks at the same time.
An Isolate is a space in your app's thread, with its own private memory and line of execution.

In the following screenshot, you can see how secondary or background processes run parallel to the main process without blocking it: the main line of execution responds to the user inputs, deals with animations, builds widgets, and in general deals with the UI:

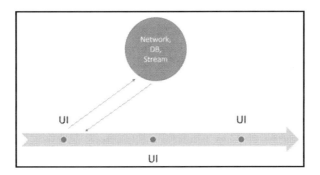

When a long-running operation, such as a network call, must be performed, this is executed in another line of execution, an Isolate in Dart. When the operation has finished running, the main Isolate receives a message, and deals with it as required.

Maybe a real-world example will make it a bit easier.

Example 1: Single-process programming

- You go to a nice restaurant; the waiter comes to your table and takes your order: a plate of spaghetti with pesto sauce.
- The waiter is also a cook, so he goes to the kitchen and prepares your dish. This takes 25 minutes.
- Meanwhile, other customers enter the restaurant.
- After the dish is ready, the waiter comes to your table and serves you the dish, which you eat with great satisfaction.
- The problem is that during the 25 minutes that were required to prepare your dish, the other customers in the restaurant were waiting, and could not place any order. So, some of them left, and some of them complained about the time it took them to place their orders.

Example 2: Asynchronous programming

- You go to a nice restaurant; the waiter comes to your table and takes your order: a plate of spaghetti with pesto sauce.
- The waiter gives the piece of paper on which they wrote your order to the kitchen, and the cook begins preparing your dish. This takes the waiter approximately 1 minute.

- Other customers enter the restaurant, and the waiter takes their orders and brings them to the kitchen.
- After 25 minutes, a bell rings from the kitchen, and the waiter comes to your table and serves you the dish, which you eat with great satisfaction.
- During the 25 minutes that were required to prepare your dish, the other customers in the restaurant placed their orders, and all of them were served within a reasonable amount of time.

The key in these two examples (which, of course, oversimplify the tasks involved in running a restaurant) is concurrency.

Concurrency happens when two or more tasks can start, run, and complete in overlapping time periods.

In our example, while the waiter was taking orders (main Isolate), the cook could prepare the dishes. The time of preparation does not change (it always takes 25 minutes), but the main execution line is always responding to the user requests, because long-running operations are executed in secondary Isolates.

When you have a long-running operation in your app, such as an HTTP connection or a database connection, you should always make it asynchronous. The logic behind that is that you may have a slow connection, so retrieving data could block your app for too long, or the time required to update your data might also take a long time, making your app unresponsive.

In Flutter, some tasks can only be performed asynchronously.

This is particularly important in mobile apps because if you run long operations in the main thread, your user would see the screen freezing, and they could not interact with your app in any way. And, after a few seconds, the operating system might give a message to the user, asking them if they want to keep waiting or close the app, and you really want to avoid this message.

In Flutter, you have two types of asynchronous results: a Future and a Stream. We'll talk about Futures later. A Stream is a sequence of results. So, going back to our previous example, a Stream is like a restaurant where plates keep coming to your table. Think of the belt carrying dishes in a sushi restaurant, or a Brazilian restaurant where dishes keep coming until you put a "stop" sign on your table.

Let's see the Stream in action in our app by executing the following steps:

1. Create a model for the `CircularPercentIndicator` that takes a text and a percentage: in the lib folder of our app, add a file called `timermodel.dart`.

2. In the `timermodel.dart` file, add a class called `TimerModel`, with two fields and a constructor that sets them both, as shown in the following code snippet:

```
class TimerModel {
  String time;
  double percent;

  TimerModel(this.time, this.percent);
}
```

3. Next, create a new file in the lib folder of the app, called `timer.dart`, and type the following code:

```
import 'dart:async';
import './timermodel.dart';

class CountDownTimer {
  double _radius = 1;
  bool _isActive = true;
  Timer timer;
  Duration _time;
  Duration _fullTime;
}
```

In the preceding code, we are creating a new class, called `CountDownTimer`, with five fields: `_radius` is what we'll use to express the percentage of completed time; the `_isActive` Boolean will tell us if the counter is active or not. When the user presses the stop button, it will become inactive.

A Timer is a class that you can use to create countdown timers. We have created a Timer called `timer`. Then, there are two Duration fields: `_time`, which we'll use to express the remaining time, and `_fulltime`, which is the beginning time (a short break, for instance—maybe 5 minutes).

4. Before returning the time that will be shown in the `CircularProgressIndicator`, we need to perform some formatting. In the `CountDownTimer`, let's create a function to do that, as follows:

```
String returnTime(Duration t) {
    String minutes = (t.inMinutes<10) ? '0' +
t.inMinutes.toString() :
     t.inMinutes.toString();
    int numSeconds = t.inSeconds - (t.inMinutes * 60);
    String seconds = (numSeconds < 10) ? '0' +
numSeconds.toString() :
```

```
      numSeconds.toString();
   String formattedTime = minutes + ":" + seconds;
   return formattedTime;
}
```

Duration is a Dart class used to contain a span of time. What happens in the preceding code is that the Duration that's passed to the function gets transformed into a String, with two digits for the minutes and two digits for the seconds, for example, "05:42".

With the `inMinutes` property, we get the minutes, and with the `inSeconds`, the total seconds in a Duration object. We make sure that, if minutes or seconds have only one digit, we add a "0" before the number, and then concatenate the two values with a ":" sign. At the end of the function, we return the formatted string.

5. Under the fields, let's create the `stream()` method. The asterisk (*) after async is used to say that a Stream is being returned, as shown in the following code block:

```
Stream<TimerModel> stream() async* {
   yield* Stream.periodic(Duration(seconds: 1), (int a) {
     String time;
     if (this._isActive) {
       _time = _time - Duration(seconds: 1);
       _radius = _time.inSeconds / _fullTime.inSeconds;
       if (_time.inSeconds <= 0) {
         _isActive = false;
       }
     }
     time = returnTime(_time);
     return TimerModel(time, _radius);
   });
}
```

The `stream()` method returns a Stream.

A Stream is generic, meaning that you can return a Stream of any type. In this case, we are returning a Stream of `TimerModel`. The method is asynchronous (async*). In Flutter, you use async (without the * sign) for Futures and async* (with the * sign) for Streams.

What's the difference between a Stream and a Future? It's that any number of events can be returned in a Stream, whereas a Future only returns once.

When you mark a function `async*`, you are creating a generator function.

6. You use the `yield*` statement to deliver a result. To make it simple, it's like a return statement, but it doesn't end the function. As stated previously, you use the "*" sign after yield because we are returning a Stream; if it were a single value, you would just use yield. The code can be seen in the following snippet:

```
yield* Stream.periodic(Duration(seconds: 1), (int a) {
```

`Stream.periodic()` is a constructor creating a Stream that emits events at the intervals specified in the first parameter. In our code, this will emit a value every 1 second.

7. Then, we declare a String called `time` and check whether the `_isActive` field is true, as follows:

```
String time;
if (this._isActive) {
```

If it is, we decrease the value of time by 1 second (it's a countdown, after all), like this:

```
_time = _time - Duration(seconds: 1);
```

8. Next, we also update the `_radius` value. This is the remaining time divided by the total time, as follows:

```
_radius = _time.inSeconds / _fullTime.inSeconds;
```

This value goes from 1, at the beginning of the countdown, to 0 at the end of the countdown.

9. Next, we check whether the `_time` field got down to 0, and, if it did, we change the value of `_isActive` to false to stop the countdown, as follows:

```
if (_time.inSeconds <= 0) {
    _isActive = false;
}
```

We call the `returnTime` method to transform the remaining Duration into a String, like this:

```
time = returnTime(_time);
```

Finally, we return a `TimerModel` object containing the time String and the `_radius` double, like this:

```
return TimerModel(time, _radius);
```

So, this function returns a Stream of `TimerModel`, decrementing the Duration every second.

Next, we need a way to start the timer and show the result in the main view.

Showing the time in the main screen: StreamBuilder

Right now, our main screen never changes, so what we need to do is show the countdown to the user, and also make sure the user can start and stop the timer whenever they need, as follows:

1. We'll begin by creating the function that will count the work time. For now, we want the work time to be 30 minutes (we'll make this editable later in this chapter). So, first, in the `CountDownTimer` class in the timer.dart file, create a field called work and set it to 30. This is the default number of minutes for the work time, and is shown in the following code snippet:

```
int work = 30;
```

2. Next, still in the `CountDownTimer` class, create a void function that will set the `_time` duration to the number of minutes contained in the work variable, and the same for the `_fullTime` field, as follows:

```
void startWork() {
  _radius = 1;
  _time = Duration(minutes: this.work, seconds: 0);
  _fullTime = _time;
}
```

3. The `startWork()` method should be called from the main screen when it loads. So, let's get back to the `main.dart` file, and import the `timer.dart file`, as follows:

```
import './timer.dart';
```

4. Then, at the top of the `MyApp` class, create a `CountDownTimer` variable called timer, like this:

```
final CountDownTimer timer = CountDownTimer();
```

5. At the top of the `build()` method of `MyApp`, call the `startWork()` method, like this:

```
timer.startWork();
```

6. Now, we can access the timer properties—time and radius—and show them on the screen: in the `CircularPercentIndicator` in the Column in the `build()` method, add the following code:

```
return Expanded(
    child: CircularPercentIndicator(
        radius: availableWidth / 2,
        lineWidth: 10.0,
        percent: timer.percent,
        center: Text( timer.time,
            style: Theme.of(context).textTheme.headline4),
        progressColor: Color(0xff009688),
));
```

If you try the app right now, you should see the timer, but the countdown is not active. That's because we are still missing an important part of the Stream, which is the `StreamBuilder`. This is what you need to use when you want to listen to events that come from Streams.

A `StreamBuilder` rebuilds its children at any change in the Stream.

Let's use it in our app, including the `Expanded` widget into a `StreamBuilder`, as follows:

1. We'll set some `initialData` to have the builder show something while it's waiting for data coming from the stream.
2. Then, we'll set the stream itself that we've created in the `TimerModel` class.
3. Finally, we need to set a builder: this takes a context and a snapshot of type `AsyncSnapshot`, and the child is what gets rebuilt every time some data comes from the stream. An `AsyncSnapshot` contains the data of the most recent interaction with a `StreamBuilder` (or a FutureBuilder).

Wrap the `CircularPercentIndicator` into a `StreamBuilder`, as shown in the following code block:

```
child: StreamBuilder(
    initialData: '00:00',
    stream: timer.stream(),
    builder: (BuildContext context, AsyncSnapshot snapshot) {
        TimerModel timer = (snapshot.data == '00:00') ? TimerModel('00:00',
            1) : snapshot.data;
            return Expanded(
                child: CircularPercentIndicator(
                radius: availableWidth / 2,
                lineWidth: 10.0,
                percent: timer.percent,
                center: Text( timer.time,
                    style: Theme.of(context).textTheme.headline4),
                progressColor: Color(0xff009688),
        ));
    })),
```

In the preceding code, note that the snapshot contains a `data` property: this is what was received from the yield* in the `stream()` method of the `CountDownTimer` class, which returned a `TimerModel` object.

If you try the app right now, the timer should work correctly. However, while the timer is working, the user cannot interact with our app right now. We need to respond when our user taps on one of the buttons. Let's add interactivity to our app next.

Enabling the buttons

First, let's make the **start** and **stop** buttons work. In order to do that, let's get back to the `timer.dart` file using the following steps:

1. Add a new `void` method, called `stopTimer`. This will only set the `_isActive` variable to false, as follows:

```
void stopTimer() {
  this._isActive = false;
  }
```

2. Next, let's write another method called `startTimer` that will check whether the remaining time is bigger than 0 seconds, and will set the `_isActive` Boolean to true, as follows:

```
void startTimer() {
    if (_time.inSeconds > 0) {
       this._isActive = true;
    }
  }
```

3. Finally, in the `main.dart` file, let's call these two new methods from the Start and Stop buttons, like this:

```
Expanded(
    child: ProductivityButton(
       color: Color(0xff212121),
       text: 'Stop',
       onPressed: () => timer.stopTimer())),
Padding(
    padding: EdgeInsets.all(defaultPadding),
),
Expanded(
    child: ProductivityButton(
       color: Color(0xff009688),
       text: 'Restart',
       onPressed: () => timer.startTimer())),
```

If you try the app now, you'll be able to stop and start the timer at will.

Now, let's deal with the upper buttons. We need to make 'Work', 'Short Break', and 'Long Break' buttons available to the user. Temporarily, we will hardcode the duration of the three buttons, but later in this chapter, we'll give the user the power to set the values. Let's look at the steps to do just that here:

1. In the `timer.dart` file, in the `CountDownTimer` class, let's declare two more variables for the times of the short and long breaks, as follows:

```
int shortBreak = 5;
int longBreak = 20;
```

2. Then, let's add a method for the short and long breaks, as shown in the following code snippet:

```
void startBreak(bool isShort) {
    _radius = 1;
    _time = Duration(
        minutes: (isShort) ? shortBreak: longBreak,
        seconds: 0);
    _fullTime = _time;
}
```

3. In the `main.dart` file, let's add the correct method to the three top buttons, as follows:

```
Expanded(
    child: ProductivityButton(
        color: Color(0xff009688),
        text: "Work",
        onPressed: () => timer.startWork())),
Padding(
        padding: EdgeInsets.all(defaultPadding),
),
Expanded(
    child: ProductivityButton(
        color: Color(0xff607D8B),
        text: "Short Break",
        onPressed: () => timer.startBreak(true))),
Padding(
    padding: EdgeInsets.all(defaultPadding),
),
Expanded(
    child: ProductivityButton(
        color: Color(0xff455A64),
        text: "Long Break",
        onPressed:() => timer.startBreak(false))),
```

Note that the `onPressed` parameter takes a function as its value. This is because, in Dart and Flutter, you can pass a function as a parameter, in a constructor or any other method.

If you try the app right now, you'll notice that all the main functions work correctly! Now, we only need to make the user choose their work and break times, and save them in the device memory. For that, we need a Settings screen, which we'll build in the next section.

Navigating to the settings route

Right now, our app is working, but there is no way for the user to change the time settings for the timer. There might be some people for whom 15 minutes is the maximum working time, or, for some tasks, 90 minutes might be better. So, in this part, we'll build a Settings screen for our app, where the user will be able to set the time chunks that work better for them. And, in building this part of the app, you'll learn one simple and effective way to save data onto a device with Flutter.

At the end of this part, the Settings screen will look like the following screenshot:

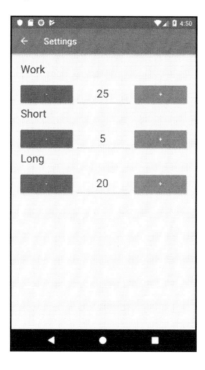

So, let's add a new file in the lib folder of our app and call it settings.dart, proceeding as follows:

1. We'll create a **SettingsScreen** StatelessWidget that, in the build() method, will return a Scaffold, with an AppBar whose title will be 'Settings', and a Container with a 'Hello World' Text that we'll use as a placeholder for now, as illustrated in the following code block:

```
import 'package:flutter/material.dart';
class SettingsScreen extends StatelessWidget {
 @override
 Widget build(BuildContext context) {
    return Scaffold(
        appBar: AppBar(title: Text('Settings'),),
        body:Container(
            child: Text('Hello World'),
        ));
    }
}
```

2. Right now, there's no way to reach the Settings route, so we need to add a function to open it from the main screen.

 In Flutter, screens or pages are called routes. We'll use the terms as synonyms in this book.

In order to do that, let's get back to the main.dart file, and, in the build() method of the TimerHomePage class, let's add the following code:

```
final List<PopupMenuItem<String>> menuItems =
List<PopupMenuItem<String>>();
 menuItems.add(PopupMenuItem(
 value: 'Settings',
 child: Text('Settings'),
 ));
```

In Flutter, a PopupMenuButton displays a menu when pressed. In its itemBuilder property, it can show a List of PopupMenuItems. That's why, in this portion of code, we have created a List of PopupMenuItems, even if the menu is just one at this time.

3. In order to make the `PopupMenuButton` show in the screen, add it to the `AppBar` in the `Scaffold,` like this:

```
appBar: AppBar(
    title: Text('My Work Timer'),
    actions: [
        PopupMenuButton<String>(
            itemBuilder: (BuildContext context) {
                return menuItems.toList();
            },
```

In the following screenshot, you can see a `PopupMenuButton` before and after clicking on it:

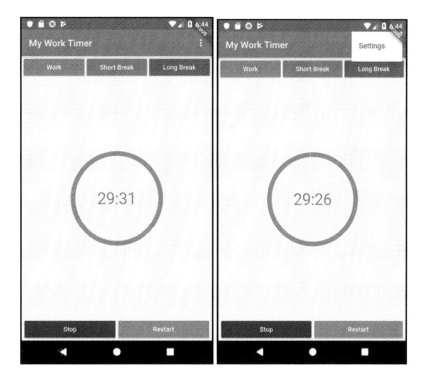

4. Next, let's create a `goToSettings` method: this is the method that actually navigates to the Settings route.

Navigation in Flutter is based on a **stack**. A stack contains the screens that an app has built from the beginning of its execution. Whenever you need to change the screen in a Flutter app, you can use the Navigator object.

Navigator has several methods that interact with the stack, but we only need to worry about two for now: the push() method and the pop() method. The push() method puts a new page at the top of the stack. The pop() method removes the page at the top of the stack so that the previous screen on your stack becomes visible again.

When you use the push() method, you need to specify a route, which is the screen you want to load. For that purpose, you use the MaterialPageRoute class, in which you specify the name of the page you want to push. Both push() and pop() require the current context.

Let's understand the navigation flow using images, with the push() and pop() methods:

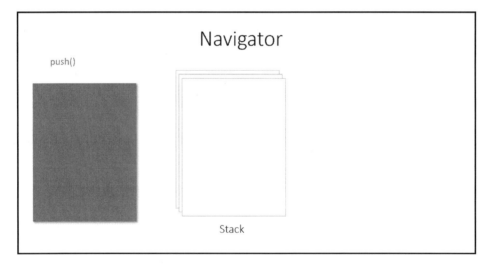

When you call the push() method of the navigator, the new route or screen gets to the top of the navigation stack, as shown in the following screenshot:

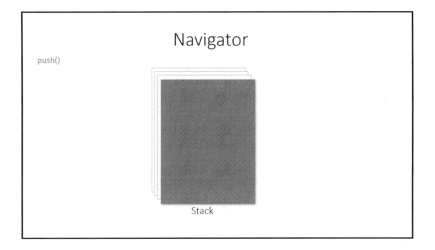

The pop() method removes the screen from the navigation stack, as shown in the following screenshot:

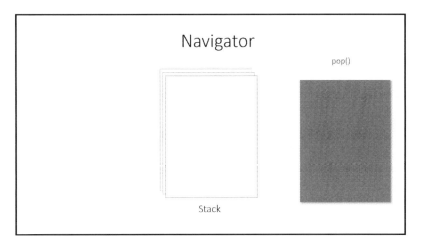

5. Moving back to our code, let's write the goToSettings() method, as shown in the following code snippet:

```
void goToSettings(BuildContext context) {
 Navigator.push(
 context, MaterialPageRoute(builder: (context) =>
SettingsScreen()));
 }
```

6. Don't forget to import the `settings.dart` file, as follows:

```
import 'settings.dart';
```

7. Then, in the `appBar` of the `Scaffold`, let's add the actions that will specify a `PopupMenuButton` with the `itemBuilder` containing our `menuItems`, as follows:

```
actions: [
    PopupMenuButton<String>(
        itemBuilder: (BuildContext context) {
            return menuItems.toList();
        },
        onSelected: (s) {
            if(s=='Settings') {
                goToSettings(context);
            }
        }
    )
],
```

Now, if you try the app, you can actually navigate from one screen to the other!

Next, we will create the layout of the Settings screen.

Building the Settings screen layout

The settings for this app will need to keep the state, so let's create a stateful widget called Settings. If you are using one of the supported editors (VS Code, IntelliJ IDEA, or Android Studio), you can just type the `stful` shortcut to save some typing: this will create the boilerplate code for a new stateful widget.

In the `settings.dart` file, at the end of the file, type `stful` and type `Settings` as the name of the widget, as shown in the following code block:

```
class Settings extends StatefulWidget {
  @override
  _SettingsState createState() => _SettingsState();
}

class _SettingsState extends State<Settings> {
  @override
  Widget build(BuildContext context) {
    return Container(

    );
```

```
    }
  }
```

In the settings page, in the next section, we will add a GridView to the Settings screen to build the UI.

Using the GridView.Count() constructor

We could use a combination of Row and Column widgets to build this screen, but we'll use a new widget here: it's the GridView.

A GridView is a scrollable, 2D array of widgets, and you can use it to show some data to your users in a tabular form.

Possible use cases for the GridView include a picture gallery, a table of songs, a list of movies, and many others. The GridView is scrollable, and has two dimensions: in other words, it's a scrollable table. It can scroll horizontally or vertically. There are several constructors for the GridView that cover several different use cases, but, for this app, we will use the GridView.Count() constructor. You can use it when you know the number of items that the grid will show on the screen, as follows:

```
class _SettingsState extends State<Settings> {
  @override
  Widget build(BuildContext context) {
    return Container(
      child: GridView.count(
        scrollDirection: Axis.vertical,
        crossAxisCount: 3,
        childAspectRatio: 3,
        crossAxisSpacing: 10,
        mainAxisSpacing: 10,
        children: <Widget>[],
        padding: const EdgeInsets.all(20.0),
      )
    );
  }
}
```

The first property that we set is the scroll direction, which is Axis.Vertical. This means that, if the content of the GridView is bigger than the available space, the content will scroll vertically.

Then, we set the `crossAxisCount` property: as we're scrolling vertically, this is the number of items that will appear on each row. The `childAspectRatio` property determines the size of the children in the GridView. The value represents the `itemWidth` / `itemHeight` ratio. In this case, by setting 3, we are saying that the width must be three times the height.

As there's no space between the children of a GridView by default, we can add some spacing for the main axis, using the `mainAxisSpacing` parameter, and giving it a value of 10.

You could do the same for the cross-axis as well, again with a value of 10. And to complete this example, we've added some padding taking an `EdgeInsets.all` of 20.

Adding custom SettingButtons to the widgets.dart file

As we did for the `ProductivityButton`, in order to avoid unnecessary code duplication, we can create a button that we can reuse several times within the Settings screen. This button has some properties that are different from the `ProductivityButton`, so we'll create a new widget using the following steps:

1. In the `widgets.dart` file, let's create a new stateless widget called `SettingButton`, like this:

   ```
   class SettingButton extends StatelessWidget {
     @override
     Widget build(BuildContext context) {
       return Container(
       );
     }
   }
   ```

   This class will have a few properties that we will use in the constructor method, as follows:

   ```
   final Color color;
   final String text;
   final int value;
   SettingsButton(this.color, this.text, this.value);
   ```

2. Next, instead of returning a Container, we'll return a `MaterialButton` that will use the properties that were set in the constructor, as follows:

   ```
   return MaterialButton(
     child:Text(
   ```

```
    this.text,
    style: TextStyle(color: Colors.white)),
    onPressed: () => null,
    color: this.color,
    );
  }
```

For now, the method in the onPressed property just returns null, but we will change that later.

1. Let's get back to the settings.dart file, so that we can place it in the GridView.

2. At the top of the build() method of the SettingsState class in the settings.dart file, let's create a TextStyle that we will use to specify the font size, as follows:

```
    TextStyle textStyle = TextStyle(fontSize: 24);
```

3. Next, in the children parameter of the GridView.count() constructor, let's insert all the widgets we need to place on the screen, as follows:

```
    children: <Widget>[
      Text("Work", style: textStyle),
      Text(""),
      Text(""),
      SettingsButton(Color(0xff455A64), "-", -1),
      TextField(
          style: textStyle,
          textAlign: TextAlign.center,
          keyboardType: TextInputType.number),
      SettingsButton((0xff009688), +", 1,),
      Text("Short", style: textStyle),
      Text(""),
      Text(""),
      SettingsButton(Color(0xff455A64), "-", -1, ),
      TextField(
          style: textStyle,
          textAlign: TextAlign.center,
          keyboardType: TextInputType.number),
      SettingsButton(Color(0xff009688), "+", 1),
      Text("Long", style: textStyle,),
      Text(""),
      Text(""),
      SettingsButton(Color(0xff455A64), "-", -1,),
      TextField(
          style: textStyle,
          textAlign: TextAlign.center,
          keyboardType: TextInputType.number),
```

```
        SettingsButton(Color(0xff009688), "+", 1,),
    ],
```

4. When you create a GridView, each cell has the same size. As we set the `crossAxisCount` property to 3, for each row of the grid there are three elements: in the first row, we just place three texts, one containing "Work", and two empty. The two empty texts are just to make sure that the following widget will end up in the second row:

```
Text("Work", style: textStyle),
Text(""),
Text(""),
```

In the second row, we have two buttons and a TextField.

A Textfield is a widget that you can use to interact with your users, as they can enter text with a hardware keyboard or with an onscreen keyboard, and you can then read the values that they typed.

5. This pattern is repeated for the next rows: basically, we use this screen to read and write three time settings: the work time, the short break time, and the long break time, as illustrated in the following code block:

```
SettingButton(Color(0xff455A64), "-", -1),
TextField(
    style: textStyle,
    textAlign: TextAlign.center,
    keyboardType: TextInputType.number),
SettingButton(Color(0xff009688), "+", 1,),
```

6. Finally, let's call the `Settings()` widget from the `build()` method of the `SettingsScreen` widget: instead of returning a Container, we'll return our Settings class, as follows:

```
return  Scaffold(
    appBar: AppBar(
        title: Text('Settings'),
    ),
    body: Settings()
);
```

7. If you try the app right now, the Settings screen should look like the following screenshot:

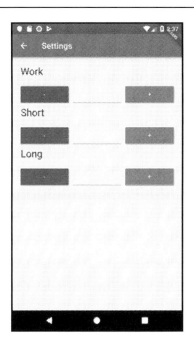

Now that we have the layout for the second screen, we need to add the logic, as we want to read and write the settings of our app.

Using shared_preferences to read and write app data

There are several ways to save data onto a mobile device: you can persist data to a file, or you can use a local database, such as SQLite, or you can use SharedPreferences (on Android) or NSUserDefaults (on iOS).

 shared_preferences should not be used for critical data as data stored there is not encrypted, and writes are not always guaranteed.

When using Flutter, you can take advantage of the `shared_preferences` library: it wraps both NSUserDefaults and SharedPreferences so that you can store simple data seamlessly in both iOS and Android without dealing with the specifics of the two operating systems.

Data is always persisted to disk asynchronously when you use `shared_preferences`.

SharedPreferences is an easy way to persist key-value data on disk. You can only store primitive data: int, double, bool, String, and stringList.

SharedPreference data is saved within the app, so, when the user uninstalls your app, the data will also be deleted.

It's not designed to store a lot of data, but, for our app, this tool is perfect. We will also see other different methods to deal with data in later chapters.

We need to include SharedPreferences in our project. So, in the `pubspec.yaml` file, let's add the dependency, as follows:

```
shared_preferences: ^0.5.6+2
```

The version number may vary when you read this book, so have a look at the library page to use the correct version, at `https://pub.dev/packages/shared_preferences`.

When you want to add a dependency in the pubspec.yaml file, you use the following syntax: package_name: version_number.
A version number is three numbers separated by dots,such as 1.2.34. It can also have an optional build (+1, +2) at the end.
The caret sign "^" is used to tell the framework that any version from the specified version up to (but not including) the next major build is allowed. For example, ^1.2.34 allows any version below 2.0.0.

Then, we need to include the library in the settings.dart file, by running the following code:

```
import 'package:shared_preferences/shared_preferences.dart';
```

Before getting into the specifics of using SharedPreferences, we need a way to read data from the TextFields when the user changes value, and write to the TextField when we load the screen and need to read from the SharedPreferences. When using TextFields, an effective way of reading and writing data is using a `TextEditingController`. Let's look at the steps:

1. Add the following code at the top of the `_SettingState` class:

```
TextEditingController txtWork;
TextEditingController txtShort;
TextEditingController txtLong;
```

2. Next, override the `InitState()` method to set the new `TextEditingControllers`, as follows:

```
@override
 void initState() {
    TextEditingController txtWork = TextEditingController();
    TextEditingController txtShort = TextEditingController();
    TextEditingController txtLong = TextEditingController();
    super.initState();
 }
```

Here, we are creating the objects that will allow us to read from and write to the TextField widgets.

Next, let's add the `TextEditingController` to the relevant TextFields, and we'll do that using the controller property of the three TextFields we have created before in the `build()` method, as follows:

1. So, we'll add the controller to the TextField of the work time, like this:

```
controller: txtWork,
```

2. Then, we do the same for the TextField of the short break, as follows:

```
controller: txtShort,
```

3. Finally, we add the controller to the TextField of the long break, like this:

```
controller: txtLong,
```

4. At the top of the `_SettingState` class, let's create the constants and variables that we'll use to interact with `shared_preferences`, as follows:

```
static const String WORKTIME = "workTime";
static const String SHORTBREAK = "shortBreak";
static const String LONGBREAK = "longBreak";
int workTime;
int shortBreak;
int longBreak;
```

5. Let's also create a variable for the SharedPreferences, still at the beginning of the `_SettingState` class, like this:

```
SharedPreferences prefs;
```

Next, we'll need to create two methods: the first one will read from shared_preferences, and the second will write any change the user makes.

Let's begin by reading the settings, as follows:

1. After the `build()` method of the `_SettingState` class, let's add a method called `readSettings()`, as illustrated in the following code block:

```
readSettings() async {
  prefs = await SharedPreferences.getInstance();
  int workTime = prefs.getInt(WORKTIME);
  int shortBreak = prefs.getInt(SHORTBREAK);
  int longBreak = prefs.getInt(LONGBREAK);
  setState(() {
  txtWork.text = workTime.toString();
  txtShort.text = shortBreak.toString();
  txtLong.text = longBreak.toString();
  });
  }
```

This will be asynchronous (async).

Asynchronous operations return Future objects (futures), which is something to be completed at a later time. To suspend execution until a Future completes, we use await in an async function.

`SharedPreferences.getInstance()` is asynchronous, so we can use the await statement to make sure prefs gets instantiated before the next lines of code are executed.

2. When we call `prefs.getInt(KEY)`, we are calling a method that returns an integer from the SharedPreferences—in particular, the integer that, as a key, has the value we pass as an argument. So, if we have a key called "work" and a value of 25, this function will return 25. If there is no value at the key you've passed, this function will return null.

We repeat this for all the values we want to store for the settings. Then, we update the state of the class by changing the text property of the textControllers.

In short, this function reads the values of the settings from SharedPreferences, and then it writes the values in the textFields.

3. Now, under the `readSettings` method, let's also create the method that writes the settings. We'll call it `updateSettings()`, as illustrated in the following code block:

```
void updateSetting(String key, int value) {
switch (key) {
```

```
            case WORKTIME:
              {
                int workTime = prefs.getInt(WORKTIME);
                workTime += value;
                if (workTime >= 1 && workTime <= 180) {
                  prefs.setInt(WORKTIME, workTime);
                  setState(() {
                    txtWork.text = workTime.toString();
      });
                }
              }
            break;
            case SHORTBREAK:
              {
                int short = prefs.getInt(SHORTBREAK);
                short += value;
                if (short >= 1 && short <= 120) {
                  prefs.setInt(SHORTBREAK, short);
                  setState(() {
                    txtShort.text = short.toString();
                  });
                }
              }
            break;
            case LONGBREAK:
              {
                int long = prefs.getInt(LONGBREAK);
                long += value;
                if (long >= 1 && long <= 180) {
                  prefs.setInt(LONGBREAK, long);
                  setState(() {
                    txtLong.text = long.toString();
                  });
                }
              }
            break;
          }
        }
```

The updateSettings() method takes two parameters: a key and a value. We want the user to update the value by clicking the + and - buttons on the screen, so the value will be 1 for the + button or -1 for the – button.

The key will be one of the constants we've declared at the top of the class. This method reads the value of the key that was passed and adds the value (+1 or -1). The following code reads the saved work time and adds `value` to it:

```
int workTime = prefs.getInt(WORKTIME);
workTime += value;
```

Next, you check whether `workTime` is within the accepted range (between 1 and 180 minutes):

```
if (workTime >= 1 && workTime <= 180)
```

The code updates the key that was passed and also updates the text property of the text controller, as follows:

```
prefs.setInt(WORKTIME, workTime);
    setState(() {
        txtWork.text = workTime.toString();
});
```

We then repeat the same steps for the other two settings: shortBreak and longBreak.

Now, the question is: when do we call those two methods?

When the screen is shown, we need to read the values immediately, as we want to show them in the TextFields. So, let's call `readSettings()` in the `initState()` method, before calling `super.initState()`, as follows:

```
@override
  void initState() {
    txtWork = TextEditingController();
    txtShort = TextEditingController();
    txtLong = TextEditingController();
    readSettings();
    super.initState();
  }
```

If everything is working as it should, the TextFields now contain the values (null the first time you try the app).

We want to update the settings every time the user changes the value pressing one of the + or - buttons. This should change the values in the relevant TextField and also update the setting in SharedPreferences.

When we press any of the buttons, a method should then be called, updating the right TextField and setting. And, in order to achieve this goal, we need to tweak our `SettingButton` widget.

Let's get back to the `widgets.dart` file and perform the following steps:

1. Before the class definition, let's also create a pointer to a function, like this:

   ```
   typedef CallbackSetting = void Function(String, int);
   ```

   In Dart, `typedef` can be used as a pointer that references a function. This is because we want to call the function, with the correct parameters, from the relevant button.

2. Now, let's tweak the `SettingButton` widget, adding two new parameters: setting and callback.

3. The updated `SettingsButton` looks like this:

   ```
   class SettingsButton extends StatelessWidget {
     final Color color;
     final String text;
     final double size;
     final int value;
     final String setting;
     final CallbackSetting callback;
     SettingButton(this.color, this.text, this.size, this.value,
   this.setting, this.callback);
     @override
     Widget build(BuildContext context) {
       return MaterialButton(
           child:Text(
             this.text,
             style: TextStyle(color: Colors.white)),
           onPressed: () => this.callback(this.setting, this.value),
           color: this.color,
           minWidth: this.size,
         );
     }
   ```

   Note that now, the `onPressed` property contains the callback of the method that gets passed, with the setting and value parameters. This is a very powerful approach that allows you to pass methods as parameters, including their arguments.

4. Now, let's actually fix the creation of the `SettingButton` widgets in the `settings.dart` file, like this:

```
SettingButton(Color(0xff455A64), "-", buttonSize, -1, WORKTIME,
updateSetting ),
SettingButton(Color(0xff009688), "+", buttonSize, 1, WORKTIME,
updateSetting),
SettingButton(Color(0xff455A64), "-", buttonSize, -1, SHORTBREAK,
updateSetting),
SettingButton(Color(0xff009688), "+", buttonSize, 1, SHORTBREAK,
updateSetting),
SettingButton(Color(0xff455A64), "-", buttonSize, -1,LONGBREAK,
updateSetting),
SettingButton(Color(0xff009688), "+", buttonSize, 1, LONGBREAK,
updateSetting),
```

If you try the app right now, you'll realize that we have an issue we still need to solve, as shown in the following screenshot:

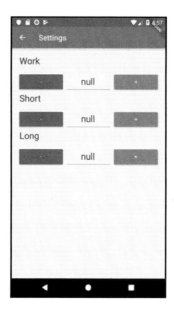

You probably guessed it: null strings shouldn't be there at all. The problem is that we haven't written anything into the SharedPreferences yet, and we are unable to do so as you cannot add any value to null. So, the first time the app is run, we need to write some default settings into the SharedPreferences so that the user will then be able to change the settings if they wish to do so.

Refactor the `readSettings()` method so that when one of the values is null, it will populate the setting with some default values, as follows:

```
readSettings() async {
    prefs = await SharedPreferences.getInstance();
    int workTime = prefs.getInt(WORKTIME);
    if (workTime==null) {
      await prefs.setInt(WORKTIME, int.parse('30'));
    }
    int shortBreak = prefs.getInt(SHORTBREAK);
    if (shortBreak==null) {
      await prefs.setInt(SHORTBREAK, int.parse('5'));
    }
    int longBreak = prefs.getInt(LONGBREAK);
    if (longBreak==null) {
      await prefs.setInt(LONGBREAK, int.parse('20'));
    }
    setState(() {
      txtWork.text = workTime.toString();
      txtShort.text = shortBreak.toString();
      txtLong.text = longBreak.toString();
    });
  }
```

The last step to complete our app is reading the setting from the `timer.dart` file as well. To do this, perform the following steps:

1. At the top of the `timer.dart` file, import the shared_preferences package, like this:

```
import 'package:shared_preferences/shared_preferences.dart';
```

2. Create a method that retrieves the settings saved in the `SharedPreferences` instance or sets default values, as follows:

```
Future readSettings() async {
    SharedPreferences prefs = await
SharedPreferences.getInstance();
    work = prefs.getInt('workTime') == null ? 30 :
prefs.getInt('workTime');
    shortBreak = prefs.getInt('shortBreak') == null ? 30 :
prefs.getInt('shortBreak');
    longBreak = prefs.getInt('longBreak') == null ? 30 :
prefs.getInt('longBreak');
  }
```

3. Add a call to the readSettings() method at the top of the startWork() method, like this:

```
void startWork() async{
    await readSettings();
    _radius = 1;
    _time = Duration(minutes: this.work, seconds: 0);
    _fullTime = _time;
}
```

If you try the app now, you'll see that it finally works! Well done—you have completed a rather rich Flutter app!

You can download the code for the finished app in the GitHub project repository for this book.

Summary

My Time is a simple app, but by building it you've covered a lot of Flutter features. In particular, you've used the GridView layout—a scrollable, 2D array of widgets that you can use to show data to your users in tabular form.

You've seen ways to implement asynchronous programming with Flutter. In particular, you've used a Stream to implement the countdown for the app, and you've used a StreamBuilder to listen to the events that came from the Stream. You've seen that the Streambuilder rebuilds its children at any change of the Stream.

Then, you've used the Navigator class to show different screens to your users, through the push() and pop() methods.

Finally, you've seen that there is a simple and effective way to store data for your apps: the SharedPreferences class, from the shared_preference library. You've also seen how to install an external library in your app using the pubspec.yaml file, and used the await statement in an async method.

Now, you are able to persist simple data in any app that you'll build, create multi-screen apps, and create streams of data.

We've covered a lot of ground in this chapter: it's time to have some fun with a game! In the next chapter, we'll build a simple game using animations and gesture control.

Questions

At the end of each project, you'll find a few questions to help you remember and review the content covered in the chapter. Please try to answer the following questions, and when in doubt, have a look at the content in the chapter itself: you'll find all the answers there!

1. Which is the cross-axis for a GridView scrolling vertically?
2. How do you retrieve a value from SharedPreferences?
3. Which instruction would you use to retrieve the width of the screen?
4. How do you open another screen in your app?
5. Which file contains all the dependencies of your app?
6. What's the difference between a Stream and a Future?
7. How do you change the value of a TextField?
8. How do you create a new Duration object?
9. How can you add a menu button to your apps?
10. What are the steps to install an external library into your app?

Further reading

This chapter has been at least partly inspired by reading Deep Work by Cal Newport. I think the author describes one of the best ways to be successful in any activity that requires thought. More information can be found at `http://www.calnewport.com/books/deep-work/`.

Many developers struggle when they are first exposed to asynchronous programming. The Dart team did a good job explaining how this model works in Dart and Flutter: you'll find a lot of content and examples here: `https://dart.dev/tutorials/language/futures`.

For specific guidance on Streams, have a look at `https://dart.dev/tutorials/language/streams`.

Currently, there's a lot of interest in functional programming, and the `typedef` declarations that we used while building this app are an important part of it for Dart. If you are interested in learning more about functional programming in Dart, have a look at `https://buildflutter.com/functional-programming-with-flutter/`.

Pong Game - 2D Animations and Gestures

4

Animations are an important feature that you can add to your apps to make them more attractive. They make it possible to add important functionality in a way that is pleasant for your users. For example, you could use animations to notify the user that an action has been completed, or you can use them to get user input. In any case, animations are often required to give your apps a polished look that can help make them successful. The good news is that Flutter has very good support for animations.

If you are like me, you probably love games, and usually, animations are what games are made of. So, in this chapter, we'll build a simplified single-player version of the ancient Pong game. We'll build a ball that will bounce through the screen, and we'll use a bat to avoid it touching the bottom part of the screen.

Building this game will give us the opportunity to see in detail how animations work in Flutter. We will also see how to add gesture detection to your widgets, another important feature. Finally, we'll add some randomness to the game to make it a bit more interesting.

As usual, we'll start from scratch. The result will probably not be something you would publish to the stores, but I believe it can be a fun way to see animations in an unconventional way and a good starting point to think about the logic of a game.

The time required for this project is approximately 2 hours and 30 minutes.

In particular, the topics we will cover include the following:

- Using Stack and Positioned to build the user interface
- Using Animation and AnimationController to build `Tween` animations
- Using GestureDetector
- Using `Random()` from the Dart Math library

Technical requirements

You'll find the completed app code in the book's Github repository at `https://github.com/PacktPublishing/Google-Flutter-Projects`.

To follow along with the code examples in this book, you should have the following software installed on your Windows, macOS , Linux, or Chrome OS device:

- The Flutter SDK.
- When developing for Android: the Android SDK, easily installed by Android Studio.
- When developing for iOS: macOS and Xcode.
- An emulator (Android), a simulator (iOS) or a connected iOS or Android device enabled for debugging.
- An editor: Visual Studio Code, Android Studio, or IntelliJ Idea are recommended. All should have the Flutter/Dart extensions installed.

Building the UI of the app

The first step toward creating the game is to build the basic components of the UI. After creating a new app, we'll build a ball, a bat, and a text for the score:

1. Let's create a new app, which we can call `simple_pong`.
2. In the `main.dart` file, in the `build()` method of the `MyApp` stateless widget, we'll return a `MaterialApp`, whose title is "Pong Demo", and, for the theme, we'll use the classic blue as `primarySwatch`.
3. In the home of `MaterialApp`, we'll place a scaffold whose `AppBar` will take a text containing "Simple Pong".
4. In the body, we'll place an empty container for now, but we will fix that later on.

   You can see the steps listed in the following code:

   ```
   import 'package:flutter/material.dart';

   void main() => runApp(MyApp());

   class MyApp extends StatelessWidget {
     @override
     Widget build(BuildContext context) {
       return MaterialApp(
         title: 'Pong Demo',
   ```

```
              theme: ThemeData(
                  primarySwatch: Colors.blue,
              ),
              home: Scaffold(
                  appBar: AppBar(
                      title: Text('Simple Pong'),
                  ),
                  body: Container()
          ));
      }}
```

There's nothing particularly new or exciting about this. As you can see, most apps tend to have the same boilerplate code. You may change colors and styles, but most of your apps are likely to have a `MaterialApp` containing a Scaffold as a starting point.

As you can see from the following screenshot, our app contains three UI elements that the user will see: the ball, the bat, and the score text. Those three elements will need to be included in a grid for the game itself:

So, let's build the UI components next.

Creating the ball

We'll deal with the ball first. This deserves a new file in our project, called `ball.dart`:

1. Create a new file called `ball.dart`, and inside it create a stateless widget, which you can call "Ball". This widget is stateless because it does not need to know its position or state during the app. The animation will change the position of the ball widget from the calling class.

 Remember that, in order to create a stateless widget, if you are using Visual Studio Code, Android Studio, or IntelliJ Idea, just type `stless`, and the boilerplate code will be created for you by the editor itself.

You can find the complete version of the file here:

```
import 'package:flutter/material.dart';

class Ball extends StatelessWidget {

@override
Widget build(BuildContext context) {
    final double diam = 50;
    return Container(
        width: diam,
        height: diam,
        decoration: new BoxDecoration(
            color: Colors.amber[400],
            shape: BoxShape.circle,
        ),);
}}
```

2. In the `Ball` class, first, we can set the diameter of the shape at 50 logical pixels. Of course, feel free to reduce or expand it based on your preferences.
3. Then we return a container, whose height and width will be the diameter we have just set, and the decoration will have the shape of `BoxShape.circle`.

When you create a container, the default shape is a rectangle. By specifying `BoxShape.circle`, you can avoid dealing with angles in an extremely easy way.

Let's also set the color to be `Colors.amber[400]`.

In the preceding example, we use `Colors.amber[400]`. Most colors have values from 100 to 900 in increments of 100, plus the color 50. Greater numbers mean darker colors. The accent colors, such as `Colors.blueAccent`, have a smaller set of values: 100, 200, 400, and 700.

And this is everything we need for the ball. In the next section, we'll deal with the bat.

Creating the bat

The bat is the shape we'll use to keep the ball from falling to the bottom of the screen. This will also require a separate file.

Create a new file called `bat.dart`:

1. This will also contain a stateless widget, as the bat does not need to know its position or deal with the user. All these actions will be performed by the caller:

```
import 'package:flutter/material.dart';
class Bat extends StatelessWidget {
  @override
  Widget build(BuildContext context) {
   return Container();
  }
}
```

2. The bat will have a width and a height that will depend on the size of the screen. These will be passed from the caller, so in the bat class, create two final double variables called `width` and `height`:

```
final double width;
final double height;
```

3. Next, create a constructor that will take two parameters, populating the two variables:

```
Bat(this.width, this.height);
```

4. Again, the `build` method will return a Container, whose width and height are the values of the parameters passed in the constructor, and will have a decoration that will set the background color to be `Colors.blue[900]`. The final code for the class is shown here:

```
import 'package:flutter/material.dart';
class Bat extends StatelessWidget {
```

```
final double width;
final double height;
Bat(this.width, this.height);
@override
Widget build(BuildContext context) {
 return Container(
    width: width,
    height: height,
    decoration: new BoxDecoration(
      color: Colors.blue[900],
    ),);
}}
```

At this time, we have the two main elements of the UI. We'll deal with the score text later on, when we incorporate the logic of the game. So now, we require a grid to contain the ball and the bat.

Creating the grid

Let's create a new file for the game: we can call this `pong.dart`. This time, we'll need to create a **Stateful** widget, as there will be several values that will change during this class life cycle:

1. Using the `stful` shortcut, let's create a new stateful widget called Pong:

    ```
    import 'package:flutter/material.dart';
    import './ball.dart';
    import './bat.dart';

    class Pong extends StatefulWidget {
      @override
      _PongState createState() => _PongState();
    }

    class _PongState extends State<Pong> {
      @override
      Widget build(BuildContext context) {
        return Container();
    }}
    ```

2. Instead of returning a `Container`, let's return a `LayoutBuilder`. This is a useful widget when you want to measure the space available in the context, including the parent constraints. We'll use this to make sure that the ball will not go out of the visible space in the app.

A `LayoutBuilder` widget requires a builder in its constructor. This takes a function with the context and the constraints. Inside this function, we'll return a `Stack`:

```
return LayoutBuilder(
        builder: (BuildContext context, BoxConstraints constraints)
    {
            return Stack();
    });
```

 There are several ways to achieve this, but among the available containers in Flutter, there is one that is perfect for our purposes, and this is the `Stack`. A `Stack` is a widget that positions its children relative to the edges of its box.

As both the ball and the bat will need to move during the lifetime of our game, we'll be able to change their position by changing their distance from the borders of the `Stack`. A `Stack` widget has a `children` property where we can place all the elements contained in the `Stack` itself. One way to position the elements inside it is by using the `Positioned` widget. Here, you can specify top, left, bottom, or right properties.

 `Positioned` is a widget that controls where a child of a stack is positioned.

Let's add the `Ball` and the `Bat` to the `Stack`. For now, we'll just put the ball at position `top:0`, which means at the top of the available space, and the bat at position `bottom:0`, which means at the bottom of the available space. The size of the bat will be an arbitrary 200 width and 50 height, but we'll change that shortly:

```
return Stack(
        children: <Widget>[
          Positioned(
            child: Ball(),
            top: 0
            ),
          Positioned(
            bottom: 0,
            child: Bat(200,25),)
        ], );
```

In order to be able to try out the layout so far, we only need to call the `Pong()` widget from the `MyApp` class in the `main.dart` file. First, we'll need to import at the top of the `MyApp` class:

```
import './pong.dart';
```

This is followed by importing the body of the scaffold:

```
body: SafeArea(
    child: Pong()
)
```

 A `SafeArea` is a widget that automatically adds some padding to its child in order to avoid intrusions by the operating system, such as the status bar at the top of the screen or the notch on a newer iPhone.

And if you try the app right now, you'll be able to see the ball and the bat in the top-left corner and bottom-left corner of the screen, respectively, as follows:

Before dealing with the animation, let's prepare this layout to be able to deal with changes in size and positions.

At the top of the _PongState class, let's create a few variables that will deal with the available space, the size of the bat, and the position of the bat and ball:

```
double width;
double height;
double posX = 0;
double posY = 0;
double batWidth = 0;
double batHeight = 0;
double batPosition = 0;
```

width and height represent the available space on the screen, posX and posY are the horizontal and vertical position of the ball, batWidth and batHeight represent the size of the bat, and batPosition is the horizontal position of the bat. The bat won't be able to move vertically, as it will remain at the bottom of the screen.

Inside LayoutBuilder, let's first set the variables that contain the height and width of the layout, and the size of the bat. These values are contained in the BoxConstraints instance that's passed as a parameter to the builder method in LayoutBuilder.

The BoxConstraints class contains four useful properties: minWidth, minHeight, maxWidth, and maxHeight. They are set at runtime and are useful whenever you need to know the constraints of the parent of a widget.

We will make the bat size relative to the dimensions of the screen. Hence, the width will be 20% of the screen (width/5), and the height 5% of the available space (height/20).

In the build() method of the _PongState class, and in the builder method of LayoutBuilder, add the following code:

```
builder: (BuildContext context, BoxConstraints constraints) {
    height = constraints.maxHeight;
    width = constraints.maxWidth;
    batWidth = width / 5;
    batHeight = height / 20;
    return Stack(
        . . .
```

Next, in the `Stack` returned by the builder, let's use these values when we build the bat:

```
return Stack(
    children: <Widget>[
        Positioned(child: Ball(), top: 0),
        Positioned(
            bottom: 0,
            child: Bat(batWidth, batHeight),
        )
    ],
);
```

With the main elements of the layout complete, we are now ready to start building the animation.

Using animations

In order to create the animation that will make our ball move inside the screen, we'll use three classes, which are the base of most animations in Flutter:

- The first class is quite predictably called `Animation`. The `Animation` class takes some values and translates them into animations. An instance of `Animation` is not bound to any widget on the screen, so it is unaware of what is happening on the screen: it has listeners that can check the state of the animation during each frame change.
- The second class is `AnimationController`. `AnimationController`, as the name implies, controls the animation objects. For example, you can use it to start an animation, give it a duration, and repeat it when needed. An `AnimationController` can control more than one animation. For the project in this chapter, we'll only use one animation.
- The last class we'll use is `Tween`. `Tween` is short for "in between", and it contains the value of the property that needs to change during the animation. For example, if you're animating the left position of a widget from 0 to 200, your `Tween` will represent the values at 1, 2, 3 ... up to 200.

In the next few steps, we'll see these three classes in action in our code to move the ball through the screen:

1. At the top of the `_PongState` class, create the variables that will contain the instances of `Animation` and `AnimationController`:

```
Animation<double> animation;
AnimationController controller;
```

2. Next, let's override the `initState()` method:

```
@override
void initState() {
    super.initState();
}
```

You may be wondering what the `initState` method is. Let's have a look at the following diagram:

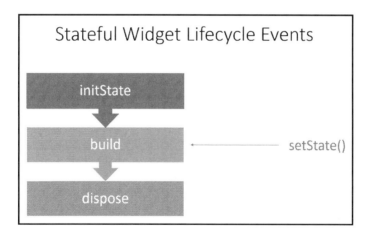

There are several event methods that are called during the life cycle of a `Stateful` widget.

The `initState` method is called when a `State` is created. You can use this method for any initialization, as it is called only once.

We've used the `build()` method several times in this and previous projects. It's worth noting that each time you call the `setState()` method, the `build()` method is automatically triggered. This is where you can put values that change, but it is useless for any initialization value, as it would get overwritten each time the `setState()` method is called. At the end of the lifetime of any stateful widget, you can override the `dispose()` method. This helps to free resources from the system.

So, from this description, you probably guessed that we'll need to set up our ball animation in the initState method, and set its position in the build method. The first animation we'll build will just move the ball from the position top: 0, left: 0 to the position top: 100, left: 100. Let's look at the steps:

1. Let's begin with initState. We are using posX for the horizontal position and posY for the vertical position of the ball. At the beginning of the animation, both will be 0.

2. Next, we will initialize AnimationController. Its duration will be 3 seconds, as we want the ball to take three seconds to get from position 0, 0 to position 100, 100.

3. An AnimationController requires a TickerProvider, which is configured using the vsync argument on the constructor. We'll set the vsync property to be this:

```
@override
void initState() {
    posX = 0;
    posY = 0;
    controller = AnimationController(
        duration: const Duration(seconds: 3),
        vsync: this, );
    super.initState();
}
```

4. You may notice that we get an error here. That is because vsync takes a TickerProvider. In order to solve this issue, we need to add the with SingleTickerProviderStateMixin clause to our state:

```
class _PongState extends State<Pong> with
SingleTickerProviderStateMixin {
```

This requires a little bit of theory. In object-oriented programming languages, a **Mixin** is a class that contains methods that can be used by other classes without having to be the parent class of those other classes. That's why we use the with clause in Flutter, because, in this way, we are including the class, not inheriting from it. In other words, Mixins are a way to reuse code in a class in multiple class hierarchies.

If you want to dive deeper in the use of mixins in Dart, there's an excellent article on Medium at the following link: https://medium.com/flutter-community/dart-what-are-mixins-3a72344011f3.

The `SingleTickerProviderStateMixin` provides one `Ticker`. In simple terms, a `Ticker` is a class that sends a signal at an almost regular interval, which, in Flutter, is about 60 times per second, or once every 16 milliseconds, if your device allows this frame rate.

5. Next, still in the `initState()` method of the `_PongState` class, under `AnimationController`, create the animation itself:

```
animation = Tween<double>(begin: 0, end: 100).animate(controller);
animation.addListener(() {
    setState(() {
    posX++;
    posY++;
});
```

Here we are using a `Tween`. As mentioned previously, a `Tween` is a linear interpolation between a beginning and ending value. The beginning value is 0, and the end value is 100. On that, we call the `animate()` method, passing the `controller` that we've just created. This returns the animation itself.

6. In the animation, we then set a listener calling the `addListener()` method. This will be called whenever the object changes.

7. Inside the `setState()` method, we just increment the horizontal and vertical positions at each iteration of the animation, so that the ball will move down 100 pixels in both directions.

8. The last step is changing the top and left parameters of the ball `Positioned` widget. They'll both take the animation value, which we defined when we created the `Tween` and is between 0 and 100. Basically, the ball will take three seconds to go from position 0, 0 to position 100, 100:

```
return Stack(
 children: <Widget>[
 Positioned(
 child: Ball(),
 top: posY,
 left: posX,
 ),
```

9. In order to start the animation, in the `initState()` method, before the `super.initState()` instruction, call the `forward()` method on the controller:

```
controller.forward();
```

10. If you try the app right now, you should be able to see the ball moving slowly to the bottom-right corner, and the final position should look similar to the following screenshot:

To summarize, we are using the animation controller to define how long the animation should run, we are using a `Tween` to set a linear value increment, and we are using the `forward()` method to start the animation.

If we left the app as it is now, this would certainly be the most boring game ever. The first thing we need to do is to keep the ball moving, and when it reaches the edges of the available space, we need it to change direction. So, let's make a few tweaks to our app.

Adding the game logic

The ball should never stop, and it should bounce at the edges of the available space. What we see as bouncing is actually a change in direction. So when the ball meets the right-hand edge, it should move left, and vice versa. The same is true for the vertical direction when it moves up. The ball should change direction and move down when it meets the top border. Also, the animation value wouldn't be useful, so we need to separate the ball position from the animation value, and use the animation only as a way to redraw the ball in the correct position. Let's look at the steps to apply this logic:

1. In the `pong.dart` file, first, let's create an `enum` for the directions, under the `import` declarations, as shown here:

   ```
   enum Direction { up, down, left, right }
   ```

   In case you've never seen it before, the `enum` keyword creates an **Enumerated** type. This is a special kind of class that you can use to represent a fixed number of constant values. In our example, we are creating an enumerator called `Direction` that can have four values: `up`, `down`, `left`, and `right`. This will allow our code to be a bit more readable, and it's an alternative to using numbers or constants for the direction.

2. Next, at the top of the `_PongState` class, let's add two variables, of type `Direction`, that will contain the vertical (`vDir`) and the horizontal (`hDir`) directions. In the beginning, the ball will need to move down and left:

   ```
   Direction vDir = Direction.down;
   Direction hDir = Direction.right;
   ```

3. Next, we need to check whether the ball has reached its boundaries. We already know the boundaries of our app, as we have set the width and height variables in the `LayoutBuilder` builder method. So, we just need to check the position of the ball to see whether it reached those boundaries. Still in the `PongState` class, let's create a method called `checkBorders()`, which will check whether the ball has reached its border, and will change the direction whenever it has:

   ```
   void checkBorders() {
       if (posX <= 0 && hDir == Direction.left) {
           hDir = Direction.right;
       }
       if (posX >= width - 50 && hDir == Direction.right) {
           hDir = Direction.left;
       }
       if (posY >= height - 50 && vDir == Direction.down) {
   ```

```
            vDir = Direction.up;
        }
        if (posY <= 0 && vDir == Direction.up) {
            vDir = Direction.down;
        }
    }
```

4. Next, we need to keep the animation going for as long as it's needed. In the `initState()` method of the `_PongState` class, let's set it to 10,000 minutes instead of 3 seconds (a very long game…) for now:

```
controller = AnimationController(
    duration: const Duration(minutes: 10000),
    vsync: this,
);
```

5. Next, let's move the ball according to the direction. Still in the `initState()` method, when we create the animation, in `addListener()`, let's change the code for `setState()` as shown here:

```
animation.addListener(() {
    setState(() {
        (hDir == Direction.right)? posX += 1 : posX -= 1;
        (vDir == Direction.down)? posY += 1 : posY -= 1;
    });
    checkBorders();
});
```

In the preceding code, we are using a ternary operator to move the ball based on the direction. If the horizontal direction is `Direction.right`, we need to increment the horizontal position, otherwise, we need to decrement it. The same logic applies to the vertical position as well: we increment `posY` when the direction is `down`, and we decrement it when the direction is `up`. After each movement, we call the `checkBorders()` method to see whether it's necessary to change direction.

You can try this out immediately, and the ball should be bouncing through the screen. You may find the ball is moving too slowly. You can adjust the speed of the ball by changing the increment of the position. In this case, we are always adding or subtracting 1. If we want to make the animation faster, we can just make it 3 or 5 instead of 1. If we want to make it slower, we can make it less than 1, for example, 0.5.

6. Now, let's create a variable to contain the increment number. For my emulator, a value of 5 works fine. At the top of the _PongState class, let's add the declaration provided here:

```
double increment = 5;
```

7. Then, let's use the increment in our code:

```
animation.addListener(() {
    setState(() {
        (hDir == Direction.right)? posX += increment :
         posX -= increment;
        (vDir == Direction.down)? posY += increment :
         posY -= increment;
    });
    checkBorders();
});
```

If you try out the app right now, you will see that the speed of the ball should be much higher. Feel free to adjust the increment value based on the speed you feel correct for the game.

Our next step will be to move the bat so that we can stop the ball from falling!

Using GestureDetector

As the name implies, GestureDetector is a widget that detects gestures.

In the body of your layout, insert a GestureDetector. This widget has properties that respond to gestures of your user. You can respond to several user gestures. The most common ones include onTap, onDoubleTap, and onLongPress. Inside each of those gesture properties, you can add the code needed to respond to the user's gestures. Generally, what you'll do is change the state of the widget, but you are certainly not limited to that.

In our case, we'll need to move the bat, so the state value that will change is the left property of the positioned widget that contains the bat. We only need to respond to the horizontal drag, as the bat won't need to move vertically. Let's look at the steps to do that:

1. In the build() method of pong.dart file, as a child of the batPositioned widget, let's add a GestureDetector, with an onHorizontalDragUpdate parameter. This will take a DragUpdateDetails object, which we can call update, containing information about the drag that's happening on the screen.

2. Inside the function, we call a method called `moveBat()`, which will take the updated value:

```
Positioned(
    bottom: 0,
    left: batPosition,
    child: GestureDetector(
        onHorizontalDragUpdate: (DragUpdateDetails update)
         => moveBat(update),
        child: Bat(batWidth, batHeight))
),
```

3. Next, at the bottom of the `_PongState` class, write the `moveBat()` method:

```
void moveBat(DragUpdateDetails update) {
    setState(() {
        batPosition += update.delta.dx;
    });
}
```

`DragUpdateDetails` has a delta property that contains the distance moved during the drag operation. `dx` is the horizontal delta. We just update the `batPosition` by adding the delta, which can be a positive or negative number.

If we try the app right now, we'll be able to move the bat horizontally across the screen.

Before giving the user the ability to interact with the game, let's override an important method in the `_PongState` class, which is `dispose()`: you should use it to release the resources used by the animation. In this case, the `dispose()` method will be automatically called when the `_PongState` object is discarded. Inside this method, we add a call to the `dispose()` method of the animation controller to prevent memory leaks:

```
@override
void dispose() {
    controller.dispose();
    super.dispose();
}
```

At this time, the ball and the bat are not linked in any way, but we're going to fix that next.

Checking the bat position

Now that we have the ball moving, and the bat responding to our gestures, we need to tell when the ball reaches the bottom of the screen without touching the bat. This is when we actually lose the game.

We need to modify the checkBorders() method. Here, we are dealing with the four borders of the screen: top, left, right, and bottom. The only change we need to make is for the bottom. It is here that we need to check whether the bat is in the correct position to make the ball bounce back up, or if the game needs to stop.

In the pong.dart file, edit the checkBorders() method, at the point where you check for Direction.down, as indicated here:

```
if (posY >= height - 50 - batHeight && vDir == Direction.down) {
    //check if the bat is here, otherwise loose
    if (posX >= (batPosition - 50) && posX <= (batPosition +
    batWidth + 50)) {
        vDir = Direction.up;
    } else {
        controller.stop();
        dispose();
    }
}
```

50 is the diameter of the ball. Instead of bouncing at the very bottom of the screen, the ball needs to bounce over the bat. So, we check when the ball reaches the bottom **minus** the diameter of the ball.

In the nested if statement, we check the horizontal position. The "ideal" position of the bat, which allows the ball to bounce, is between batPosition, which is the horizontal starting position of the bat, and batPosition + batWidth, which is the horizontal end position of the bat. To this, again, we add the diameter of the ball. If the position of the ball is included in these two values, the ball bounces back up. Otherwise, we stop the animation and free the system resources.

As we are using number 50 several times, let's add a variable, and use that instead:

1. So, at the top of the checkBorders method, let's add the following:

   ```
   double diameter = 50;
   ```

2. Use the diameter variable for our checks. The final `checkBorders` method is shown here:

```
void checkBorders() {
    double diameter = 50;
    if (posX <= 0 && hDir == Direction.left) {
      hDir = Direction.right;
    }
    if (posX >= width - diameter && hDir == Direction.right) {
      hDir = Direction.left;
    }
    if (posY >= height - diameter - batHeight && vDir ==
    Direction.down) {
      //check if the bat is here, otherwise loose
      if (posX >= (batPosition - diameter) && posX <= (batPosition
      + batWidth + diameter)) {
        vDir = Direction.up;
      } else {
        controller.stop();
        dispose();
      }
    }
    if (posY <= 0 && vDir == Direction.up) {
      vDir = Direction.down;
    }
}
```

When we call the `dispose()` method on an object, the object is no longer usable. Any subsequent call will raise an error. To prevent getting errors in our app, we can create a method that, prior to calling the `setState()` method, will check whether the controller is still mounted and the controller is active:

1. Add the following code at the end of the `_PongState` class:

```
void safeSetState(Function function) {
    if (mounted && controller.isAnimating) {
      setState(() {
        function();
      });
    }
}
```

The `mounted` property checks whether the state object is currently mounted. A state object is "mounted" before calling `initState()` and until `dispose()` is called. Calling `setState()` when mounted is not true will raise an error.

2. In the `initState()` method, in `animation.addListener`, call the `safeSetState()` method instead of `setState()`:

```
animation.addListener(() {
    safeSetState(() {
       (hDir == Direction.right) ? posX += increment :
        posX -= increment;
       (vDir == Direction.down) ? posY += increment :
        posY -= increment;
    });
    checkBorders();
```

3. In the `moveBat()` method, also call `safeSetState()`:

```
void moveBat(DragUpdateDetails update) {
   safeSetState(() {
      batPosition += update.delta.dx;
   });
}
```

If you try the app, you'll finally be able to play the game!

There are still a couple of fixes we need to add, and we'll do that in the next section, but still, the basics are all there.

Adding randomness to the game

One of the basic ingredients that make a game interesting is the random element. There are two moments in our game where we can add some randomness. One is the bouncing angle: it doesn't need to be exactly 45 degrees each time it bounces. Making the bouncing less regular will make the game less predictable. And we can also work with the speed of the ball.

Let's consider the perfect bouncing we are using now to be 1. If the bouncing could take a value between 0.5 and 1.5, the bouncing would be less regular, but still keep a degree of realism:

1. In order to use random values in Flutter and Dart, we need to import the `math` library. In the `pong.dart` file, add the import statement as shown here:

```
import 'dart:math';
```

2. Then, in the `_PongState` class, let's write a method, called `randomNumber()`, which returns a random double number between 0.5 and 1.5:

```
double randomNumber() {
  //this is a number between 0.5 and 1.5;
  var ran = new Random();
  int myNum = ran.nextInt(101);
  return (50 + myNum) / 100;
}
```

The `Random` class generates random bool, int, or double values. Its `nextInt` method returns a random **integer** from 0, inclusive, and the parameter you pass, exclusive. In this case, it will be a number between 0 and 100 inclusive.

To that, we add 50 and we add the generated integer, obtaining a number between 50 and 150, and we then divide it by 100. So, the function will return a number between 0.5 and 1.5.

3. Next, at the top of the `_PongState` class, let's create two variables, one for the vertical direction and one for the horizontal, which will contain the random number. As you can see, at the beginning of the execution, the value for both `randX` and `randY` is 1:

```
double randX = 1;
double randY = 1;
```

4. Every time the ball bounces, we want to change the value of the random number, based on the border that is reached. So, when the ball bounces left or right, we want to change the `randX` value; when the ball bounces at the top or the bottom, we want to change `randY`.

Modify the `checkBorders()` function, adding the calls to the `randomNumber()` method:

```
void checkBorders() {
    double diameter = 50;
    if (posX <= 0 && hDir == Direction.left) {
      hDir = Direction.right;
      randX = randomNumber();
    }
    if (posX >= width - diameter && hDir == Direction.right) {
      hDir = Direction.left;
      randX = randomNumber();
    }
    //check the bat position as well
      if (posY >= height - diameter - batHeight  && vDir ==
```

```
    Direction.down) {
    //check if the bat is here, otherwise loose
    if (posX >= (batPosition - diameter) && posX <= (batPosition
    + batWidth + diameter)) {
      vDir = Direction.up;
      randY = randomNumber();
    } else {
      controller.stop();
      dispose();
    }}
    if (posY <= 0 && vDir == Direction.up) {
      vDir = Direction.down;
      randY = randomNumber();
    }  }
```

5. Finally, go back to the Tween defined in the initState() method, and replace the animation definition so that, instead of incrementing the position by a fixed value, we'll use the random number to vary the speed as well:

```
animation = Tween<double>(begin: 0, end: 100).animate(controller);
  animation.addListener(() {
    safeSetState(() {
      (hDir == Direction.right)
          ? posX += ((increment * randX).round())
          : posX -= ((increment * randX).round());
      (vDir == Direction.down)
          ? posY += ((increment * randY).round())
          : posY -= ((increment * randY).round());
    });
    checkBorders();
  });
```

If you play the game now, you'll notice that the speed and bounce of the ball are less regular, making the game a bit more unpredictable. Of course, you could also increase or decrease the random element by returning a different range in the randomNumber function.

There is one last element that every game should have, and this is the score. Let's add this to our app.

Adding the score and completing the game

A game wouldn't be complete without a way to measure performance. In this case, the action to perform is pretty obvious. Every time the ball touches the bat, we can add one point to the score. Let's look at how we can apply this action:

1. Let's create a variable that will contain the score, at the top of the `_PongState` class:

   ```
   int score = 0;
   ```

2. Next, in the `build()` method, add a new `Positioned` widget to the stack. This will contain a `Text` with the score:

   ```
   return Stack(
       children: <Widget>[
           Positioned(
               top: 0,
               right: 24,
               child: Text('Score: ' + score.toString()),
           ),
   ```

3. Then, in the `checkBorders()` method, update the score each time the ball touches the bat:

   ```
   if (posX >= (batPosition - diameter) && posX <= (batPosition +
   batWidth + diameter)) {
       vDir = Direction.up;
       randY = randomNumber();
       safeSetState(() {
           score++;
       });
   }
   ```

If you try this out, you should see that the score is now visible in the top-right corner of the screen, as shown here:

Now, let's add a final touch to our app: when the player loses, we want to give them a message asking whether they want to play again, and, if so, we start the animation again:

1. Let's create a new method in the _PongState class. We can call it showMessage. What we want to achieve is a dialog over the screen, as shown in the following screenshot:

2. This will call the `showDialog` method, which displays a dialog window above the screen, with material design animations. This method takes a builder method, where you build a `Dialog` widget and take the current `BuildContext`:

```
void showMessage(BuildContext context) {
    showDialog(
      context: context,
      builder: (BuildContext context) {
        return AlertDialog(
        );});
}
```

3. In our app, we'll use `AlertDialog` to ask the user whether they want to play again. The alert dialog takes a `title`, `content`, and `actions`.

4. In the `showMessage` method, we have the following:
    - `title` shows on top of the dialog window.
    - `content` is the main content of the dialog.
    - `actions` is an array of widgets that specify the actions that users will be able to perform: in our app, we'll use two buttons, one for **YES** and one for **NO** as actions.

5. If the user presses the **YES** `FlatButton`, we'll call the `setState` method to place the ball at position 0,0, and reset the score to 0 as well.

6. The `pop` method of `Navigator` will remove the dialog from the screen and the `controller.repeat` method will play the animation again. Complete the `AlertDialog` with the following code:

```
return AlertDialog(
    title: Text('Game Over'),
    content: Text('Would you like to play again?'),
    actions: <Widget>[
        FlatButton(
            child: Text('Yes'),
            onPressed: () {
                setState(() {
                    posX = 0;
                    posY = 0;
                    score = 0;
                });
                Navigator.of(context).pop();
                controller.repeat();
            },
        ),
        FlatButton(
            child: Text('No'),
```

```
        onPressed: () {
            Navigator.of(context).pop();
            dispose();
        },
    )
],
);
```

7. Finally, in the `checkBorders()` method, instead of calling the `dispose()` method of `controller`, we'll call the `showMessage()` method:

```
controller.stop();
showMessage(context);
```

If you try this out, you'll see the dialog whenever you lose.

This completes this project. There are several features you could add to improve this game, including the creation of a wall of fame, saving the best scores to the device, adding bricks at the top of the screen, adding sound, changing the angle of bouncing based on the position of the bat, and adding a second bat for a second player. If you want to test yourself, try adding some of these functions to this app. It might be a fun way to improve your Flutter skills.

Summary

In this chapter, you've built a simple game, based on animation and on detecting a user's gestures.

Animations in Flutter are fast and relatively easy to implement. The moving parts involved in the animation are the `Animation` class, which takes in some values and translates them into animations, `AnimationController`, which controls the animation objects, `Tween`, which contains the value of the property that needs to change during the animation, and `Ticker`, which calls its callback once per animation frame.

Enclosing any widget in a `GestureDetector` will allow you to listen to several gestures the user performs over your user interface. This allowed a moving bat to be constructed on the screen, leveraging the `onHorizontalDragUpdate` property of `GestureDetector`.

Adding some randomness generally makes a game more interesting. We've also seen how to use the `Random` class to generate a random integer value with the `nextInt` method.

While building the game, you've also seen how to use `LayoutBuilder` to get the available space on a screen, and a `Stack` to control exactly how widgets should be positioned on the screen of your app.

To give some feedback to the user, and have them perform a choice, you've also used an `AlertDialog`, setting its `title`, `content`, and `actions`.

In the next chapter, we'll create a movies app that will connect to a web service using the HTTP library service.

Questions

At the end of each project, you'll find a few questions to help you remember and review the content covered in the chapter. Please try to answer the following questions and, when in doubt, have a look at the content in the chapter itself: you'll find all the answers there!

1. Which child widget can you use inside a `Stack` to decide exactly its position relative to the borders of the `Stack`?
2. What's the difference between the `initState` and `build` methods?
3. How can you set the duration of an animation?
4. How can you use a `Mixin` class in your own classes?
5. What is a `Ticker`?
6. What's the difference between an `Animation` and an `AnimationController`?
7. How do you stop a running animation? And how do you free its resources?
8. How can you generate a random number between 0 and 10?
9. If you wanted to respond to a tap of the user over one of your widgets, for example, a container, which widget could you use?
10. How do you show an `AlertDialog` in an app?

Further reading

The first place to consult if you want to use animations in your apps is the official Flutter guide, which you can find at the following link: `https://flutter.dev/docs/development/ui/animations`. Another great resource with videos, examples, and step-by-step guides is `https://buildflutter.com/functional-programming-with-flutter/`.

In this chapter, we've built a game starting from scratch. This is probably not the most common scenario for a real-world game, as there are several libraries and toolkits that you can leverage to create complex apps and games. If you are serious about creating compelling animations, there's a third-party tool, called Rive, that allows you to create incredible animations and add them to your Flutter apps. More on this can be found at `https://rive.app/`.

There's a great example on how to build a multi-platform game with Flutter at `https://medium.com/flutter-community/from-zero-to-a-multiplatform-flutter-game-in-a-week-8245da931c7e`. Also, have a look at `https://flutterawesome.com/high-performance-animations-and-2d-games-with-flutter/` to find ideas and see what's possible with Flutter.

Even though Flutter is very young, there are already several libraries that make it easier to create games and animations in Flutter without starting from scratch, and projects are added very frequently. For example, have a look at Flame, at `https://pub.dev/packages/flame`. You'll also find great tutorials and documentation on creating games with Flutter.

5
Let's Go to the Movies - Getting Data from the Web

Who doesn't like movies?

In this chapter, we'll build a movie app. As soon as the user opens the app, it will show a list of movies that are about to come out in cinemas. I love this project for several reasons: it's easy to read, does not require a huge amount of code, and at the same time, contains many incredibly important concepts. These include asynchronous programming in Flutter, reading JSON data from the web, using `ListView` widgets, and passing data from one screen to another. In short, this project is packed with concepts you're likely to use very often if you keep dealing with Flutter. And you'll be building a full stack real-world app that deals with both the client side and the server side, or the frontend/backend as many people call them.

In particular, the topics we'll cover include the following:

- Using the HTTP library to retrieve data from a web service
- Parsing JSON data and transforming it into model objects
- Adding a ListView to show data
- Showing a detail screen and passing data through screens

Technical requirements

You'll find the completed app code on this book's GitHub repository at `https://github.com/PacktPublishing/Flutter-Projects`.

To follow the code examples in this book, you should have the following software installed on your Windows, Mac, Linux, or Chrome OS device:

- The Flutter SDK
- When developing for Android, the Android SDK, which is easily installed using Android Studio
- When developing for iOS, MacOS and Xcode
- An emulator (Android), simulator (iOS), or a connected iOS or Android device enabled for debugging
- An editor: Visual Studio Code, Android Studio, or IntelliJ IDEA are recommended and should all have the Flutter/Dart extensions installed

Project overview

In this chapter, we'll build a Movies app. As soon as the user opens it, the app will show a list of movies that are about to come out in cinemas. The user will also be able to search for movies by title on the same screen, like so:

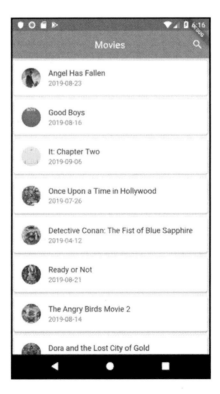

If they tap on one of the movies, the app will show a second screen, which is a more detailed view of the movie with a bigger image and an overview:

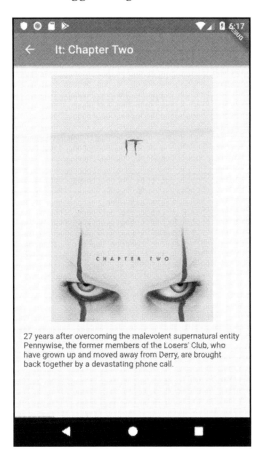

To retrieve the data, the app will use an open web service, which is **The Movie Database API.**

By the end of this chapter, you'll have built a fully functional app that connects to the web and retrieves data from a remote web service.

The time required for this project is approximately three hours.

Connecting to a web service and retrieving data with HTTP

Very few mobile apps are completely independent of external data: think of the apps you use for weather forecasts, listening to music, reading books, news, or emails. They all have something in common: they rely on data taken from an external source. The most common source to get data from a mobile (or any client) app is called a **web service** or **web API**.

What happens is that a client app connects to a web service, makes a **request** to get data, and if the request is legitimate, the web service **responds** by sending the data to the app, which then will parse the data for its features. The advantage of this approach is that developers only need to create and maintain one source of data and can have as many clients as needed. Actually this pattern (client/server) is nothing new, but it's extremely common when designing apps.

In the following, you can see a diagram showing this pattern. At the center, you have a remote server, which is the data source, and all around it are the clients, such as your mobile app, that connect to the server to retrieve data:

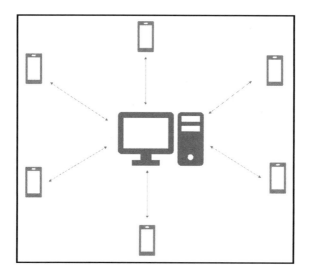

Web services generally expose data in two formats: *JSON* or *XML*. They are both text formats that can represent mostly the same kind of data, but as JSON is a bit more compact, it's a format you'll probably find more often when using web services.

In the following screenshot, you can see an example of each format:

In both formats, you can see an example of a movie, with the title, the year it was produced, the genre, and the actors. We don't need to get into the details of these formats; just note that both formats allow you to express complex data, and in Flutter, you can easily retrieve and parse both JSON and XML. The service we'll use in this chapter delivers JSON.

We won't deal with creating web services; we'll just use the one inside our app, but don't worry, you'll see how to create a server-side data source with Firebase in a later chapter.

In particular, we'll be using the Movie Database API (`https://www.themoviedb.org`). This is a community-built database with huge amounts of data that provides movies and TV information in several languages.

Before making your first connection to the database, you'll need to get an API key. You can obtain an API key by creating an account at `https://www.themoviedb.org/`, then clicking the API link in the bar on the left-hand side of your account page. This is free but requires a valid email to activate the account. Having an API key is also required to follow along with the examples in this chapter.

In the following sections, we'll create the app and retrieve the first set of data from the Movie Database web service.

Creating the app and connecting to the API with the HTTP library

Let's create a new Flutter app. We will call it Movies:

1. The first thing to do is to open the `pubspec.yaml` file and add a dependency to the HTTP library, which we'll use to make HTTP requests. Please check the latest available version at `https://pub.dev/packages/http`.
Add the `http` library under the `flutter` dependency, as follows:

   ```
   dependencies:
     flutter:
       sdk: flutter
     http: ^0.12.0+4
   ```

2. Then, let's create a new file, called `http_helper.dart`, that we'll use to create the settings and methods that we'll use to connect to the web service. In the new file, let's import the HTTP library:

   ```
   import 'package:http/http.dart' as http;
   ```

   With the `as http` command, we are giving the library a name and therefore, we'll be using all functions and classes of the HTTP library through the `http` name.

3. Then, let's create a new class, which we'll call `HttpHelper`:

   ```
   class HttpHelper {}
   ```

4. The next step is creating the address `url` to connect to the service. This will require a few strings, which we'll concatenate as needed to retrieve data from the service. Add the following declarations at the top of the `HttpHelper` class:

   ```
   final String urlKey = 'api_key=YOUR API KEY HERE';
   final String urlBase = 'https://api.themoviedb.org/3/movie';
   final String urlUpcoming = '/upcoming?';
   final String urlLanguage = '&language=en-US';
   ```

To make it easier to retrieve the values of these strings, all of them begin with a url prefix. The first string, urlKey, contains the value, api_key =, and the API key you've obtained from the Movie Database service. The urlBase string is the beginning of every address we'll be using. urlUpcoming is the part of the URL that's specific for the upcoming movies. Finally, urlLanguage contains an optional parameter that allows you to specify which language you want to use for the results of your queries.

5. We are now ready to write the first method of this class, which we'll use to retrieve a list of 20 upcoming movies:

```
Future<String> getUpcoming() async { }
```

You may notice an unfamiliar syntax here. The getUpcoming() function returns a future and is signed as async. These two elements are both related to asynchronous programming.

In Chapter 3, *My Time – Listening to a Stream of Data*, you have already used asynchronous programming with streams. In this chapter, you'll see how to use **Futures**.

Generally speaking, when you run your code, for example, in a method, each line executes from the first to the last, in order. If there are 10 lines of code in your function, line 5 executes only after line 4 has finished executing.

On the other hand, we generally take for granted that our devices can do more than one thing at the same time. When you are listening to music on your device, you also expect to be able to browse your playlist or adjust the volume. You would be very disappointed if you had to wait for the song to finish before being able to adjust the volume!

The thing is, by default, every single action is executed is a single thread, generally called the main thread, or the UI thread.

You should avoid an unresponsive UI at all costs: after a few seconds, both Android and iOS will ask the user if they want to kill your app.

What we can do to solve this issue in Flutter is create different isolates, or lines of execution, when we have long-running tasks in our app so that, for example, our network tasks run at the same time (or **concurrently**) as our main thread.

Concurrency is what happens when two or more tasks can start, run, and complete in overlapping time periods.

In other words, asynchronous operations let your program complete work while waiting for another operation to finish. Here are some common asynchronous scenarios:

- Retrieving data from the web
- Reading and writing data to a file
- Reading and writing to a local database

To perform asynchronous operations in Flutter, you can use the `Future` class and the `async`, `await`, and `then` keywords.

A `Future` is used to represent a potential value, or error, that will be available at some time in the future. Basically, when a function returns a `Future`, it means that it takes a while for its result to be ready, and the result will be available in the future. The `Future` itself is returned immediately and its underlying object is returned at some time in the future.

Writing `Future<String>` means that the function will immediately return a `Future` without interrupting the code, and then, when it completes retrieving all of the data, it will return `String`.

In the `getUpcoming()` method, we are adding the `async` keyword. In Dart and Flutter, you must add `async` when you use an `await` keyword in the body of the function. Any method returning a `Future` is asynchronous anyway, whether or not you mark it with `async`.

Let's retrieve some data from the web service:

1. In the `getUpcoming` method, let's add a string to create the URL that we'll use during the connection:

   ```
   final String upcoming = urlBase + urlUpcoming + urlKey +
   urlLanguage;
   ```

2. Next, let's use the HTTP library to create a connection to the URL we've built:

   ```
   http.Response result = await http.get(upcoming);
   ```

   The `get` method of the `http` class returns a `Future` that contains `Response`. The `http.Response` class contains the data that has been received from a successful HTTP call.

The `await` keyword, which only works in functions marked as `async`, waits for a `Future` to complete. It won't go to the next line of its thread until it completes this line, behaving a lot like synchronous code, but remember, this happens on a secondary line of execution, so it won't stop the UI thread.

3. Now, how do we read the response? Let's write the following code:

```
if (result.statusCode == HttpStatus.ok) {
    String responseBody = result.body;
        return responseBody;
}
else {
    return null;
}
```

4. The `HttpStatus` class requires the `dart:io` library. At the top of the `http_helper.dart` file, add the required import:

```
import 'dart:io';
```

`Response` has `statusCode` and `body` properties. The status code may express a successful response, which is a code 200 of `HttpStatus.ok` or an error. You may be familiar with error 404; in Dart, you would just express it with `HttpStatus.notFound`.

In the preceding code, if the response has a valid status code, we read the body of the response, which is a string containing all of the data that was retrieved by the `http.get` method, and we return it to the caller.

To sum it up, we now have an asynchronous function that makes an HTTP request and returns a `Future` containing a string. Now we need to call this function from the `main` method and show the result to the user. Let's do that next.

Parsing JSON data and transforming it into model objects

We are now ready to show the data that was retrieved from the web service in the UI:

1. Open the `main.dart` file, delete the default code of the app, and create a basic empty app like this:

```
import 'package:flutter/material.dart';
void main() => runApp(MyMovies());
```

```
class MyMovies extends StatelessWidget {
  @override
  Widget build(BuildContext context) {
    return MaterialApp(
      title: 'My Movies',
      theme: ThemeData(
        primarySwatch: Colors.deepOrange,
      ),
      home: Home(),
    );
  }
}

class Home extends StatelessWidget {
  @override
  Widget build(BuildContext context) {
   return MovieList();
  }
}
```

2. There's nothing new in this code. Just notice that we chose `ThemeData`, with `Colors.deepOrange primarySwatch`, and in `Home StatelessWidget`, we are calling the `MovieList` class, which we haven't created yet. Let's immediately fix this by adding a new file in our `lib` folder called `movie_list.dart` and adding a `MovieList` stateful widget:

```
import 'package:flutter/material.dart';

class MovieList extends StatefulWidget {
  @override
  _MovieListState createState() => _MovieListState();
}

class _MovieListState extends State<MovieList> {
  @override
  Widget build(BuildContext context) {
    return Container();
  }
}
```

3. Let's import this new file in the `main.dart` file to fix the error we are receiving right now:

```
import 'movie_list.dart';
```

4. Now, we need to show the data retrieved by the `getUpcoming()` async method in the `HttpHelper` class. To do that, first, let's import the `http_helper.dart` file at the top of the `movie_list.dart` file:

```
import 'http_helper.dart';
```

5. In the `_MovieListState` class, let's create `String` that will contain the data that we need to show an `HttpHelper` called `helper`:

```
String result;
HttpHelper helper;
```

6. Let's override the `initState` method and create an `HttpHelper` instance:

```
@override
  void initState() {
    helper = HttpHelper();
    super.initState();
  }
```

7. Then, in the `build` method, we'll call the `getUpcoming` asynchronous method, and when the results are returned (this is the `then` method), we call the `setState` method to update the result string with the value that was returned:

```
@override
  Widget build(BuildContext context) {
    helper.getUpcoming().then(
      (value) {
        setState(() {
          result = value;
        });
      }
    );
    return Scaffold(
      appBar: AppBar(title: Text('Movies'),),
      body: Container(
      child: Text(result)
    ));
  }
```

8. Next, we'll return `Scaffold` that, in its body, shows `Container` with a `Text` child, containing the result string.

9. If you try the app right now, the end result should look similar to this:

Here, you have some text that takes up all of the available space on the screen and contains all of the JSON code retrieved from the Movies API. This is probably not the most user-friendly way to show data to your users, but we'll fix that next!

Adding the Movie model class

In object-oriented languages, a common pattern when dealing with data, especially structured data, is creating classes that will serve as an interface between the data and the application. This is to make our code easier to both read and maintain, so we'll follow this pattern and create a `Movie` class that will contain the movie properties that we want to show to our user.

There are several pieces of data in the JSON file we received from the Movies API, but we'll just select a few of them: the ID, the title, the average votes, the release date, the overview (which is a description of the movie), and the poster path (this will contain the path of the image to show in our app, if one is available).

In the next few steps, we'll create the properties and methods of the `Movie` class and update the `HttpHelper` class to start parsing the data received from the web service:

1. Let's create a new file, called `movie.dart`, and in the file, let's create a `Movie` class, as follows:

```
class Movie {
   int id;
   String title;
   double voteAverage;
   String releaseDate;
   String overview;
   String posterPath;
}
```

2. Next, let's also create a constructor that will set all of the fields in the class:

```
Movie(this.id, this.title, this.voteAverage, this.releaseDate,
   this.overview, this.posterPath);
```

3. When we get the data from the web API, we want to transform it into a `Movie`. So, we need a method to get data in JSON format and output a `Movie` object. Let's write the following code:

```
Movie.fromJson(Map<String, dynamic> parsedJson) {
      this.id = parsedJson['id'];
      this.title = parsedJson['title'];
      this.voteAverage = parsedJson['vote_average']*1.0;
      this.releaseDate = parsedJson['release_date'];
      this.overview = parsedJson['overview'];
      this.posterPath = parsedJson['poster_path'];
   }
```

This named constructor will return a `Movie` object. As a parameter, it will take a `Map`, which is a **key-value pair set**. The key will be a string (for example, `"title"`), and the value needs to be `dynamic`, as it can be text or a number.

When you get a `Map`, you can access its values with square brackets and the key name. That's why we can access the value of the title key by writing `parsedJson['title']`.

We now have a function that can transform a `Map` into a `Movie`. But at this moment, we don't have any `Map`, we just have a `String` containing all of the text that we retrieved from the web service.

4. Let's get to the `httpHelper getUpcoming()` function and parse the JSON content that we receive, as shown here:

```
Future<List> getUpcoming() async {
    final String upcoming = urlBase + urlUpcoming + urlkey
     + urlLanguage;
    http.Response result = await http.get(upcoming);
    if (result.statusCode == HttpStatus.ok) {
      final jsonResponse = json.decode(result.body);
      final moviesMap = jsonResponse['results'];
      List movies = moviesMap.map((i) =>
      Movie.fromJson(i)).toList();
      return movies;
    }
    else {
      return null;
    }
}
```

5. This will require importing the `convert.dart` library and `movie.dart` at the top of the file:

```
import 'dart:convert';
import 'movie.dart';
```

OK, let's see what's happening there. You might remember that the body property of a `Response` object is a string. To make it easy to parse the result of our request, we want to transform this string into an object:

```
final jsonResponse = json.decode(result.body);
```

The type returned by `json.decode` is `dynamic`. This means that it can contain any type at runtime.

If you have a look at the JSON text retrieved from the web service, it contains a header with information about the response, and a `results` node that contains an array with all of the movies that were returned. We are not interested in the header, so we just need to parse the `'results'` array:

```
final moviesMap = jsonResponse['results'];
```

From there, we call the `map()` method. You can call the `map()` method over an `Iterable` (which basically means a set of objects). This will iterate each element of the set (in this case, `i`), and for each object inside `moviesMap`, it will return `Movie`, as returned by the `fromJSON` constructor of the `Movie` class. Yes, several different things are happening in this single line of code:

```
List movies = moviesMap.map((i) => Movie.fromJson(i)).toList();
```

Sometimes, I explain this concept with an example that may be a bit more familiar: imagine that you want to make 10 glasses of lemonade. You go to the store and the seller gives you a box with the content description (10 lemons) and, of course, the 10 lemons inside. When you go home, you take the 10 lemons from the box, throw the box away, and cut the lemons so that you can squeeze them to prepare 10 glasses of lemonade. This is what we are trying to achieve here: we get the full JSON (*the lemon box*) from the web service (*the store*) with `http.get(upcoming)`; we only take the movies (*only the lemons, we don't need the box*) with `jsonResponse['results'];`. We then transform the dynamic objects into movies (*from lemon to lemonade*) with `moviesMap.map((i) => Movie.fromJson(i)).toList()`.

Now we have a list of movies. In the next section, we'll show those movies to the user in a `ListView`.

Adding a ListView to show data

Instead of showing a single piece of text, with no user interaction whatsoever, for the UI, we'll use one of the most common widgets that deals with data: the ListView. This will allow our user to scroll vertically through the movies. And as the ListView can contain any type of widget, it will give us the freedom to show data in any way we want:

1. So, let's open the movie_list.dart file, and at the top of the _MovieListState class, let's create two variables, which will contain the list of movies and the number of movies that were retrieved:

   ```
   int moviesCount;
   List movies;
   ```

2. Then, create a new method, called initialize. It returns a future and is marked as async.

3. Inside the method, call the getUpcoming method from the httpHelper class, and then call the setState method so that we can set moviesCount and the movie's properties:

   ```
   Future initialize() async {
       movies = List();
       movies = await helper.getUpcoming();
       setState(() {
         moviesCount = movies.length;
         movies = movies;
       });
   }
   ```

4. In the build() method of the class, delete the call to the getUpcoming method and the text containing the result string. The new build method should look like this:

   ```
   @override
   Widget build(BuildContext context) {
       return Scaffold(
         appBar: AppBar(title: Text('Movies'),),
         body: Container()
       );
   }
   ```

5. Instead of returning a `Container`, we want to return a `ListView` showing the `Movies` objects returned by the `getUpcoming()` method. So, in the body of the `Scaffold`, let's write the following code:

```
body: ListView.builder (
        itemCount: (this.moviesCount==null) ? 0 : this.moviesCount,
        itemBuilder: (BuildContext context, int position) {
        })
```

As we've already mentioned, a `ListView` is a scrolling widget: it displays its children one after another either horizontally or vertically, and its default direction is vertical. The `ListView.builder` constructor that we're using here makes it easy to create a `ListView` and is very performant, as it creates items as they're scrolled onto the screen. This is recommended whenever you have long lists.

The `itemCount` parameter of the builder constructor takes the number of items that the `ListView` will contain. In our code, we are using a ternary operator. If the `moviesCount` property is null, then the number of items will be 0, otherwise, it will be the `moviesCount` property set in the `initialize()` method.

The second parameter is `itemBuilder`. This is an iteration method for each item in the `ListView` and takes `BuildContext` and the current position. It's here that we'll decide what to show to our user.

6. Let's return a `Card`, which is a container widget with slightly rounded corners and a shadow. When using a `Card`, you can choose a color and an elevation. In this case, let's set the color to `white` and the elevation to `2.0`.

7. In the child of a `Card`, let's put a `ListTile` as follows:

```
itemBuilder: (BuildContext context, int position) {
        return Card(
        color: Colors.white,
        elevation: 2.0,
        child: ListTile(
          title: Text(movies[position].title),
          subtitle: Text('Released: '
          + movies[position].releaseDate + ' - Vote: ' +
          movies[position].voteAverage.toString()),
        ));
        })
```

`ListTile` is another material widget that can contain one to three lines of text with optional icons at the beginning and end.

8. Let's also call the `initialize` method in the `initState` method so that we can try out the app:

```
@override
  void initState() {
    helper = HttpHelper();
    initialize();
    super.initState();
  }
```

9. The result should look similar to this (the titles should be different, as movies come out every day!):

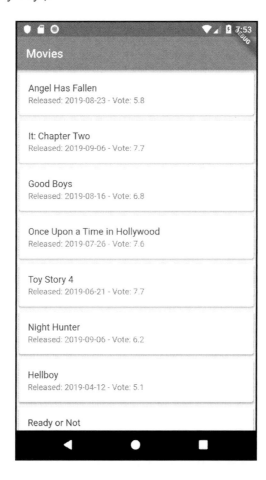

As you can see, the results are much more readable now; your user will be able to scroll through the movies vertically and will only see the information that we have decided they should see. Now let's add a small poster image to the left of the text.

Showing a trailing icon in a ListTile

Most movies have a poster image. We want to add the poster image at the left of the title and subtitle in `ListTile`. Let's look at how we can do that:

1. In the Movie Database API, there's a path for the poster icons. Let's add it at the top of the `_MovieListState` class:

```
final String iconBase = 'https://image.tmdb.org/t/p/w92/';
```

2. If there is no poster image, we want to show a default image. Let's also create a `final String` for it at the top of the class:

```
final String defaultImage =
'https://images.freeimages.com/images/large-previews/5eb/movie-clap
board-1184339.jpg';
```

3. In the build method, let's declare a `NetworkImage` called `image`; then, in the `itemBuilder`, before returning `Card`, let's set the image depending on the path of the movie:

```
Widget build(BuildContext context) {
    NetworkImage image;
    return Scaffold(
      appBar: AppBar(title: Text('Movies'),),
      body: ListView.builder (
      itemCount: (this.moviesCount==null) ? 0 : this.moviesCount,
      itemBuilder: (BuildContext context, int position) {
        if (movies[position].posterPath != null) {
          image = NetworkImage(
              iconBase + movies[position].posterPath
            );
          }
        else {
          image = NetworkImage(defaultImage);
        }
```

4. The image variable contains a `NetworkImage`, either the one specified in the `posterPath` string or the default image. Now we need a way to show the image inside the `ListTile`. To do that, we can add a `leading` parameter that contains a `CircleAvatar` widget. Add the following code in the `ListTile` widget in the `build()` method:

```
leading: CircleAvatar(
            backgroundImage: image,
        ),
```

5. `CircleAvatar` is a circle that can contain an image or some text. Even if it's typically used for user's images, we can certainly adapt it for our movies.

6. The result is as follows:

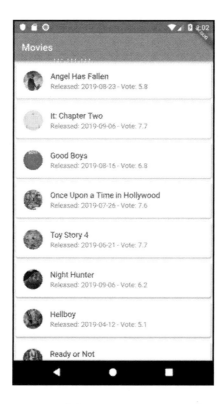

Well done! The UI of the first screen of the app is now complete. Of course, you could play with the text style or the size of `CircleAvatar`, but I'll leave this up to your preferences. What we need to do next is adding the second screen of our app: the Movie Detail screen.

Showing the detail screen and passing data through screens

The detail screen of the app will show a bigger poster image and an overview of the movie. All of the required data, except the image, has already been downloaded and parsed from the web service, so we won't need to use the HTTP library for this screen.

The steps required to complete this part are as follows:

1. Create the second screen, with the widgets that will need to receive the movie data to set the title, the image, and the overview of the movie.
2. Respond to the tap of the user in the ListView.
3. Pass the movie data from the first screen to the second screen.

So let's create a new file, called movie_detail.dart, in the lib folder of the app. Here, we'll only need to import the material.dart library to access the material widgets, and our movie.dart file for the Movie class:

```
import 'package:flutter/material.dart';
import 'movie.dart';
```

The question we need to answer now is: *do we use a stateless or a stateful widget for this screen?* As you already know, you use stateful widgets when the state of a widget changes during its life cycle. You might be tempted to think that as the image, title, and overview of a movie can change, we need a stateful widget here, but this is not the case. When the user clicks on one of the items of the ListView, we will always build a new instance of the screen, passing the movie data. So this screen will not need to change during its life cycle:

1. Create a stateless widget using the stless shortcut. We can call this class MovieDetail:

   ```
   class MovieDetail extends StatelessWidget {
     @override
     Widget build(BuildContext context) {
       return Container(
       );
     }
   }
   ```

2. When we call `MovieDetail`, we want to pass a `Movie`. So, at the top of the `MovieDetail` class, create a `movie` property, and mark it as `final` as this is a stateless widget:

```
final Movie movie;
```

3. Then, create a constructor that sets the `movie` property of our `Widget` class:

```
MovieDetail(this.movie);
```

4. In the `build()` method, instead of returning a `Container`, return a `Scaffold`. Its `appBar` will contain the title of the `Movie`, and in the body, we'll place a `SingleChildScrollView`. This widget will make its child scrollable if it doesn't fit the screen.

5. In the `SingleChildScrollView`, we'll place a `Center` widget, whose child will be a `Column` containing `Text` with the movie overview:

```
return Scaffold(
    appBar: AppBar(
      title: Text(movie.title),
    ),
    body:SingleChildScrollView(child: Center(child:Column(
    children: <Widget>[
      Container(
        padding: EdgeInsets.only(left: 16, right: 16),
        child: Text(movie.overview),
      )],
    )))));
```

6. Now we only need to add the image of the poster. Let's create a `final String` containing the path of the image under the movie declaration:

```
final String imgPath='https://image.tmdb.org/t/p/w500/';
```

7. Then, let's use the same logic we've used in the MovieList screen: if the image is available, we'll show it; otherwise, we'll only show a default picture. So, at the top of the build method, add the code to set the path of the image:

```
String path;
if (movie.posterPath != null) {
    path= imgPath + movie.posterPath;
}
else {
    path =
'https://images.freeimages.com/images/large-previews/5eb/movie-clap
board-1184339.jpg';
}
```

8. Still in the build method, to decide the size of the image, we'll get the height of the screen:

```
double height = MediaQuery.of(context).size.height;
```

9. Then, in the column, above the overview, let's add a Container that, as child, will have the correct image, shown by calling the Image.network constructor. We'll also add some padding, and the height of the image will be the context height divided by 1.5:

```
Container(
    padding: EdgeInsets.all(16),
    height: height / 1.5,
    child: Image.network(path)
),
```

10. The UI of the detail view is ready. We only need to call it from the ListView. So let's get back to the movie_list.dart file and import the movie_detail.dart file:

```
import 'movie_detail.dart';
```

11. Then, let's add the onTap parameter to the ListTile in the build method. Here, we'll declare MaterialPageRoute that will get to MovieDetail, but in its builder, we'll also pass the movie at the current position. This is how easy it is to pass data to another widget in Flutter!

12. Then, we just call the Navigator.push method to actually add the MovieDetail route to the Navigator stack:

```
onTap: () {
    MaterialPageRoute route = MaterialPageRoute(
```

```
                    builder: (_) => MovieDetail(movies[position]));
            Navigator.push(context, route);
        },
```

13. And if you try the app now, you'll be able to tap on any movie on the screen and see the Detail view, as shown here:

Now our app is almost complete. We only need to add a search function and we'll close this project!

Adding the search feature

By leveraging the Movie Database web service search feature, we'll allow our users to search any movie by title. What we want to do is show a search icon button in the `AppBar`. When the user taps on the button they will be able to enter part of a movie title into a `TextField`, and when they press the search button on the keyboard, the app will call the web service to retrieve all movies that contain the user's input.

Let's add the logic that we'll use to implement the search feature and call the Movie Database web API with the title we want to search:

1. In the http_helper.dart file, in the HttpHelper class, let's declare a final String, containing the beginning of the URL required to perform a movie search. Obviously each API has its own URL structure, but most public web services have thorough documentation that will help you to build the correct URLs:

   ```
   final String urlSearchBase =
   'https://api.themoviedb.org/3/search/movie?api_key=[YOUR API KEY
   HERE]&query=';
   ```

I generally recommend creating a settings structure in your files. For example, in this project, we set all of the URL constants at the beginning of the httpHelper class. It's usually not a good idea to build the URLs when you need to use them, as your code gets harder to debug.

2. Next, let's create a new function, called findMovies, that will return a List of Movies, and will take a string containing the title or part of the title:

   ```
   Future<List> findMovies(String title) async {
       final String query = urlSearchBase + title ;
       http.Response result = await http.get(query);
       if (result.statusCode == HttpStatus.ok) {
         final jsonResponse = json.decode(result.body);
         final moviesMap = jsonResponse['results'];
         List movies = moviesMap.map((i) =>
         Movie.fromJson(i)).toList();
         return movies;
       }
       else {
         return null;
       } }
   ```

3. In the findMovies() function, we first create the query to pass to the web API, which is a concatenation of urlSearchBase and the title that was passed to the function.

4. Then we call the http.get method, passing the query and getting back a Response object, which we call result.

If the status code of `result` is `HttpStatus.ok`, we decode and parse the body of the result and create and return a `List` of `Movies` based on the result. The process is very similar to the `getUpcoming` method, but here we are passing a query based on the user input.

5. Next, we need to implement the search function in the UI. There are several ways we could achieve this, but what we'll do is leverage the `AppBar` widget, which can contain not only text but also icons, buttons, and several other widgets, including a `TextField`.

6. Let's get back to the `movie_list.dart` file. We'll create two properties in the `_MovieListState` class: one for the visible icon (the search icon when the screen is loaded) and the second a generic widget that at the beginning will be a `Text` widget containing `Movies`:

```
Icon visibleIcon = Icon(Icons.search);
Widget searchBar= Text('Movies');
```

7. Next, in the `appBar` of the `Scaffold` in the `build()` method, let's change the title to take the `searchBar` widget, and let's add an `actions` parameter. This takes an array of widgets that are displayed after the title. Usually, they are buttons representing common operations. This will only contain a single `IconButton` containing `Icons.search`:

```
title: searchBar,
actions: <Widget>[
  IconButton(
  icon: visibleIcon,
  onPressed: () {}
),]),
```

8. For the `onPressed` function of `IconButton`, we'll call the `setState` method so that we can show the `TextField` and change the icon when the user presses the search button:

```
onPressed: () {
    setState(() {
        if (this.visibleIcon.icon == Icons.search) {
            this.visibleIcon = Icon(Icons.cancel);
            this.searchBar = TextField(
                textInputAction: TextInputAction.search,
                style: TextStyle(
                color: Colors.white,
                fontSize: 20.0, ),
            ); }
        else {
```

```
            setState(() {
            this.visibleIcon = Icon(Icons.search);
            this.searchBar= Text('Movies');
    });}});},
```

A few notes about the preceding code: `Icons.search` and `Icons.cancel` are two graphics that should help to make it clear what actions can be expected in the app. You can find a full updated list of the available Flutter icons at `https://api.flutter.dev/flutter/material/Icons-class.html`.

The `textInputAction` property of `TextField` allows you to specify the main action of the soft keyboard. `TextInputAction.search` should show a magnifying glass on the keyboard, but the end result always depends on the operating system you're using.

If you try the app right now, you'll notice that the search button is visible at the top right of the screen, and if you tap on it, input text will appear on `AppBar`, allowing you to type some text.

Now, we only need to call the `findMovies` method from the `HttpHelper` class when the user presses the search button on the keyboard.

9. In the `_MovieListState` class, let's write a method to do that: we can call it `search`. It will be asynchronous, as it will be calling an async function, and it takes the text that's been typed by the user:

```
Future search(text) async {
    movies = await helper.findMovies(text);
    setState(() {
      moviesCount = movies.length;
      movies = movies;
    });
  }
```

The purpose of the `search` method is to call the `HttpHelper findMovies` method, wait for its result, and then call the `setState` method to update the `moviesCount` and `movies` properties so that the UI will show the movies that were found.

10. Finally, in the `TextField` in the `AppBar`, let's call the `search()` method when the user submits the query:

```
onSubmitted: (String text) {
    search(text);
},
```

11. And if you try the app now, you'll be able to search for any movie you want:

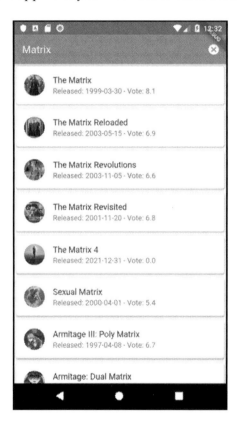

Well done, your app is now complete! And by the way, if you have a look at the titles on the screen, you'll notice that there's a **The Matrix 4** movie there: this is how I discovered that there would be a fourth installment of that movie!

Summary

With the project we've built in this chapter, you are now able to read data from an external source in any app that you'll design. This opens up literally endless opportunities for your creations.

In particular, we've seen how to leverage the `get()` method of the `http` library to retrieve data from a URL. We've seen an example of JSON, used the `decode` method, and seen how to deal with an `http.Response` object. We've checked the `Response` status with the `HttpStatus` enumerator and parsed some JSON content using the `map()` method.

We've dealt with a powerful tool in Dart and Flutter, which is asynchronous programming: using the `async`, `await`, and `then` keywords, together with the `Future` object, we've created a set of functions and features that do not block the main execution thread of your app. Hopefully, you now understand how to leverage multi-threading in your Flutter apps.

We've also downloaded images from the web with `Image.network()` and `NetworkImage`.

For the UI, we've seen how to use a `ListView` using the builder constructor. By setting the `itemCount` and `itemBuilder` parameters, we created a nice, scrolling list in an efficient way. We've also added `ListTile` widgets, with their `title`, `subtitle`, and `leading` properties.

We've seen how easy it is to pass data through screens in Flutter by leveraging the `MaterialPageRoute builder` constructor and hence creating a second screen for the details of a `Movie` without having to download any data.

Finally, we've added a search feature to our app. Using `AppBar` again, we've changed the widgets dynamically based on the user actions and performed a search over the Movie Database web service.

You've added a powerful tool to your Flutter toolkit: the ability to retrieve data from an outside service.

In the next chapter, you'll see how to store data inside your device in a relational database. Used together, these two features make most of what's needed to build a successful business app.

Questions

At the end of each project, you'll find a few questions to help you to remember and review the contents covered in each chapter. Please try to answer the following questions, and when in doubt, have a look at the content in this chapter: you'll find all of the answers there!

1. Is this code correct?

   ```
   String data = http.get(url);
   ```

   If not, why?

2. What are the JSON and XML formats used for?
3. What is a thread?
4. Can you name a few common asynchronous scenarios?
5. When should you use the `async/await` keywords?
6. What's the difference between `ListView` and `ListTile`?
7. How can you use the `map` method to parse data and create a list?
8. How do you pass data from one screen to another?
9. When should you use the `json.decode` method over the body of a `Response` object?
10. What is `CircleAvatar`?

Further reading

As retrieving data from the web is a hot topic, you'll find plenty of resources that deal with it. A good starting point is a short article on the official website explaining the process with a simple example. You can find it at `https://flutter.dev/docs/cookbook/networking/fetch-data`.

Multi-threading and asynchronous programming might be confusing for many developers when they first deal with it. There's a really useful guide at `https://dart.dev/codelabs/async-await` that thoroughly explains the main concepts of how to use this pattern with several examples and use cases.

Parsing JSON content can get complicated when data is complex. You can find a complete guide to it at `https://flutter.dev/docs/development/data-and-backend/json`.

For a deeper understanding of the `ListView` widget, a necessary step is reading the content at `https://api.flutter.dev/flutter/widgets/ListView-class.html`.

Even if, for this project, we haven't added any testing features, when you're adding complexity, it's always a good idea to use automated testing systems. A great place to start is `https://flutter.dev/docs/cookbook/testing/unit/introduction`.

6
Store That Data - Using Sq(F)Lite To Store Data in a Local Database

The project we'll build in this chapter will be a simple **Shopping List** app: if you are like me, you might forget things now and then, and while this project will probably not solve your memory issues, it might help you come back from the supermarket with all the groceries you need.

In `Chapter 5`, *Let's Go to the Movies - Getting Data from the Web*, you've seen how to retrieve data from a web service. In this chapter, you'll learn how to store data in the device itself. Together, HTTP methods and storing data cover the core functionalities of most business apps: think of an app that keeps an inventory of a store, or an app to keep track of your personal expenses, or a fitness app that measures your exercise time. All these apps have something in common: they store data.

By the end of this chapter, you'll build a fully functional database app, and you'll learn how to do the following:

- Use SQLite in Flutter.
- Create model classes.
- Show data to users of the app.
- Use singletons, and perform **Create, Read, Update and Delete** (CRUD) actions on a local database.

Following the project described in the next few pages, you'll be able to create an app with Flutter that stores data in a local relational database.

The time required to build the project described here is approximately 3 hours.

Technical requirements

You'll find the completed app code on the book's GitHub repository at https://github.com/PacktPublishing/Flutter-Projects.

To follow along with the code examples in this book, you should have the following software installed on your Windows, Mac, Linux, or Chrome OS device:

- The Flutter **software development kit (SDK)**.
- When developing for Android: the Android SDK, easily installed by Android Studio.
- When developing for iOS: macOS and Xcode.
- An emulator (Android), a simulator (iOS), or a connected iOS or Android device enabled for debugging.
- An editor: Visual Studio Code, Android Studio, or IntelliJ IDEA are recommended. All should have the Flutter/Dart extensions installed.
- For this chapter, some knowledge of relational databases will be helpful, even if not strictly required.

Essential theory and context

According to the official site (SQLite.org), SQLite is a *"small, fast, self-contained, high-reliability, full-featured, SQL database engine"*.

Let's see what that means to us, as Flutter mobile developers: first of all, SQLite is an SQL database engine. That means that you can use the SQL language to build queries, so if you are already familiar with SQL, you can leverage your knowledge. If you are totally new to databases, I suggest you have a look at the excellent W3Schools SQL tutorial at https://www.w3schools.com/sql/default.asp: you'll find it much easier to follow along with the project in this chapter.

The main features of SQLite are as follows:

- **Small and fast**: Developers have extensively tested SQLite speed and file size, and it outperformed several other technologies, both as space on disk and for its speed of retrieval of data. More information is available at: https://sqlite.org/fasterthanfs.html and https://sqlite.org/footprint.html.

- **Self-contained** means that SQLite requires very few external libraries, making it the perfect choice for any lightweight, platform-independent app. SQLite reads and writes directly from the database files on disk, so you don't have to set up any client-server connection in order to use it.
- **High reliability**: SQLite has been used without problems in several billions of mobile, **Internet of Things (IoT)**, and desktop devices for over a decade, proving itself extremely reliable.
- **Full-featured**: SQLite has a full-featured SQL implementation, including tables, views, indexes, triggers, foreign key constraints, and several standard SQL functions.

SQLite is a very good choice for persisting data in Android and iOS because it's easy to implement, and is secure, in the public domain, cross-platform, and compact.

 There are two schools of thought about how to pronounce SQLite: "Ess-Cue-El-Ight" or "See-Quel-Light". The creator of SQLite, Richard Hipp, generally uses the first one, but he also says that you can pronounce it however you want, and adds that there's no "official" pronunciation.

In order to add the SQLite features in Flutter, we will use the `sqflite` plugin, which is the SQLite plugin for Flutter that currently supports both iOS and Android, and contains asynchronous helper methods for SELECT, INSERT, UPDATE, AND DELETE queries. We'll see the steps required to use the `sqflite` plugin library throughout this chapter.

The database that we will create has two tables: lists and items. This can be seen in the following screenshot:

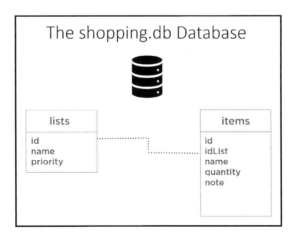

The **lists** table has three fields: **id** (integer), **name** (text), and **priority** (integer).

The **items** table has an **id** (integer), a **name** (text), a **quantity** (text), a **note** (text), and an **idList** (integer) that will be a foreign key constraint that points to the **id** of the list. As you can see, the schema is very simple, but it will allow us to experiment with many of the features that are needed in order to build a database app.

Project overview

The Shopping List app we'll build in this chapter is made of two screens. The first screen, which the user will see when they open the app, shows a shopping list, as illustrated in the following screenshot:

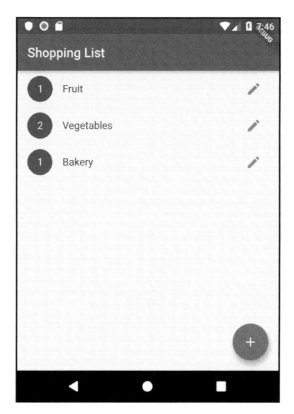

Each item on the list has a priority, which is the number you see on the left of the preceding screenshot, a name (**Bakery**, **Fruit**, and so on), and an edit button on the right. When you swipe on any of the items in the list, the item will be deleted, and when you tap on the edit button, the app will show an edit dialog screen, allowing you to edit the **Shopping List** name and priority, as illustrated in the following screenshot:

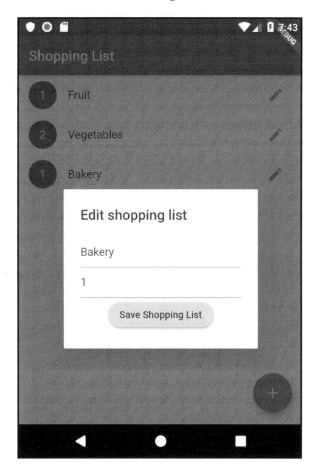

When you tap on one of the shopping lists, you'll get to the second screen of the app, which shows another list: the items contained in the shopping list you selected. For example, if you tap on the **Fruit** shopping list, you'll see the items: **Oranges** and **Apples**, as shown in the following screenshot:

Each item on the list will have a name, a quantity, and a note. The functionality of the screen will be similar to the first screen: you'll be able to add new items by tapping on the **Floating Action Button (FAB)**, edit items by tapping on the edit button, and delete items from the list by swiping any element of the list.

As usual, we'll create a new project from scratch, and in the next section, you'll see how to add a SQLite database to your Flutter app.

Using sqflite databases

In this section, we'll create a new project, add the `sqflite` dependencies, and create our database through a SQL raw query. Then, we will test the database we've created by adding some mock data and printing it in the debug console. This will require a few methods to insert and retrieve data from the database.

Creating an sqflite database

Let's create a new Flutter project from your editor. We can call it `shopping`. Follow the steps given here:

1. As `sqflite` is a package, the first step to perform in order to be able to use it in our project is adding the dependency in the `pubspec.yaml` file.

   In order to find the latest version of the dependency, please visit `https://pub.dev/packages/sqflite`. The dependencies that we are going to use in this project are shown in the following code block:

   ```
   dependencies:
     flutter:
       sdk: flutter
     sqflite: ^1.2.0
     path: ^1.6.4
   ```

2. In the `lib` folder, create a subfolder called `util`. Here, we'll create a new file: `dbhelper.dart`. This file will contain the methods to create the database, and to retrieve and write data.

3. At the top of the file, we'll import `sqflite.dart` and `path.dart`. `path.dart` is a library that allows you to manipulate file paths. This is useful here, as each platform (iOS or Android) saves the file in different paths. By using the `path.dart` library, we don't need to know how files are saved in the current operating system, and we can still access the database using the same code. Import the `path` and `sqflite` libraries at the top of the `dbhelper.dart` file, as follows:

   ```
   import 'package:path/path.dart';
   import 'package:sqflite/sqflite.dart';
   ```

4. Create a class that can be called from other parts of our code: quite predictably, we can call it `DbHelper`, as shown in the following snippet:

```
class DbHelper {}
```

5. Inside the class, create two variables: an integer called `version` and a database called `db`. `version` contains a number that represents the version of the database, which at the beginning is `1`. This will make it easier to update the database when you need to change something in its structure. `db` will contain the SQLite database itself. Place the two declarations at the top of the `DbHelper` class, like this:

```
final int version = 1;
Database db;
```

6. Create a method that will open the database if it exists, or create it if it doesn't; we can call it `openDb`.

7. As database operations may take some time to execute, especially when they involve dealing with a large quantity of data, they are asynchronous. Therefore, the `openDb` function will be asynchronous and return a `Future` of type `Database`. Let's place the following code at the end of the `DbHelper` class:

```
Future<Database> openDb() async {}
```

8. Inside the function, first, we need to check whether the `db` object is null. This is because we want to avoid opening a new instance of the database unnecessarily. In the `openDb()` method, let's add the following code:

```
if (db == null) {}
```

9. If `db` is null, we need to open the database. The `sqflite` library has an `openDatabase` method. We'll set three parameters in our call: the path of the database to be opened, the version of the database, and the `onCreate` parameter. The `onCreate` parameter will only be called if the database at the path specified is not found, or the version is different. The code for this is shown in the following block:

```
if (db == null) {
    db = await openDatabase(join(await getDatabasesPath(),
    'shopping.db'),
      onCreate: (database, version) {
    database.execute(
        'CREATE TABLE lists(id INTEGER PRIMARY KEY, name TEXT,
          priority
```

```
        INTEGER)');
    database.execute(
        'CREATE TABLE items(id INTEGER PRIMARY KEY,
            idList INTEGER, name TEXT, quantity TEXT,
            note TEXT, ' + 'FOREIGN KEY(idList)
            REFERENCES lists(id))');
}, version: version);
}
```

The function inside the `onCreate` parameter takes two values: a `database` and a `version`. In the function, we call the `execute()` method, which performs raw SQL queries in a database. Here, we are calling it twice: the first time to create the lists table, and the second time for the items table.

You may notice that we are using only two data types: `INTEGER` and `TEXT`.

 In SQLite, there are only five data types: `NULL`, `INTEGER`, `REAL`, `TEXT`, and `BLOB`. Note that there are no Boolean or Date data types.

The quantity field of the items table is a `TEXT` and not a number because we want to allow the user to insert the measure as well, such as "5 lbs" or "2 kg".

 When an integer field is called `id` and is a primary key, when you provide `NULL` while inserting a new record, the database will automatically assign a new value, with an auto-increment logic. So, if the greatest ID is 10, the next record will automatically take 11.

10. Finally, let's return the database at the end of the `openDb()` method, like this:

```
return db;
```

To sum up, what happens here is that if a database named `shopping.db` exists and has a version number of 1, the database gets opened. Otherwise, it gets created.

Let's check if everything works as expected, next.

Testing the database

At this time, even if we called the `openDb()` method, we would have no way of knowing whether the database has been correctly created or not.

In order to test the database, we'll create a method in the `DbHelper` class that will insert one record in the lists table, one record in the items table, and then will retrieve both and print them in the debug console. Finally, we'll refactor the main method so that it calls the testing method. This way, we'll be sure that the database has been created correctly and we can read and write data to it. Follow these steps:

1. Create a new method in the `DbHelper` class, called `testDb()`, that will insert some mock data into our database, and then retrieve the data and print it into the debug console. All database methods are asynchronous, so `testDb()` returns a `Future`, and is marked `async`, as follows:

```
Future testDb() async { }
```

For a refresher on `Future`, `async` and `await`, see `Chapter 5`, *Let's Go to the Movies - Getting Data from the Web*.

2. Insert a record inside this method in the lists table, as shown in the following code block:

```
Future testDb() async {
    db = await openDb();
    await db.execute('INSERT INTO lists VALUES (0, "Fruit", 2)');
    await db.execute('INSERT INTO items VALUES (0, 0, "Apples",
    "2 Kg",
    "Better if they are green")');
    List lists = await db.rawQuery('select * from lists');
    List items = await db.rawQuery('select * from items');
    print(lists[0].toString());
    print(items[0].toString());
}
```

Let's see what's happening in the preceding code:

- First, we await the `openDb()` method, which returns the database: db = await openDb();. The first time you call this method, the database is created.
- Then, we call the `execute` method twice: `await db.execute`. We call this the first time to insert a record into the **lists** table, and the second time, we call it to insert a record into the **items** table. In both cases, we are using the SQL language, with an `insert` query.

- Next, we read from the tables in the database using the `rawQuery` method and passing a `select` query.
  `Select *` takes all the values from the specified table. We return the retrieved values into a `List`.
- Finally, we print into the debug console the first element of the two lists we have populated with the `rawQuery` method: `lists` and `items`.

3. Now, we need to call the `testDb()` method from the main method of our app. Go to the `main.dart` file and remove the default code created by the framework, leaving only the basic code, as shown in the following block:

```dart
import 'package:flutter/material.dart';

void main() => runApp(MyApp());

class MyApp extends StatelessWidget {
  @override
  Widget build(BuildContext context) {
    return MaterialApp(
      title: 'Shoppping List',
      theme: ThemeData(
        primarySwatch: Colors.blue,
      ),
      home: Container()
    );
  }
}
```

4. At the top of the file, import `dbhelper.dart`, as follows:

```dart
import './util/dbhelper.dart';
```

5. At the beginning of the `build()` method of the `MyApp` class, create an instance of the `DbHelper` class, called `helper`, and then call its `testDb()` method, like this:

```dart
DbHelper helper = DbHelper();
helper.testDb();
```

We are now ready to try the app: if you run it and have a look at the **debug console**, you should see the result of the SELECT query that we performed over the database. In the following code snippet, you can see an example of the debug console content:

```
I/flutter ( 4766): {id: 0, name: Fruit, priority: 2}
I/flutter ( 4766): {id: 0, idList: 0, name: Apples, quantity: 2 Kg, note:
Better if they are green}
```

This means that we successfully inserted and retrieved data from the two tables—lists and items—in our database. That's a good starting point, but right now, our app is just showing a white screen. In the next sections of the chapter, we'll have to make the app more interactive, allowing our users to view and edit data from the app itself.

 Please note that if you run the app more than once, you will get an SQL exception due to a constraint failure, as you'll insert records with the same unique row key into the tables. Just change the ID value in the insert statement to add more data.

In the next section, we'll begin the process by creating the model classes that we'll use in our code to interact more efficiently with the database.

Creating the model classes

A common approach when dealing with a database from an **Object-Oriented Programming** language (or **OOP** for short) is to deal with objects that mirror the structure of the tables in a database: this makes the code more reliable, easier to read, and helps prevent data inconsistencies.

Our shopping.db structure is extremely simple, so we'll just have to create two model classes, containing the same fields that are now in the tables, and a map method to simplify the process of inserting and editing data into the database. Follow these next steps to create a model class:

1. We'll begin with the lists: create a new folder, called models.
2. Inside the models folder, create a new file called shopping_list.dart.
3. Inside the file, create a class called ShoppingList that will contain three properties: the id integer, the name String, and the priority integer, as shown in the following code snippet:

```
class ShoppingList {
  int id;
  String name;
```

```
    int priority;
}
```

4. Next, create a constructor that will set the three properties, as follows:

```
ShoppingList(this.id, this.name, this.priority);
```

5. Finally, we'll create a `toMap()` method that will return a `Map` of type `String, dynamic`. A map is a collection of key/value pairs: the first type we specify is for the key, which in this case will always be a string. The second type is for the value: as we have different types in the table, this will be dynamic. In a `Map`, you can retrieve a value using its key. Add the code below to create the method:

```
Map<String, dynamic> toMap() {
    return {
        'id': (id==0)?null:id,
        'name': name,
        'priority': priority,
    };
}
```

In an SQLite database, when you provide a `null` value when you insert a new record, the database will automatically assign a new value, with an auto-increment logic. That's why for the `id`, we are using a ternary operator: when the `id` is equal to `0`, we change it to `null`, so that SQLite will be able to set the `id` for us.

For the other two fields, the `Map` will take the values of the class.

Now, we can repeat the same steps for the `Items` model class. Follow these next steps:

1. Create a new file called `list_items.dart` in the `models` folder.
2. Inside the file, create a class called `ListItem` that will contain five properties: an `id` (an integer), the ID of the `List` (again, an integer), the `name` (a `String`), `quantity` (an integer), and `note` (a `String`), as follows:

```
class ListItem {
    int id;
    int idList;
    String name;
    String quantity;
    String note;
}
```

3. Then, we'll create a constructor that will set all the properties, like this:

```
ListItem(this.id, this.idList, this.name, this.quantity,
this.note);
```

4. Create a toMap() method that will return a Map of type String, dynamic, using the same ternary operator to make the ID null when its value is 0, as follows:

```
Map<String, dynamic> toMap() {
 return {
 'id': (id==0)?null:id,
 'idList': idList,
 'name': name,
 'quantity': quantity,
 'note': note
 };
 }
```

Now, in the DbHelper class, we need to create two methods that will make use of the model classes to insert data into the shopping.db database.

5. Import the two model classes into the DbHelper class in the dbhelper.dart file, like this:

```
import '../models/list_items.dart';
import '../models/shopping_list.dart';
```

6. We'll begin with the insertList() method, which will insert a new record into the **lists** table. As with every database operation, this will be an asynchronous function, and it will return a Future of type int, as the insert method will return the ID of the record that was inserted. This method will take an instance of the ShoppingList model class as a parameter, called list, as shown in the following code snippet:

```
Future<int> insertList(ShoppingList list) async {}
```

7. Inside the insertList() method, we will call the insert() method of the database object: this is a specific helper method exposed by the sqflite library that takes three arguments, as shown in the following screenshot:

```
                   sqflite insert helper method

int id = await db.insert(        ←Call the insert helper method

        'items',                 ←Pass the name of the table

        item.toMap(),
                                 ←Pass the data to be inserted as a
);                                 Map
```

The `insert()` method allows you to specify the following parameters:

- The name of the table where we want to insert data—`lists`, in this case.
- A `Map` of the data that we want to insert: in order to get that, we'll call our `toMap()` function of the list parameter.
- Optionally, the `conflictAlgorithm` specifies the behavior that should be followed when you try to insert a record with the same ID twice. In this case, if the same list is inserted multiple times, it will replace the previous data with the new list that was passed to the function.

8. So, in our app, let's write the following code in the `insertList()` method:

```
int id = await this.db.insert(
    'lists',
    list.toMap(),
    conflictAlgorithm: ConflictAlgorithm.replace,
);
```

`insert()` is an asynchronous method, so we'll call it with the `await` command; the `id` will contain the ID of the new record that was inserted.

9. Finally, let's return the `id` by using the following code statement:

```
return id;
```

10. Still in the DbHelper class, create a second method, called insertItem, with exactly the same behavior as the insertList() method, which will insert a ListItem into the items table, as shown in the following code snippet:

```
Future<int> insertItem(ListItem item) async {
    int id = await db.insert(
      'items',
      item.toMap(),
      conflictAlgorithm: ConflictAlgorithm.replace,
    );
    return id;
}
```

11. We are now ready to test those two methods: we'll call them from the main.dart file. At the top of the file, let's import our two model classes, as follows:

```
import './models/list_items.dart';
import './models/shopping_list.dart';
```

We'll need to do some refactoring here, because the content of the main screen will change during the lifetime of the app, and therefore we'll need a stateful widget to redraw the content of the screen. So, it's probably worth doing it now when we only have little code here.

12. At the bottom of the main.dart file, after the MyApp class, let's create a new stateful widget, using the stful shortcut. We'll call this ShList, as shown in the following code snippet:

```
class ShList extends StatefulWidget {
  @override
  _ShListState createState() => _ShListState();
}
class _ShListState extends State<ShList> {
  @override
  Widget build(BuildContext context) {
    return Container();
  }
}
```

13. At the top of the _ShListState class, create an instance of the DbHelper class by adding the following code:

```
DbHelper helper = DbHelper();
```

14. **Remove** the following code from the `build()` method of the `MyApp` class: we don't need it here anymore:

```
DbHelper helper = DbHelper();
helper.testDb();
```

15. Inside the `_ShListState` class, add an async method called `showData()`. Later on, this method will actually show the data on the screen, but for now, we'll just use it to test our new `insertList` and `insertItem` methods. The following code snippet shows this:

```
Future showData () async {}
```

16. Inside the `showData()` function, we'll call the `openDb` method over the `helper` object. Using the `await` command makes sure the database has been opened **before** we try to insert data into it. This is illustrated in the following code snippet:

```
await helper.openDb();
```

17. Create a `ShoppingList` instance, and call the `insertList()` method on the `helper` object. We'll put the value returned by `insertList` into a `listId` integer, as follows:

```
ShoppingList list = ShoppingList(0, 'Bakery', 2);
int listId = await helper.insertList(list);
```

18. Let's repeat the same for a `ListItem`: here, the list ID will be taken from the `listId` variable, as follows:

```
ListItem item = ListItem(0, listId, 'Bread', 'note', '1 kg');
int itemId = await helper.insertItem(item);
```

19. Finally, let's print into the debug console the values that were retrieved, to make sure everything is working as expected, as follows:

```
print('List Id: ' + listId.toString());
print('Item Id: '+ itemId.toString());
```

20. The last step for this section is to call the `showData()` method. In the `build()` method of the `_ShListState` class, let's call the `showData()` method, like this:

```
showData();
```

21. In the `home` property of the `MaterialApp`, in the `build()` method of the `MyApp` class, let's create a `Scaffold` whose body calls the `ShList` class, as follows:

```
home: Scaffold(
    appBar: AppBar(title: Text('Shopping List'),),
    body: ShList()
));
```

We are now ready to run the app.

If everything worked as expected, you should now see the IDs of the records that we've inserted in the database (the numbers you see may vary based on the number of records in your database), as follows:

```
I/flutter ( 4589): List Id: 2
I/flutter ( 4589): Item Id: 3
```

Well done! We've created the model classes that will make it easier to deal with the database and used the `insert` helper method to insert data into our tables. It's now time to show that data to our user, which we'll do next!

Showing database data to the user

Now that we have added some data into our `shopping.db` database, it's time to show that data to the user. We'll begin by showing the available shopping lists on the first screen, in a `ListView`. After the user taps on any item of the list, they'll get to the second screen of the app, which will show all the items in the shopping list.

First, we'll create a function that retrieves the content of the lists table in our database, using a `sqflite` helper method, as follows:

1. In the `DbHelper` class, add a new method called `getLists()` that will return a `Future` of a `List`, containing a `ShoppingList`. As usual, this will be asynchronous. The following code snippet illustrates this:

```
Future<List<ShoppingList>> getLists() async {}
```

2. Inside the function, call the `query` helper method on the database. As this will retrieve all the data in the lists table, the only required parameter here is the name of the table, as shown in the following code snippet:

```
final List<Map<String, dynamic>> maps = await db.query('lists');
```

Note that the `query()` helper method returns a `List` of `Map` items. In order to use them easily, we need to convert the `List<Map<String, dynamic>` into a `List<ShoppingList>`. We can do that by calling the `List.generate()` method, which you can use to generate a list of values. The first parameter specifies the size of the list, and the second is a function that generates the values of the list.

3. Add the following code given in the `getLists()` function:

```
return List.generate(maps.length, (i) {
    return ShoppingList(
      maps[i]['id'],
      maps[i]['name'],
      maps[i]['priority'],
    );
});
```

The return value here is a `List` of `ShoppingList` objects, which is what we wanted to obtain. Once we've got the `List` of `ShoppingList` objects, we need to show those on the first screen of our app.

4. In the `main.dart` file, at the top of the `_ShListState` class, create a `shoppingList` property that will be a `List` of `ShoppingList` items, as follows:

```
List<ShoppingList> shoppingList;
```

5. In the `showData()` method, delete all the test code except the `await helper.openDb();` line. Under that, we'll call the `getLists()` function of our `helper` object, as follows:

```
shoppingList = await helper.getLists();
```

6. Call the `setState()` method to tell our app that the `ShoppingList` has changed, like this:

```
setState(() {
    shoppingList = shoppingList;
});
```

7. Now that we have retrieved all the needed data, we need to show it on the screen. In the `build()` method of the `_ShListState` class, return a `ListView.builder`, which will contain the number of items available in the `shoppingList` property. If `shoppingList` is `null`, then the `itemCount` of the `ListView` will be 0. In order to achieve this, as usual, we'll use the ternary operator syntax, which is shown in the following code snippet:

```
return ListView.builder(
    itemCount: (shoppingList != null)? shoppingList.length : 0,
);
```

8. In the `itemBuilder`, return a `ListTile` whose title will be the `name` property of the `shoppingList` list, at position `index`, like this:

```
itemBuilder:(BuildContext context, int index) {
 return ListTile(
 title: Text(shoppingList[index].name));
});
```

9. If everything worked as expected, if you try the app right now, you should see a list of the names of the shopping lists that we've inserted up to this point. This can be seen in the following screenshot:

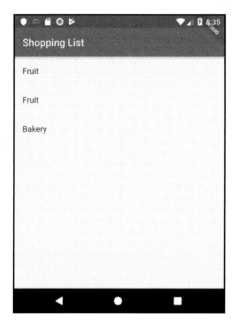

In order to complete this screen, we'll add a few more data for our items, as follows:

1. First, to make the **user interface (UI)** a bit more appealing, add a
   CircleAvatar to the leading property the ListTile, containing the priority,
   as follows:

```
return ListTile(
    title: Text(shoppingList[index].name),
    leading: CircleAvatar(child:
Text(shoppingList[index].priority.toString()),),
);
```

2. Then, still in the ListTile, add a trailing icon that we'll use later on to edit
   the shoppingList, like this:

```
trailing: IconButton(
    icon: Icon(Icons.edit),
    onPressed: (){},
)
```

Now that we can see the **Shopping List**, let's also show the items on each list. For this, we'll
need a new file, as follows:

1. In order to organize better our code, create a new folder called ui that will
   contain the UI files of our projects, except main.dart, which will remain in the
   lib folder.
2. In the ui folder, create a new file called items_screen.dart. Inside the new
   file, first, import the files that we'll need in order to show the items, as follows:

```
import 'package:flutter/material.dart';
import '../models/list_items.dart';
import '../models/shopping_list.dart';
import '../util/dbhelper.dart';
```

3. Create a stateful widget, called `ItemsScreen`, like this:

```
class ItemsScreen extends StatefulWidget {
  @override
  _ItemsScreenState createState() => _ItemsScreenState();
}
class _ItemsScreenState extends State<ItemsScreen> {
  @override
  Widget build(BuildContext context) {
    return Container();
  }
}
```

Each time we'll get to this screen, it will be because we have selected a `ShoppingList` object. We will never need to call this screen independently. So, it makes sense that when we create the `ItemsScreen` widget, we expect a `ShoppingList` to be passed.

4. At the top of the `ItemsScreen` class, create a final `ShoppingList` called `shoppingList`, and let's also create a constructor that will set the `shoppingList` property, as follows:

```
final ShoppingList shoppingList;
ItemsScreen(this.shoppingList);
```

5. We'll do the same for the `State`: at the top of the `_ItemsScreenState` class, declare a `ShoppingList`, and create the constructor that sets it, as follows:

```
final ShoppingList shoppingList;
_ItemsScreenState(this.shoppingList);
```

6. Now, when calling the `createState()` method, add the `shoppingList` argument, like this:

```
@override
_ItemsScreenState createState() =>
_ItemsScreenState(this.shoppingList);
```

7. Now that we have set the `shoppingList`, in the `build()` method of the `_ItemsScreenState` class, return a `Scaffold` that, in the `AppBar` title, shows the name of the `shoppingList`, as follows:

```
@override
Widget build(BuildContext context) {
    return Scaffold(
      appBar: AppBar(
        title: Text(shoppingList.name),
      ),
      body:Container()
    );
}
```

8. In order to test the app, call `ItemsScreen` when the user taps on one of the items in the `ListView` of the main screen. So, back to the `main.dart` file, first, we'll import the `items_screen.dart` file, like this:

```
import './ui/items_screen.dart';
```

9. Then, in the `build()` method of the `_ShLstState` class, inside the `ListTile` of the `ListView`, add an `onTap` parameter. Inside it, call the `Navigator.push()` method to call the `ItemsScreen`, passing the object in the `shoppingList` at position `index`, as follows:

```
onTap: (){
  Navigator.push(
  context,
  MaterialPageRoute(builder: (context) =>
  ItemsScreen(shoppingList[index])),
  );},
```

10. If you try this out, when you tap on one of the items in the `ListView`, you'll get to the second screen, which right now only shows the title of the `shoppingList`, as shown in the following screenshot:

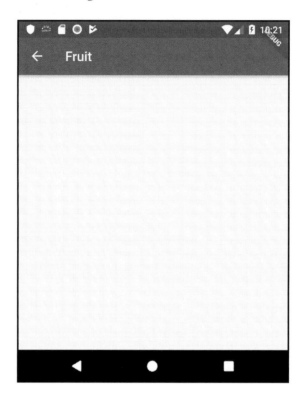

The next step we need to perform is showing the list into the second screen, which will contain the items in the shopping list that were selected from the first screen. Therefore, we need to create a method that queries the database in the `items` table, passing the ID of the `ShoppingList` that was selected, and returns all the retrieved elements. We'll add this method in the `DbHelper` class, together with all the other methods that deal with the database. Let's look at the steps to achieve that, as follows:

1. As usual, this will be an asynchronous method that will return a `Future` of type `List<ListItem>`, as shown in the following code snippet:

```
Future<List<ListItem>> getItems(int idList) async { }
```

2. Then, as we did for the `getLists()` method, we'll call the `query` method over the database, passing the name of the table, `Items`, as the first argument. But we'll also set a second argument, named `where`, that will filter the results based on a specific field—in this case, `idList`. The `idList` variable will be equal to the value that we'll set into the `whereArgs` named parameter. In this case, the `idList` will have to be equal to the value that was passed to the `getItems()` function. As you may recall, this will return a `List<Map<String, dynamic>>`. We'll place the result of the query on a variable called `maps`, as shown in the following code snippet:

```
final List<Map<String, dynamic>> maps =
    await db.query('items',
        where: 'idList = ?',
        whereArgs: [idList]);
```

3. Convert the `List<Map<String, dynamic>>` into a `List<ListItem>`, and return it to the caller, like this:

```
return List.generate(maps.length, (i) {
        return ListItem(
          maps[i]['id'],
          maps[i]['idList'],
          maps[i]['name'],
          maps[i]['quantity'],
          maps[i]['note'],
        );
});
```

4. It's now time to show the items to the user: back in the `items_screen.dart` file, at the top of the `_ItemsScreenState` class, we'll create two properties: one will be the `DbHelper`, and another one will contain all the `ListItems` that will be shown, as follows:

```
DbHelper helper;
List<ListItem> items;
```

Now, if you think about it, we don't need to have multiple instances of the `DbHelper` class throughout the app. Having a single connection to the database is what we actually need.

In Dart and Flutter, there is a feature called "**factory constructors**" that overrides the default behavior when you call the constructor of a class: **instead of creating a new instance, the factory constructor only returns an instance of the class**.

In our case, this means that the first time the factory constructor gets called, it will return a new instance of DbHelper. After DbHelper has already been instantiated, the constructor will not build another instance, but just return the existing one.

Add the following code in the DbHelper class to make the magic happen:

```
static final DbHelper _dbHelper = DbHelper._internal();

DbHelper._internal();

factory DbHelper() {
    return _dbHelper;
}
```

In detail, first, we are creating a private constructor named _internal. Then, in the factory constructor, we just return it to the outside caller.

In Dart and Flutter, factory constructors are used for implementing the "singleton" pattern, which restricts the instantiation of a class to one "single" instance. This is useful whenever just one object is needed in your app. As an example, you could use those with databases, as here, or with connections to a web service, or in general, whenever you need to access a resource that is shared by the entire app.

5. In the items_screen.dart file in the _ItemsScreenState class, we'll create an asynchronous method named showData() that will take the ID of the ShoppingList that was passed to the class.

6. Inside the class, first, call the openDb() method to make sure the database is available and open, then the getItems() method from the helper object passing idList. The result of the getItems() method will be placed in the items property.

7. Next, call the setState() method to update the State of the items property, so that the UI will be redrawn, as shown in the following code snippet:

```
Future showData(int idList) async {
    await helper.openDb();
    items = await helper.getItems(idList);
    setState(() {
      items = items;
    });
}
```

8. Still in the _ItemsScreenState class, at the top of the build() method, set helper as a new instance of DbHelper(), and then call the showData() method, passing the ID of the shoppingList, as follows:

```
helper = DbHelper();
showData(this.shoppingList.id);
```

Next, let's create the UI, using the following steps:

1. In the body of the Scaffold returned by the build() method of the _ItemsScreenState class, we'll place a ListView, calling its builder constructor. As we did previously for the ListView of ShoppingList, for the itemCount parameter, we'll use a ternary operator. When the items property is null, the itemCount will be set to 0; otherwise, it will be set to the length of the items list. The following code snippet shows this:

```
ListView.builder(
        itemCount: (items != null) ? items.length : 0,
        itemBuilder: (BuildContext context, int index) {}
)
```

2. In the itemBuilder, we'll return a ListTile.

3. Here, we want to show the name, quantity, and note for each of the items on the list. We'll place the name in the title of the ListTile, and the subtitle will contain both quantity and note.

4. We'll also set the onTap parameter to an empty method, and we'll place a trailing icon, with an edit icon. When the user clicks this, they will be able to edit the item in the ShoppingList. For now, we'll leave it empty. The following code block illustrates this:

```
itemBuilder: (BuildContext context, int index) {
    return ListTile(
        title: Text(items[index].name),
        subtitle: Text(
            'Quantity: ${items[index].quantity} - Note:
            ${items[index].note}'),
        onTap: () {},
        trailing: IconButton(
        icon: Icon(Icons.edit),
        onPressed: () {}, ), );
})
```

If you try this out, you should be able to see each item in the shopping list, with a trailing edit icon, as shown in the following screenshot:

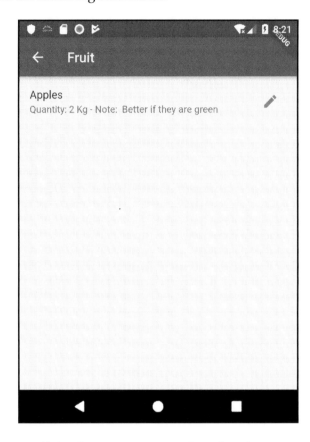

Our app is now showing all the data to our user: when they first enter the app, they immediately see the saved shopping lists; then, if they click on one of the items, they get to the second screen, which contains the item details of the list.

Right now, though, our user cannot insert, edit, or delete any data, so this is what we will work on next.

Inserting and editing data

We now need to allow our users to insert new data and edit or delete existing records in the database. Both the insert and edit functions require some UI that can contain the text that the user types, and for that, we'll use dialog boxes, which are ideal when you need some information from the user, and then come back to the caller when they are finished.

So, we'll create two new files, one for the `ShoppingList` and one for the `ListItems`. We'll call these `shopping_list_dialog.dart` and `list_item_dialog.dart`. We'll place both in the `ui` folder of the app.

Let's begin with the `shopping_list_dialog.dart` file. What we want to achieve here is showing our user a dialog window that allows them to insert or edit a `ShoppingList`, as shown in the following screenshot:

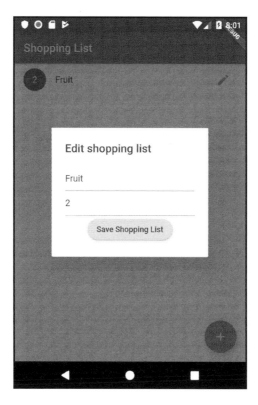

This dialog will always be called from the main screen. You can follow the steps given next to accomplish this:

1. Import the required dependencies: the inevitable `material.dart`, our `dbHelper`, and the `listItems.dart` file, as follows:

```
import 'package:flutter/material.dart';
import '../util/dbhelper.dart';
import '../models/shopping_list.dart';
```

2. Create the class that will contain the UI for the dialog. We'll call it `ShoppingListDialog`, as follows:

```
class ShoppingListDialog   {}
```

3. For this class, we want to show the user two textboxes, one for the title of the `ShoppingList` and one for the priority that the user will choose. So, at the top of the `ShoppingListDialog` class, create two `TextController` widgets that will contain the name and priority of the `ShoppingList`. Quite predictably, we can call them `txtName` and `txtPriority`, as shown in the following code snippet:

```
final txtName = TextEditingController();
final txtPriority = TextEditingController();
```

4. Then we'll create a method called `buildDialog()` that will take the current `BuildContext` (which in Flutter is required to show a dialog window), the `ShoppingList` object that we want to manipulate, and a Boolean value that will tell whether the `list` is a new `list` or if we need to update an existing `list`. The `buildDialog()` method will return a `Widget`, as follows:

```
Widget buildDialog(BuildContext context, ShoppingList list, bool
isNew) {}
```

5. Inside the `buildDialog()` method, call the `DbHelper` class. Here, we don't need to call the `openDb()` method, as from this window we already know that it's been called previously, and we are receiving an existing instance of the class. The following code snippet illustrates this:

```
DbHelper helper = DbHelper();
```

6. Next, we'll check whether the instance of `ShoppingList` that was passed is an existing `list`. If it is, we'll set the text of the two `TextControllers` to the values of the `ShoppingList` that were passed, as follows:

```
if (!isNew) {
  txtName.text = list.name;
  txtPriority.text = list.priority.toString();
}
```

7. Finally, we can return the `AlertDialog` that will contain the UI that our users will see, as follows:

```
return AlertDialog();
```

8. We'll use the `title` to inform whether this dialog is used to insert a new list or to update an existing one. For simplicity, here, we can use a ternary operator. Add the following code in the `AlertDialog()`:

```
return AlertDialog(
    title: Text((isNew)?'New shopping list':'Edit shopping list'),
);
```

9. The `content` will contain all the UI for this dialog window. We'll place all the widgets into a `SingleChildScrollView`, to make scrolling available in case the widgets do not fit into the screen. Add the following code in the `AlertDialog()`:

```
content: SingleChildScrollView()
```

10. Inside the `SingleChildScrollView`, we'll place a `Column`, as we want the widget in this dialog to be placed vertically, as follows:

```
child: Column(children: <Widget>[]),
```

11. The first elements inside the `Column` will be two `TextField` widgets, one for the `name` and one for the `priority`. After setting the relevant controller for both the `TextFields`, we'll set the `hintText` of an `InputDecoration` object to guide the user in using the UI. Add the widgets into the `Column`, as shown in the following code block:

```
TextField(
    controller: txtName,
    decoration: InputDecoration(
        hintText: 'Shopping List Name'
    )
```

```
        ),
        TextField(
            controller: txtPriority,
            keyboardType: TextInputType.number,
            decoration: InputDecoration(
                hintText: 'Shopping List Priority (1-3)'
            ),
        ),
```

12. Next, place a `RaisedButton` that will save the changes. The child of the button will be a `Text` with `'Save Shopping List'`. In the `onPressed` method, first, we will update the list object with the new data coming from the two `TextFields`, and then, we'll call the `insertList()` method of our `helper` object, passing the `list`. Add the following code into the `Column`, under the two `TextField` widgets:

```
RaisedButton(
    child: Text('Save Shopping List'),
    onPressed: (){
        list.name = txtName.text;
        list.priority = int.parse(txtPriority.text);
        helper.insertList(list);
        Navigator.pop(context);
},),
```

13. We'll also change the shape of the `Dialog` to a `RoundedRectangleBorder`, rounding its corners with a `borderRadius` of `30.0`. Add the `shape` property to the `AlertDialog`, as follows:

```
shape: RoundedRectangleBorder(
    borderRadius: BorderRadius.circular(30.0)
)
```

Before we try this out, we need to call the `alertDialog` from the main screen, using the following steps:

1. At the top of the `main.dart` file, we'll import the `shopping_list_dialog.dart` file, like this:

```
import './ui/shopping_list_dialog.dart';
```

2. In the _ShListState class, let's first declare a ShoppingListDialog, called dialog, then override the initState() method to create an instance of the class, as follows:

```
ShoppingListDialog dialog;
@override
void initState() {
    dialog = ShoppingListDialog();
    super.initState();
}
```

3. For the edit functionality, in the onPressed parameter of the edit button in the ListTile, call the showDialog method. In its builder, let's call the buildDialog() method that we've created, passing the context, the current ShoppingList, and false, as this is an edit and not an insert, as follows:

```
onPressed: (){
    showDialog(
        context: context,
        builder: (BuildContext context) =>
        dialog.buildDialog(context, shoppingList[index], false)
    );
},
```

We can already try this out. Just press any edit button in the List, and you should be able to edit the name and priority of the ShoppingList.

Now, we only need to add the UI necessary to insert a **new** ShoppingList. We could consider this the primary action on the first screen of our app.

 According to the *Material Design* guidelines, a **FAB** represents the **main action of a screen**.

As this is such an important action for our screen, we'll use a FAB to insert a new ShoppingList.

This will require a small refactoring of the `main.dart` file, necessary to pass the correct context to the dialog screen. We just need to move the `Scaffold` that is now in the `MyApp` stateless widget to the `ShList` stateful widget, as follows:

1. In the `home` parameter of the `MaterialApp`, just call the `SHList` widget, like this:

   ```
   home: ShList()
   ```

2. In the `build()` method of the `_ShListState` widget, instead of returning a `ListView.builder`, we'll return a `Scaffold`, whose `body` contains the `ListView.builder`, as follows:

   ```
   Widget build(BuildContext context) {
       ShoppingListDialog dialog = ShoppingListDialog();
       showData();
       return Scaffold(
           appBar: AppBar(
             title: Text("Shopping List"),
           ),
           body: ListView.builder(
   [...]
   ```

3. Now, under the `body` of the `Scaffold`, add a `FloatingActionButton`. For the function in the `onPressed` parameter, we'll call the `showDialog()` method, passing the current context. In its builder, we'll call the `dialog.buildDialog()` method, again passing the context, a new `ShoppingList`, whose `id` will be 0, an empty name and a `priority` of 0, and `true`, to tell the function that this is a new `ShoppingList`, as illustrated in the following code block:

   ```
   floatingActionButton: FloatingActionButton(
       onPressed: () {
           showDialog(
               context: context,
               builder: (BuildContext context) =>
                   dialog.buildDialog(context,  ShoppingList(0, '',
                   0), true),
           ); },
       child: Icon(Icons.add),
           backgroundColor: Colors.pink,
   ),
   ```

If you try this out and press the FAB, you'll be able to insert new shopping lists to the database, as shown in the following screenshot:

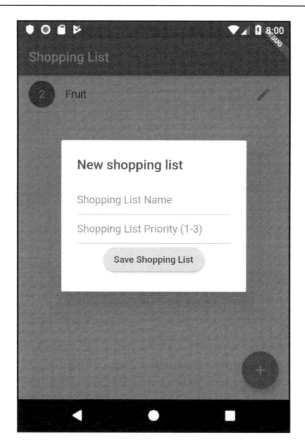

CRUD: Create, Read, Update, and Delete are the four basic functions for storing data.

Each letter in the acronym can map to a SQL statement (INSERT, SELECT, UPDATE, and DELETE) or HTTP method (POST, GET, PUT, and DELETE).

We can now create, read, and update `ShoppingLists`. The last verb of the CRUD acronym is **Delete**. Let's have a look at it next.

Deleting elements

One of the touch gestures that has won a wide adoption over time in mobile apps is the "swipe-to-delete" gesture, in which you simply drag a finger across an item, and swipe it left—or in some cases, also right.

This was introduced by Apple in the Mail app, and today it's widely spread in both iOS and Android systems.

What we want to achieve here is to delete an item in the ListView by swiping left or right. The first step is creating a method in our DbHelper class that will actually delete a record from the database, as follows:

1. We'll call this method deleteList(). As usual, it will be asynchronous and will return a Future of type int, and take the ShoppingList object that needs to be deleted.

2. Inside the method, we need to perform two actions: first, we will delete all the items that belong to the ShopppingList, and then, we'll delete the ShoppingList itself.

3. So, inside the function, we'll call the delete method of the database object, passing the name of the table (items), and a where named parameter: this will take the name of the field we want to use as a filter. In this case, we want to delete all the items that have an idList that equals the id of the ShoppingList that was passed, so we'll specify idList = ?, where the question mark will be set by the whereArgs named parameter.

4. whereArgs will take an array with a single element, which is the id of the list.

5. The delete() method returns the id of the deleted record, and that's what we'll return, as shown in the following code snippet:

```
Future<int> deleteList(ShoppingList list) async {
  int result = await db.delete("items", where: "idList = ?",
    whereArgs: [list.id]);
  result = await db.delete("lists", where: "id = ?", whereArgs:
  [list.id]);
  return result;
}
```

Now that the deleteList() method is complete, we can call it when the user swipes an item on the main screen.

There's a very useful widget in Flutter that's perfect when you want to use this pattern to delete an item: it's called Dismissible.

You could also use the swipe action to bring out a contextual menu: this can help you avoid cluttering your UI with elements that are not always needed. This equates to bringing out a contextual menu with the mouse right-click on a classic PC.

By providing the `Dismissible` widget, Flutter makes the task of deleting an item by swiping very easy. Dragging a `Dismissible` widget in the implemented `DismissDirection` makes an item slide out of view, with a nice animation.

Let's see how to use a `Dismissible` widget in our code to delete a `ShoppingList` from the main screen, as follows:

1. In the `itemBuilder` parameter of the `ListView.builder` in the body of the `Scaffold`, let's return a `Dismissable` widget.
2. The `Dismissible` widget takes a key. This allows Flutter to uniquely identify widgets, and it's a required parameter.
3. Then, set the `onDismissed` parameter. This gets called when you swipe in the specified direction. In this case, we don't care about the direction: we'll delete the item for both left and right swipes.
4. Inside the function, in the `onDismissed` parameter, we can get the name of the current item, which we'll use to give some feedback to the user.
5. Then, we'll call the `helper.deleteList` method, passing the current item in the `ListView`.
6. Next, we'll call the `setState` method, removing the current item from the list.
7. Finally, we'll call the `showSnackBar` method of the current `Scaffold`, telling the user that the `ShoppingList` was removed.

A `SnackBar` is a widget that shows messages at the bottom of your app. Generally, you use a `SnackBar` to inform your users that an action has been performed. It's particularly useful when you want to give some visible feedback for a successful task. In a real-world app, you should also give your users the option to undo the action.

The code for the `Dismissible` widget is shown in the following code block. Add it to the `itemBuilder` in the `ListView`:

```
itemBuilder:(BuildContext context, int index) {
        return Dismissible(
          key: Key(shoppingList[index].name),
          onDismissed: (direction) {
            String strName =  shoppingList[index].name;
            helper.deleteList(shoppingList[index]);
```

```
              setState(() {
                shoppingList.removeAt(index);
              });
              Scaffold
                .of(context)
                .showSnackBar(SnackBar(content: Text("$strName deleted")));
              },
            child: ListTile(
    [...]
```

The `delete` function is now complete. If you try the app and swipe left or right any item on the main screen, you should see the element of the list disappearing and the `SnackBar` at the bottom of the screen, as shown in the following screenshot:

There's only one last step in order to complete the app: completing the CRUD functionality for the items as well, and for this, it's time for a challenge.

Challenge – completing the Items Screen functionality

At this time, the second screen in our app lists the items that are available in the **items** table in the database, but we have no way to insert, delete, or update items in the table. Basically, the steps required to complete the implementation are the same as those you already performed for the `ShoppingList`, with a few tweaks. As a challenge and a useful exercise, I recommend you try to implement those features yourself.

The steps required to complete this challenge are as follows:

1. Create the UI that will allow the user to insert and update items, as shown in the following screenshot:

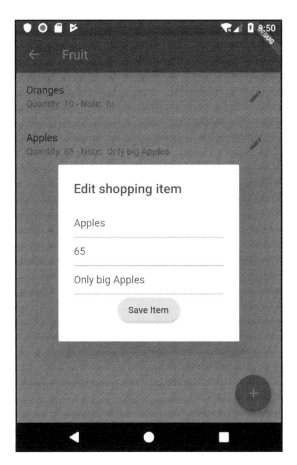

2. Add a trailing edit `IconButton` to the `ListTile`, to allow the user to edit an existing item.
3. Add a FAB to the items screen, to allow the user to insert a new item.
4. Create a function in the `DBHelper` class, called `deleteItem()`, that deletes the `ListItem` that's passed as an argument.
5. Add a `Dismissable` widget that allows the user to delete an existing item.
6. Test the functionalities you've just added to make sure they work correctly.

In the next section, you'll find the completed solution in case you want to have a look at the final implementation of the app to check your code or for a little help during the exercise.

Challenge solution – completing the Items Screen functionality

Each step of the challenge is explained here. For each task, the key points will be highlighted at the beginning of the step, then the complete code will be shown.

Step 1

Key points:

- Create a `TextEditingController` widget for each `TextField` that the user will see.
- Use the same UI both for insert and update. The `isnew` Boolean value will help decide which task to perform.
- It's always a good idea to place widgets in scrolling widgets. Here, we use the `SingleChildScrollView` widget.

Solution:

Create the `ListItemDialog` class in the `list_item_dialog.dart` file, as follows:

```
import 'package:flutter/material.dart';
import '../models/list_items.dart';
import '../util/dbhelper.dart';

class ListItemDialog {
  final txtName = TextEditingController();
  final txtQuantity = TextEditingController();
  final txtNote = TextEditingController();
```

```
Widget buildAlert(BuildContext context, ListItem item, bool isNew) {
  DbHelper helper = DbHelper();
  helper.openDb();
  if (!isNew) {
    txtName.text = item.name;
    txtQuantity.text = item.quantity;
    txtNote.text = item.note;
  }
  return AlertDialog(
    title: Text((isNew)?'New shopping item':'Edit shopping item'),
    content: SingleChildScrollView(
      child: Column(children: <Widget>[
        TextField(
          controller: txtName,
          decoration: InputDecoration(
            hintText: 'Item Name'
          )
        ),
        TextField(
          controller: txtQuantity,
          decoration: InputDecoration(
            hintText: 'Quantity'
          ) ,
        ),
        TextField(
          controller: txtNote,
          decoration: InputDecoration(
            hintText: 'Note'
          ) ,
        ),
        RaisedButton(
          child: Text('Save Item'),
          onPressed: (){
              item.name = txtName.text;
              item.quantity = txtQuantity.text;
              item.note = txtNote.text;
              helper.insertItem(item);
              Navigator.pop(context);
          },
          shape: RoundedRectangleBorder(
            borderRadius: BorderRadius.circular(30.0)
          ) ) ],),        ),    );  }}
```

Now that the `ListItemDialog` is complete, let's add it to the `ItemsScreen`.

Step 2

Key points:

- Use the trailing parameter or the `ListTile` to place the edit icon.
- In the `onPressed` parameter of the `IconButton`, and in its builder parameter, call the `buildAlert` method of a `ListItemDialog` instance.

Solution:

1. In the `build()` method in the `items_screen.dart` file, create an instance of the `ListItemDialog` class called `dialog`, like this:

   ```
   ListItemDialog dialog = new ListItemDialog();
   ```

2. Update the `ListTile` in the `itemBuilder`, in the `ListView.builder` of the same method, like this:

   ```
   return ListTile(
       title: Text(items[index].name),
       subtitle: Text(
           'Quantity: ${items[index].quantity} - Note:
   ${items[index].note}'),
       onTap: () {},
       trailing: IconButton(
       icon: Icon(Icons.edit),
       onPressed: () {
           showDialog(
               context: context,
               builder: (BuildContext context) =>
                   dialog.buildAlert(context, items[index], false));
       }, ), )
   ```

In the next step, let's add a FAB to the screen.

Step 3

Key points:

- Use the `floatingActionButton` parameter of a `Scaffold` to show a FAB to the user.
- Respond to the click of the user by creating a function in the `onPressed()` parameter in the call to the `FloatingActionButton` constructor.

Solution:

In the `Scaffold` returned by the `build()` method of the `_ItemsScreenState` class, add a `FloatingActionButton`, as follows:

```
floatingActionButton: FloatingActionButton(
    onPressed: () {
      showDialog(
        context: context,
        builder: (BuildContext context) => dialog.buildAlert(
          context, ListItem(0, shoppingList.id, '', '', ''), true),
      );
    },
    child: Icon(Icons.add),
    backgroundColor: Colors.pink,
  ),
```

Next, let's write the method to delete an item from the items table.

Step 4

Key points:

- The `delete` helper method of a database object is asynchronous, as with every database task.
- In the `delete` method, use the `where` and `whereArgs` named parameters to filter the data you want to delete.

Solution:

In the `DbHelper` class of the `dbhelper.dart` file, add a `deleteItem` method, as follows:

```
Future<int> deleteItem(ListItem item) async {
    int result = await db.delete("items", where: "id = ?", whereArgs:
    [item.id]);
    return result;
  }
```

Let's add a `Dismissible` widget to the items screen, next.

Step 5

Key points:

- Use a `Dismissible` widget to allow an item in a list to be deleted.
- Each `Dismissable` **must have a unique** `key`.
- You can use a `SnackBar` to give feedback to your users.

Solution:

In the `itemBuilder` of the `ListView.builder`, in the `build()` method of the `_ItemsScreenState` class in the `items_screen.dart` file, add a `Dismissible` widget, as follows:

```
itemBuilder: (BuildContext context, int index) {
       return Dismissible(
           key: Key(items[index].name),
           onDismissed: (direction) {
             String strName = items[index].name;
             helper.deleteItem(items[index]);
             setState(() {
               items.removeAt(index);
             });
             Scaffold.of(context)
                 .showSnackBar(SnackBar(content: Text("$strName
                 deleted")));
           },
           child: ListTile(
```

The app is now complete. There's only one more step to perform: making sure that it works as expected.

Step 6

Key points:

Trying out your app after adding new features might be the most rewarding part of your development, especially when everything works perfectly the first time... which is to say: almost never!

Usually, you need to debug and fine-tune your code several times before it works exactly as you want. But remember: you really learn to code by trial and error. If something's wrong, you have several tools at your disposal, but arguably, your first stop should be a good use of breaking points to check what's really happening with your code.

Solution:

Try adding new items in the Items screen, then edit them several times. Try adding unexpected values and see how your app behaves.

Try also deleting items by swiping right and left.

Summary

Storing data into a device is a key skill in Flutter development. In this chapter, we have created a data-driven app, leveraging the SQLite database.

In order to add the SQLite features in Flutter, we used the sqflite library, which contains asynchronous helper methods for SELECT, INSERT, UPDATE, and DELETE queries.

We used the openDb method, which returns a database object. The first time we called this method, the database was created with the specified name and version, and the following times, it was only opened.

We called the execute method to use the SQL language to insert records, and the rawQuery method to use a SELECT statement against the database.

We've created model classes that mirrored the structure of the tables in a database to make the code more reliable, easier to read, and to prevent data inconsistencies.

We used the insert, update, and delete helper methods specifying the where and whereArgs parameters, and used Map objects to deal with the data.

We've seen factory constructors, which allow you to override the default behavior whenever you call the constructor of a class. Instead of creating a new instance, the factory constructor only returns an instance of the class, thus implementing the "singleton" pattern, which restricts the instantiation of a class to one "single" instance.

We've used the showDialog() method to build parts of the UI to interact with our user, and leveraged the Swipe action with the Dismissible objects to delete data.

Now, you know how to store data into your device and read data from an internet connection. Let's leverage this knowledge, and add new features with Firebase in the next chapter!

Questions

At the end of each project, you'll find a few questions to help you remember and review the content covered in the chapter. Please try to answer the following questions, and, when in doubt, have a look at the content in the chapter itself: you'll find all the answers there!

1. What happens when you call the `openDatabase()` method?
2. What's the difference between the `rawQuery()` and `query()` methods of a `database` object?
3. How do you use a factory constructor? When should you use it?
4. What's the purpose of a `Dismissible` widget?
5. How do we use the `where` and `whereArgs` parameters of a `query()` method?
6. When should you use model classes in an app?
7. When would you use a `SnackBar`?
8. What's the syntax of an `insert()` method on an SQLite database?
9. What is the purpose of the `key` in a `Dismissable` widget?
10. When would you use a FAB?

Further reading

If you are serious about developing data-driven apps in Flutter, you should study some database concepts. In particular, if you're interested in SQLite, you should have a look at `https://www.sqlitetutorial.net/`. Here, you'll find an extensive tutorial, with examples and use cases.

If you've never heard of SQL before, or you want to study the language itself, there's a great free guide/tutorial at `https://www.w3schools.com/sql/default.asp`.

The singleton pattern is a fascinating topic: should you want to investigate it further, a good starting point is the Wikipedia entry at `https://en.wikipedia.org/wiki/Singleton_pattern`.

7
Firing Up the App - Integrating Firebase into a Flutter App

Let's face it: developers tend to be lazy, so they always look for ways to build solid and maintainable software with the least possible effort. The good news is that Flutter and Firebase work well together so you can to build full-stack apps in record time, and this is what we'll be covering in this chapter.

The app we'll build in this project is an event app. Your user will be able to see the program of an event— for example, a developers' conference, a concert, or a business meeting—and, once authenticated, they will be able to select their favorite parts of the schedule. All the data will be saved remotely, in a Cloud Firestore database.

The following topics will be covered in this chapter:

- Creating a Firebase project
- Adding Firebase and Firestore to your app
- Reading data from a Firestore database and showing it in your Flutter app
- Implementing an authentication screen and connecting it to Firebase
- Writing data to a Firestore database (**create, read, update, delete** (CRUD))

Technical requirements

You'll find the completed app code on the book's GitHub repository at `https://github.com/PacktPublishing/Flutter-Projects`.

To follow along with the code examples in this book, you should have the following software installed on your Windows, Mac, Linux, or Chrome OS device:

- The Flutter **Software Development Kit (SDK)**.
- When developing for Android: the Android SDK, easily installed by Android Studio.
- When developing for iOS: macOS and Xcode.
- An emulator (Android), a simulator (iOS), or a connected iOS or Android device with debugging enabled.
- An editor: **Visual Studio Code (VS Code)**, Android Studio, or IntelliJ IDEA are recommended. All should have the Flutter/Dart extensions installed.
- For this chapter, a Google account is required to use Firebase.

Introducing Firebase

Firebase is a set of tools with which to build scalable applications in the cloud. Among those tools, you'll find authentication, storage, databases, notifications, and hosting.

You can actually choose between two databases: the **Firebase Realtime Database** and **Cloud Firestore**. In this chapter, we'll be using the Cloud Firestore database, which is a NoSQL document database that simplifies storing, querying, and updating data in the cloud. More importantly in the context of this book, you can use it as the backend of your iOS and Android apps, with no need to write the code for a web service and, in many cases, without writing any code at all for your server-side service.

Relational databases use tables to store data, with a fixed schema that all records must follow. For example, if you store user data, you can create a `users` **table** with three **fields**: `user_id`, `name`, and `password`. Each **record** in the table will follow the constraints (rules) you define when you design your table.

 In relational databases, you store data in tables. The "columns" of the tables are called fields, and the "rows" of the table are called records. For example, if you store `users`, the table name might be `Users`, and the fields might be "`Name`" and "`Surname`". "`John`" - "`Doe`" and "`Bill`" - "`Smith`" are records.

A NoSQL database, on the other hand, is self-describing, so it does not require a schema. All its documents are JSON documents, and, theoretically, each document could have different fields and values (or key-value pairs). In the example we mentioned previously, in the users collection, the first user might have a user_id, name, and password, but the following could also contain a "user_role" field or a "user_age" field. Both documents would still be valid.

Another huge difference is the language used. SQL databases use Structured Query Language to define and manipulate data. This makes SQL databases easy to use and wide spread, but SQL requires you use predefined schemas to design the structure of your data.

In a NoSQL database, you have a dynamic schema and data is unstructured, and can be stored in many different ways.

Generally speaking, when you need to perform complex queries in multiple tables and you have structured data, SQL is the best option. When you don't need to perform queries that require several "JOINS" between tables and you want an easily scalable and fast solution, you would probably choose a NoSQL database.

As an added bonus, a backend created with Firebase can scale over Google server farms, so it's virtually limitless.

Project overview

The app we'll build in this chapter is an event app where the user will be able to see the program of an event, with the details of the schedule. All data will be hosted remotely, in a Firebase project. The events will be stored in a Cloud Firestore database.

Once authenticated, the user will be able to choose their favorite parts of the event by pressing a star icon. In this way, the "favorites" will be also saved remotely.

The following screenshot shows the app's main screen:

Another interesting aspect of the app is dealing with authentication. This is generally a cumbersome process, but the good news is that dealing with authentication with Firebase and Flutter is rather straightforward. You can see the app's authentication screen in the following screenshot:

Building the project should take about 3 hours.

Adding Firebase to your Flutter project

As mentioned before, Firebase is a set of tools that you can use to build applications in the cloud. As it's a cloud service, you won't need to install any software on your device. Firebase is operated by Google, so you will need a Google account to create your first project.

What are the advantages of using Firebase, instead of following the traditional approach of writing a client-side app, and a server-side (or backend) service?

The tools that are available within Firebase cover most of the services that you would typically have to build yourself, including **authentication**, **databases**, and **file storage**, just to name a few. The client that connects to Firebase—in our case, a Flutter app—interacts with these backend services directly, without any middleware server-side service. This means that, when you use the Firestore database, you'll write queries directly in your Flutter app! This is totally different from traditional app development, which usually requires both client and server software to be written, and it's probably the main advantage of using Firebase when developing an app that requires a backend service. You won't need to write, install, or maintain a web service using PHP, or Java, or C#. You'll deal with Firebase directly from your Flutter app.

Every project that involves the use of Firebase begins with the **Firebase console**. You can reach it at the following address: `https://console.firebase.google.com/`.

You will be asked to authenticate yourself before accessing the console. In the remote chance that you do not have any Google accounts, you can create one for free from the authentication page. So, let's begin, as follows:

1. The container of all services in Firebase is a **project**. So, we'll begin building our app by creating a new Firebase project.

> A **Firebase project** is the top-level entity for Firebase. Each Firebase feature, including Cloud Firestore and Authentication, belongs to a Firebase project, and the connection from client apps is made through the project itself.

2. Once you click on the **Add Project** button (or **New Project**, depending on the console interface), you'll need to choose a project name. Let's call it Events, as shown in the following screenshot:

3. Next, just press **Continue** to keep configuring the new project and accept the Terms and Conditions.

4. In the next screen, you'll be asked to set up Google Analytics for your Firebase project. In the context of this chapter, this is not necessary as we won't use it, but it's generally recommended or real-world projects.

5. Click **Continue** again, and after a few seconds your project will be created. We now have the Firebase project that we'll use in our app. At the end of the process, you should see a page similar to the one in the following screenshot:

This is the Firebase **Project Overview** page, which contains the name of the project (**Events**, in this case) and the billing plan (**Spark plan** means that it's a **free** plan); on the left side of the page, you have the main tools you can add to your project.

Firebase is free for apps with relatively little traffic, but as your apps grow and require more power, you'll be asked to pay, based on your app's usage. For details about Firebase prices, have a look at the following page: https://firebase.google.com/pricing.

Now that our Firebase project has been built, let's create a Firestore database and add some data that we'll read in our app.

Creating a Firestore database

In the previous chapter, we've built an app that used a SQL database. The Firestore database is a NoSQL database. These two have very different ways of storing data and change the way you design a storage solution. In Firebase, you have two different database tools: the Cloud Firestore and the Realtime Database. Both are **NoSQL** databases, but their architecture is rather different. The Cloud Firestore is the most recent, and it's the recommended choice for most new projects as it features a more intuitive data model, with faster queries and enhanced scaling options.

If you want to learn more about the differences between Cloud Firestore and Realtime Database, have a look at the guide available at the following address: https://firebase.google.com/docs/database/rtdb-vs-firestore.

Let's see how to create a Cloud Firestore database first, and then we'll highlight a few tips on how to think about data in a NoSQL database. To create a Cloud Firestore database, perform the following steps:

1. On the left side of the Firebase **Project Overview** page, click on the **Database** link.
2. From there, under the **Cloud Firestore** pane, click on the **Create Database** button.

3. In the **Create database** window, choose **Start in test mode**, as this is the option that allows access to data **without authentication**, as shown in the following screenshot:

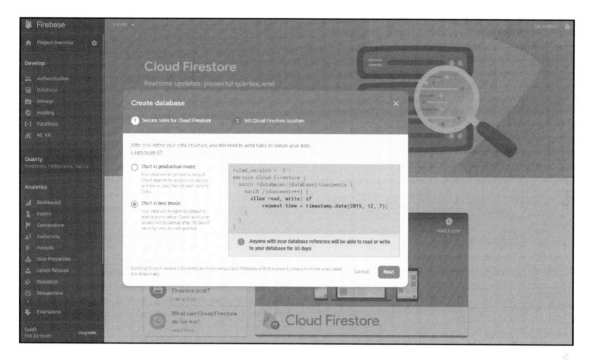

Later on, we'll also add authentication to the project.

4. Click **Next**. You'll be asked to choose among the locations of the Cloud Firestore. Choose one that is close to where you and your users will access data. For example, as I live in Europe, I'll choose one of the **europe-west** options.
5. Finally, click **Done**.

You have now created a Cloud Firestore database, and should see a page like the one shown in the following screenshot:

We'll now insert some data, as follows:

1. Click on **Start collection**. A Collection is a container for a set of documents. Call this container `event_details`, and click **Next**.
2. From there, in the **Document ID** option, click on **Auto-ID**, then add a few fields and values, as shown in the following screenshot, then click **Save**:

3. Repeat the process for another couple of documents, using the same fields and changing the values in line with your preferences.

There are a few rules when dealing with collections and documents in the Cloud Firestore database, as follows:

- **Collections can only contain documents**, not other collections, strings, or blobs.
- Documents must take up less than 1 MB, which is OK for most use cases but you'll need to split the content into several documents when they take more than 1 MB.
- A document cannot contain another document.
- **A document CAN contain a sub-collection**, which can then contain other documents.
- The Firestore root can only contain collections and not documents.

Now that we have created our Firebase project, a Cloud Firestore database, and inserted some data, it's time to create our Flutter app and integrate Firebase into it.

Integrating Firebase into a Flutter app

There are a few steps required in order to integrate a Cloud Firestore database into a Flutter app, as follows:

1. Create a Firebase project. You can do this in the Firebase console. You'll need to log in. If you already have any Google account, such as Gmail, you can use that for your Firebase projects.
2. Create a Firestore database instance, then insert collections and documents as required.
3. Register your Android and/or iOS app in your project, and download the configuration file that will be created in the process. If you are planning to release your app on both platforms, you'll need to repeat the process for each operating system.
4. Create your Flutter project and add the configuration files downloaded previously.
5. Add Google services to your projects (platform-specific).
6. Add dependencies to the `pubspec.yaml` file.

We have already performed *Steps 1* and *2* in the task list outlined at the end of the previous section, so let's now see how to deal with the remaining steps.

Configuring your Android app

Let's create a new Flutter project, calling it `events`, and update the `main.dart` file so that it looks like the following code:

```
import 'package:flutter/material.dart';
void main() => runApp(MyApp());

class MyApp extends StatelessWidget {
  // This widget is the root of your application.
  @override
  Widget build(BuildContext context) {
    return MaterialApp(
      title: 'Events',
      theme: ThemeData(
        primarySwatch: Colors.orange,
      ),
      home: Scaffold(),
    ); } }
```

When targeting Android devices, we'll need to register our app as an Android app in the Firebase console. First, we need to set a package name, and we can do that by setting `applicationId` in the app `build.gradle` file, as follows:

1. Open the file at the following path:

   ```
   <project-name>/android/app/build.gradle
   ```

2. In it, in the `defaultConfig` node, you should find an `applicationId` key, with a `com.example.events` as a value. This is a **unique identifier for your Android app**, and you should change it to your own domain name, if you have one, or to a name that uniquely identifies you. For example, in my case, I'll change it to the following:

   ```
   it.softwarehouse.events_book
   ```

3. This is needed to actually register the app with Firebase and to eventually publish the app into the Google Play Store if you wish to do so later on.

4. Next, let's get to the **Project Overview** page in Firebase. There, under the **Project Name**, click on the **Add App** button, and select **Android**.

5. You'll be asked to insert the **Android package name**. Insert it, with an optional nickname, as shown in the following screenshot:

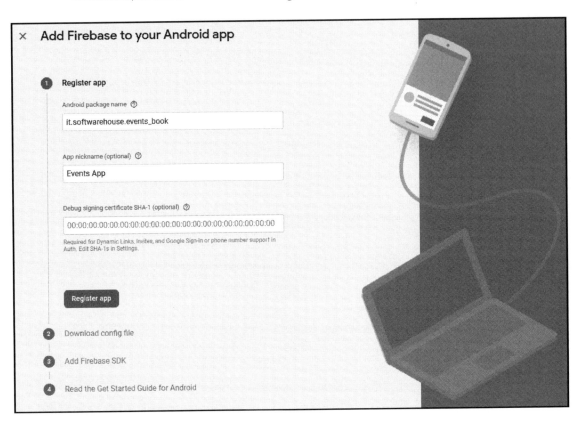

 The app nickname isn't visible to users, but it's used throughout the Firebase console to represent your app.

6. Click on the **Register app** button, and download the `google-services.json` file, then put the file into the `android/app` folder of your project.

7. Next, add the `google-services` plugin to the Gradle files.

8. In your project-level Gradle file (`android/build.gradle`), add the following rule (please check the latest version of the `google-services` plugin at the following address: `https://developers.google.com/android/guides/google-services-plugin`):

```
dependencies {
    // ...

    // Add the line below:
    classpath 'com.google.gms:google-services:4.3.2'    }
```

9. Next, let's open the `pubspec.yaml` file and add the required dependencies. For our app, we'll need the Firebase `firebase_auth` code dependency for authentication, and `cloud_firestore` to store data (don't forget to check more recent versions of the dependencies at the address: `https://firebaseopensource.com/projects/firebaseextended/flutterfire/`):

```
# Firebase dependencies
  firebase_core: ^0.4.0+9
  firebase_auth: ^0.14.0+5
  cloud_firestore: ^0.12.9+5
```

That's it. You're now ready to use Firebase for your Android app! Let's now see how to configure your app for iOS.

Configuring your iOS app

In your Mac, from your favorite editor, open the Flutter project that you have created, and make sure you update the `main.dart` file, as shown at the beginning of the previous section.

Next, we'll need to change the bundle Id of our Flutter project. This is the **value that identifies your iOS app**. Let's see how to do this here:

1. Open the app in Xcode (you may just open the iOS folder of your app), then access the **General** tab in the top-level Runner directory.

2. Next, change the **Bundle Identifier** value to a string that uniquely identifies your project, as shown in the following screenshot:

If you have a domain name, you can use that (for example, mine is it.softwarehouse.events). This is needed to register the app with Firebase and to eventually publish the app to the App Store if you wish to do so later on.

3. Save your project and get back to the Firebase console.

4. Next, let's get to the **Project Overview** page in Firebase. There, under the **Project Name**, click on the **Add App** button, and select **iOS**.

5. You'll be asked to insert the **iOS bundle ID**. Insert it, as shown in the following screenshot, then press the **Register app** button:

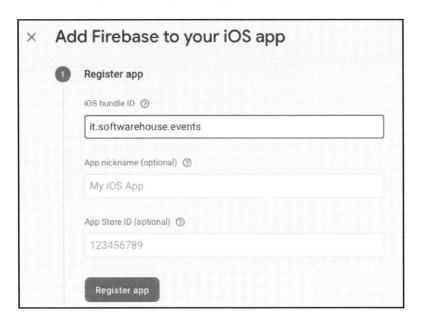

6. Click **Download GoogleService-Info.plist** to get the Firebase iOS configuration file, named `GoogleService-Info.plist`.

7. Next, from Xcode, move the downloaded file into the `Runner` directory of your Flutter app, as shown in the following screenshot:

Back in the Firebase console, click **Next**. You can skip the remaining steps of the configuration.

Testing Firebase integration with your app

Now that we have completed the app configuration to use Firebase, we need to test whether we can connect to the Firestore database. Let's begin, as follows:

1. In the `pubspec.yaml` file, make sure you have the latest `FlutterFire` dependencies.

 FlutterFire is a set of Flutter plugins that enable Flutter apps to use Firebase services. You can find the latest versions of the FlutterFire libraries at the following address: `https://firebaseopensource.com/projects/firebaseextended/flutterfire/`.

`firebase_core` is always required in order to use Firebase. `firebase_auth` is for the Authentication service, and `cloud_firestore` is rather self-explanatory.

2. In the `main.dart` file, add the following import to use the Cloud Firestore package:

```
import 'package:cloud_firestore/cloud_firestore.dart';
```

3. Then, create an asynchronous method, called `testData()`, that will attempt to connect to the Cloud Firestore database and print some data in the Debug console, as follows:

```
Future testData() async {}
```

4. Inside the method, we'll create an instance of a Firestore database and call it `db`, as illustrated in the following code snippet:

```
Firestore db = Firestore.instance;
```

5. Then, we'll call the `getDocuments()` asynchronous method on the collection called `event_details`. This method will get all the available data from the specified collection. We'll put the results into a `data` variable, as follows:

```
var data = await db.collection('event_details').getDocuments();
```

6. If `data` is not null, we'll get the documents contained into the details variable, and place them into a `List` called `details`, as follows:

```
var details = data.documents.toList();
```

7. For each item in the `details` list, we'll print the `documentId` of the item. `documentId` is the unique identifier inside a Firestore collection. The code for this can be seen in the following snippet:

```
details.forEach((d) {
    print(d.documentID);
});
```

8. Add the call to the `testData()` method in the `build()` method of `MyApp`, as follows:

```
testData();
```

9. Try the app. If everything worked as expected, in the Debug console you should see a line like the following:

```
I/flutter (11381): n9qGRgBsOleb0FV0cSx4
```

This means that we can retrieve data from the Cloud Firestore, and import it into our app!

In Android, you might receive an error relating to the number of references in your app. In this case, you need to add the following code in your `app.gradle` file, at the end of the `defaultConfig` node:

```
defaultConfig {
...
        multiDexEnabled true
}
```

Now that we've successfully connected our app to Firebase, let's design the **user interface (UI)** so that the user will be able to see a list of event details on the screen.

The EventDetail model class

Now our app successfully reads data from the Cloud Firestore database, but we can only see a `Scaffold` with a blank body. We need to create a list with all the detail events, but first we will create a model for a single event detail, in the same way we did when creating the database app, as follows:

1. In the `lib` folder of our app, we'll create a new folder called `models`. In it, we'll create a new file, called `event_detail.dart`.
2. There, we'll create a class called `EventDetail`.
3. In this, we'll create fields that mirror the fields we've specified in the Firestore documents, as follows:

   ```
   class EventDetail {
     String id;
     String _description;
     String _date;
     String _startTime;
     String _endTime;
     String _speaker;
     String _isFavorite;
   }
   ```

4. Inside the class, we'll also create a constructor that takes all the fields we have defined previously, as follows:

   ```
   EventDetail(this.id, this._description, this._date,
     this._startTime, this._endTime, this._speaker, this._isFavorite);
   ```

You may have noticed that all the fields in the EventDetail class, except for the id, have an underscore (_). When fields begin with an underscore, they can only be accessed **in the same file** where they are defined.

5. As all fields except id are private, we'll need to create the getters for the EventDetail properties that we want to make readable, by running the following code:

```
String get description => _description;
String get date => _date;
String get startTime => _startTime;
String get endTime => _endTime;
String get speaker => _speaker;
String get isFavourite => _isFavourite;
```

6. Next, let's create a named constructor, called fromMap(), that will take a dynamic object and transform it into EventDetail, as follows:

```
EventDetail.fromMap(dynamic obj) {
    this.id = obj['id'];
    this._description = obj['description'];
    this._date = obj['date'];
    this._startTime = obj['start_time'];
    this._endTime = obj['end_time'];
    this._speaker = obj['speaker'];
    this._isFavourite = obj['is_favourite'];
}
```

7. We also need to create a method that transforms the EventDetail object into Map. You might recall that Map in Dart is a collection of key-value pairs. These are an excellent way to share data when interacting with web services.

We'll call this method toMap(). It will return a Map instance of type String, dynamic. This is because the key is always a String, and the value may be any type of data as, in the EventDetail class, we are using both a String and Boolean as data types. The code is shown in the following block:

```
Map<String, dynamic> toMap() {
    var map = Map<String, dynamic>();
    if (id != null) {
      map['id'] = id;
    }
    map['description'] = _description;
    map['date'] = _date;
```

```
map['start_time'] = _startTime;
map['end_time'] = _endTime;
map['speaker'] = _speaker;
return map;
```

The EventDetail class is now complete. We need to use it when we retrieve data from the Cloud Firestore database and show the data to our user.

Creating the Event Detail screen

When the app is completed, users will interact with two screens: a list of event details, which is the program of the event, and a second screen for authentication.

We'll now create the event detail screen, as follows:

1. First, let's create a new folder in the lib folder of the app, called screens.
2. Next, we'll add a new file to the screens folder, called event_screen.dart.
3. In the event_screen.dart file, let's import the material.dart library, and then create a stateless widget called EventScreen, as shown in the following code block:

```
import 'package:flutter/material.dart';
class EventScreen extends StatelessWidget {
  @override
  Widget build(BuildContext context) {
    return Container(
    );
  }
}
```

4. In the build() method of the EventScreen class, let's return Scaffold. In Scaffold, in appBar, we'll create a new AppBar titled Event, as shown in the following code snippet:

```
return Scaffold(
    appBar: AppBar(
        title: Text('Event'),
),
```

5. In the body of the Scaffold, we'll place a widget called EventList, as follows:

```
body: EventList()
```

6. Outside the `EventScreen` class, we'll create a new stateful widget called `EventList`.

The end result of the steps we've yet outlined is shown in the following code block:

```
import 'package:flutter/material.dart';

class EventScreen extends StatelessWidget {
  @override
  Widget build(BuildContext context) {
    return Scaffold(
      appBar: AppBar(title: Text('Event'),),
      body: EventList()
    );
}}

class EventList extends StatefulWidget {
  @override
  _EventListState createState() => _EventListState();
}
class _EventListState extends State<EventList> {
  @override
  Widget build(BuildContext context) {
    return Container();
}}
```

When this screen loads, we want to retrieve the event details from the Cloud Firestore database and show them to the user in a `ListView`. Let's look at the steps to do that, as follows:

1. At the top of the `_EventsScreenState` class, we'll declare a final instance of `Firestore` and a `List` of `EventDetails` that will be populated with the data taken from the instance, as follows:

```
final Firestore db = Firestore.instance;
List<EventDetail> details = [];
```

Of course, don't forget the required imports, which are shown in the following code snippet:

```
import 'package:cloud_firestore/cloud_firestore.dart';
import '../models/event_detail.dart';
```

2. Now, let's create a method that will retrieve the data. We can call this `getDetails()`. It will be asynchronous and will return a `List` instance of `EventDetails`, as follows:

```
Future<List<EventDetail>> getDetailsList() async {}
```

3. Inside the `getDetailList()` method, we'll retrieve all the documents in the event_details collection, as follows:

```
var data = await db.collection('event_details').getDocuments();
```

4. Then, if the `data` variable is not `null`, we'll call the `map()` method on the documents retrieved by the `getDocuments()` method, and there we'll create a list of `EventDetail` objects, calling the `fromMap` constructor that we created previously, as shown in the following code snippet:

```
if (data!= null) {details = data.documents.map((document) =>
EventDetail.fromMap(document)).toList();
```

5. Next, for each `EventDetail` in the `details` list, we'll set `id` as the `documentID` instance of the document (this is because the `id` is saved at a higher level than the object itself). Finally, we'll return the details, as follows:

```
int i = 0;
details.forEach((detail){
    detail.id = data.documents[i].documentID;
    i++;
});
    }
    return details;
}
```

6. We now need to call the `getDetails()` method, but we cannot call it from the `build()` method. This is because, whenever the state changes, the `build()` method is automatically called. As we are calling `setState` from `getDetails()`, this will automatically trigger `build()`; if the build contains a call to `getDetails()`, you get an infinite call loop.

So, the best place to call the `getDetails()` method is in the `initState()` method, which is called only once, when the widget is created.

7. As the `getDetailsList()` returns Future, and not the details themselves, we'll call the `then` method on `Future`; inside its function, after checking the widget is mounted, we'll call `setState()` and set the details as the result of the `getDetailsList()` call. Add the following code in the `initState()` method of the `_EventListState` class:

```
@override
void initState() {
    if (mounted) {
        getDetailsList().then((data){
            setState(() {
                details = data;
            });
        });
    }
    super.initState();
}
```

So, when the screen is loaded, we call the `getDetailsList()` method and, after some time, the `details` list is updated and contains the `EventDetail` object of the event we are viewing.

8. The only remaining step to perform is showing the results to the user, and we'll do this in the `build()` method of the `_EventListState` class. In the `build()` method, instead of returning a `Container`, we'll return a `ListView.builder` that, as `itemCount`, will have the length of the `details` list. The `itemBuilder` parameter takes a function that returns a `ListTile`, as follows:

```
@override
  Widget build(BuildContext context) {
    return ListView.builder(
      itemCount: (details!= null)? details.length : 0,
      itemBuilder: (context, position){
        return ListTile();
      },
    );
  }
```

9. In the `ListTile`, for now, we'll just specify a `title` and a `subtitle`. We'll set the `title` to contain the description of the `EventDetail`, and for the `subtitle`, we'll concatenate the date, start time, and end time of the event detail, as shown in the following code snippet:

```
@override
Widget build(BuildContext context) {
  return ListView.builder(
    itemCount: (details!= null)? details.length : 0,
    itemBuilder: (context, position){
      String sub='Date: ${details[position].date} - Start:
${details[position].startTime} - End:
${details[position].endTime}';
      return ListTile(
      title: Text(details[position].description),
      subtitle: Text(sub),
      );
    },
  );
}
```

10. Before trying out the app, in the `main.dart` file, we need to call the `EventScreen` widget, like this:

```
home: EventScreen(),
```

Now, if you run the app, you should see a screen like the one shown in the following screenshot:

Well done! Now that we have seen the program of our event, let's talk about the authentication with Firebase for our app, and how to improve it by adding a login screen.

Adding authentication to your app

Most apps need to know the identity of users. For example, in the app we are building in this chapter, we want the user to be able to select their favorite parts of the event program and save that data remotely. In order to do this, we need to know who the user is.

Identifying users generally means two different tasks:

- Authentication means confirming the user's identity.
- Authorization means the user is allowed to access different parts of the app or the data behind the app.

Firebase Authentication provides several services you can leverage in order to provide authentication to your apps, including:

- Authentication through a username and password, or providers such as Google, Microsoft, Facebook, and several others. Basically, you can delegate the authentication process to an external provider, and your user won't have to remember another username and password to access your data.
- Creation of user identities.
- Methods such as Login, Logout, Signup, and Reset password.
- Integration with other services in Firebase, so you can easily deal with authorization rules once the identity has been created.

In our app, we'll add authentication with a username and password, and we'll allow our users to sign up and sign in. Then, we'll set a rule so that only authenticated users will be able to access the data in our Cloud Firestore database. Also, from our app, we'll give each user the ability to read and write their favorite event details. So, let's see how it's done, as follows:

1. In order to enable authentication, we'll need to get back to the Firebase console. From there, we'll get to the **Authentication** option inside the **Develop** section of the Firebase project dashboard and click on the **Sign-in method** tab.
2. You'll notice that all authentication methods are disabled by default. At this time, we'll only need to enable the **Email/Password** authentication method. Since we're enabling this provider, we'll be able to sign up and log in with an email and password. In many apps, you may wish to add other providers, such as Google or Facebook, to sign in.
3. The final result should look similar to the following screenshot:

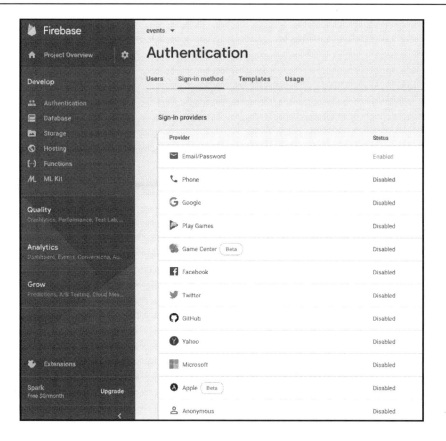

If you want to learn more about signing in with other providers, have a
look at the *Further reading* section at the end of this chapter.

4. Make sure you have added the latest version of `firebase_auth`, the official
   plugin for authentication maintained by the Firebase team, in the `pubspec.yaml`
   file, as follows (for the latest version of the plugin, check `https://pub.dev/`
   `packages/firebase_auth`):

```
dependencies:
  [...]
  firebase_auth: ^0.15.5+2
```

Now that authentication is enabled in our Firebase project, we are ready to create the login
screen in our app.

Adding the login/signup screen

The login screen will serve two purposes: it will allow our user to log in to our app, or to sign up and obtain an identity. We'll use email and password authentication, so we'll need to design a screen that allows the input of a login and a password. We won't need or use any other data from our users. We will proceed as follows:

1. Back in the app code, let's create a new file in the screens folder and call it login_screen.dart.

2. Inside the login_screen.dart file, we'll import the material.dart library, and create a new stateful widget using the stful shortcut. We'll call this widget LoginScreen.

3. Inside the _LoginScreenState class, we'll create a few state-level variables, such as those shown in the following code block:

```
bool _isLogin = true;
String _userId;
String _password;
String _email;
String _message;
```

_userId, _password, and _email are the variables that will contain the authentication data. When the _islogin Boolean is used, we'll perform a login, and when it's false, we'll enable signup. The _message String holds a message for any error that might occur during login or signup.

The screen will contain a column with five widgets: two TextFormField widgets for the email and password, two buttons, and a Text for the message. For each of those widgets, we'll create a method so that our code is easier to read and maintain.

You can see the end result of the login screen in the following screenshot:

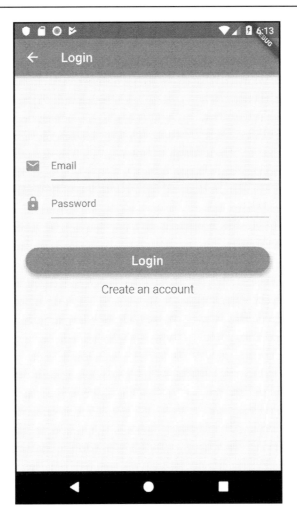

4. Let's begin with email input. We'll create a method that returns a widget called emailInput, as follows:

```
Widget emailInput() {
    return Padding(
      padding: EdgeInsets.only(top:120),
      child: TextFormField(
       controller: txtEmail,
        keyboardType: TextInputType.emailAddress,
        decoration: InputDecoration(
          hintText: 'email',
          icon: Icon(Icons.mail)
        ),
```

```
            validator: (text) => text.isEmpty ? 'Email is required' :
                '',
        )
    );
}
```

The `emailInput()` method returns a `Padding`, with some spacing at the top, and in its child contains a `TextFormField`. This is a widget that wraps a `TextField` into a `FormField` and allows easy validation. You may have noticed that we added a `keyboardType`, showing the specific keyboard for emails, and we added an `InputDecoration` with a `hintText` and an `Icon`.

5. This also needs a `TextEditingController` widget that we can declare at the top of the `State` class and then call `txtEmail`, as shown in the following code snippet:

```
final TextEditingController txtEmail = TextEditingController();
```

6. We'll repeat the same pattern for the `passwordInput()` method, changing `keyboardType` and `Icon`, and adding the `obscureText` parameter, and setting it to `true`, so that the characters are not visible while typing, as follows:

```
Widget passwordInput() {
    return Padding(
      padding: EdgeInsets.only(top:120),
      child: TextFormField(
        controller: txtPassword,
        keyboardType: TextInputType.emailAddress,
        obscureText: true,
        decoration: InputDecoration(
          hintText: 'password',
          icon: Icon(Icons.enhanced_encryption)
        ),
        validator: (text) => text.isEmpty ? 'Password is required'
        : '',
      )
    );
}
```

7. In this case, the TextEditingController is called txtPassword, as can be seen in the following code snippet:

```
final TextEditingController txtPassword = TextEditingController();
```

8. Now, let's add the two buttons. Based on the _isLogin field, we'll show a different main button and a secondary button. This is because, when _isLogin is true, the user needs to log in, and the primary button will be the login action, while the secondary button will enable the signup process. When _isLogin is false, the primary button will be the signup submit action, and the secondary button will bring us to the login process.

When pressed, the main button will call the submit() method (which we will create shortly); this will validate and submit the data that was typed by the user. It will be positioned right below the two text fields.

9. To make it a bit nicer, we'll give it a RoundedRectangleBorder shape, with a circular radius. We'll also give it a background color, taken from the current theme, so that, when the theme changes, the button color will also be updated, as shown in the following code block:

```
Widget mainButton() {
    String buttonText = _isLogin ? 'Login' : 'Sign up';
    return Padding(
      padding: EdgeInsets.only(top: 120),
      child: Container(
        height: 50,
        child: RaisedButton(
          shape: RoundedRectangleBorder(borderRadius:
           BorderRadius.circular(20)),
          color: Theme.of(context).accentColor,
          elevation: 3,
          child: Text(buttonText),
          onPressed: submit,
        )
      )
    );
}
```

The secondary button will switch from the login to the signup function, and vice versa. When pressed, it will call the setState() method, using the value of _isLogin like a toggle. That is, if _isLogin is true, it will become false, and if it's false, it will become true.

Its position will be under the main button and it will be slightly smaller, as the main button is the most important action of the screen. The code is shown in the following snippet:

```
Widget secondaryButton() {
  String buttonText = !_isLogin ? 'Login' : 'Sign up';
  return FlatButton(
    child: Text(buttonText),
    onPressed: () {
      setState(() {
        _isLogin = !_isLogin;
      });
    },
  );
```

10. The last widget of the screen is the `Text` containing the error message, which is activated when the user doesn't insert any data in the email or password fields. If there is no validation error, nothing will show. We'll call this last method `validationMessage()`, and it will return a `Text`, as shown in the following code snippet:

```
Widget validationMessage() {
  return Text(_message,
    style: TextStyle(
      fontSize: 14,
      color: Colors.red,
      fontWeight: FontWeight.bold),);
}
```

11. Now that we have completed the widgets, we need to compose the screen UI in the `build()` method of the `_LoginScreenState` class.

As usual, the `build()` method will return a `Scaffold`, with an `appbar` and a `body`. In the body of the `Scaffold`, we will place a `Container` with a `Form` widget. A `Form` in Flutter is a field container, and it makes it easier to validate fields.

12. In the `Form`, we'll place a scrolling `Column` with all the widgets we have created previously, as shown in the following code block:

```
Widget build(BuildContext context) {
  return Scaffold(
    appBar: AppBar(title: Text('Login'),),
    body: Container(
      padding: EdgeInsets.all(24),
      child:SingleChildScrollView(
```

```
child: Form(child: Column(
  children: <Widget>[
    emailInput(),
    passwordInput(),
    mainButton(),
    secondaryButton(),
    validationMessage(),
  ],),),),),),);
```

Now that we have completed the UI of the LoginScreen, we need to add the authentication logic and interact with Firebase Authentication.

Adding the authentication logic

We'll place the authentication logic in a new class. This class will contain four methods:

- A method to log in
- A method to sign up
- A method to log out
- A method to retrieve the current user

Let's begin adding our login, as follows:

1. Create a new folder in the lib folder of our app and call it shared. Inside the shared folder, let's also create a new file called authentication.dart.

2. In this file, we'll import the firebase_auth package and async.dart.

3. Next, we'll create a new class called Authentication, as follows:

```
import 'dart:async';
import 'package:firebase_auth/firebase_auth.dart';
class Authentication {}
```

4. In the Authentication class, we'll declare an instance of FirebaseAuth, which is the object that enables the use of Firebase Authentication's methods and properties, as follows:

```
final FirebaseAuth _firebaseAuth = FirebaseAuth.instance;
```

 All methods in FirebaseAuth are asynchronous.

5. Then, we'll create a method that will allow our users to log in. It will be asynchronous, will return a `Future` of type `String`, and will take two strings, one for the username and one for the password, as follows:

```
Future<String> login(String email, String password) async {}
```

6. Inside the `login()` method, we just need to call the `signInWithEmailAndPassword()` method, which does exactly what its name implies, as follows:

```
AuthResult authResult = await
_firebaseAuth.signInWithEmailAndPassword(
    email: email, password: password
  );
```

7. Next, let's create a `FirebaseUser` object. The `FirebaseUser` represents a user and has several properties that can be used by the app, such as `uid`, which is the user ID, and `email`. In this case, the function returns the user's `uid`, as shown in the following snippet:

```
FirebaseUser user = authResult.user;
return user.uid;
```

For a full list of properties for the `FirebaseUser` class, have a look at the documentation page at `https://pub.dev/documentation/firebase_auth/latest/firebase_auth/FirebaseUser-class.html`.

8. The signup process is very similar. We'll create an asynchronous method called `signUp()` and, instead of calling the `signInWithUserNameAndPassword()` method, we will call the `createUserWithUserNameAndPassword()` method, which will create a new user in our Firebase project. The code for this method is shown in the following snippet:

```
Future<String> signUp(String email, String password) async {
    AuthResult authResult = await
    _firebaseAuth.createUserWithEmailAndPassword(
      email: email, password: password
    );
    FirebaseUser user = authResult.user;
    return user.uid;
  }
```

9. We now need to create a method that will sign out the logged-in user. This is extremely simple, as we'll only need to call the `signOut()` method on the `FirebaseAuth` instance, as follows:

```
Future<void> signOut() async {
  return _firebaseAuth.signOut();
}
```

10. The last method we'll add to the `Authentication` class is a method that retrieves the current user. This will be useful when we need to check whether a user is logged in or not. We'll call it `getUser()` and it will call the `FirebaseAuth.currentUser()` method, as illustrated in the following code snippet:

```
Future<FirebaseUser> getUser() async {
  FirebaseUser user = await _firebaseAuth.currentUser();
  return user;
}
```

Now that we have completed the authentication logic, we need to add the methods of the `Authentication` class in the authentication screen. Also, when the user enters the app for the first time, they should see the authentication screen. Once logged in, the user should see the event screen.

In order to make this possible, we can use the `getUser()` method to check whether a `CurrentUser` is available or not. We'll do that from a new screen, called `LaunchScreen`. This screen's task will be to show a loading animation while the user data is retrieved. It will then redirect the user to the appropriate screen—that is, either the authentication screen or the event screen.

Let's create the launch screen for our app, as follows:

1. Let's create a new file in the `screens` folder, called `launch_screen.dart`. At the top of the file, we'll import `material.dart`, the two screens that may be opened by the launch screen, the `firebase_auth` package, and the `cloud_firestore` package.

2. Next, we'll create a stateful widget called `LaunchScreen`. In the `build()` method of the `_launchScreenState` class, we'll show a `CircularProgressIndicator` widget, which shows a nice animation while data is loading, as follows:

```
import 'package:flutter/material.dart';
import 'package:firebase_auth/firebase_auth.dart';
import 'package:cloud_firestore/cloud_firestore.dart';
```

```
import 'login_screen.dart';
import 'event_screen.dart';

class LaunchScreen extends StatefulWidget {
  @override
  _LaunchScreenState createState() => _LaunchScreenState();
}

class _LaunchScreenState extends State<LaunchScreen> {
  @override
  Widget build(BuildContext context) {
    return Scaffold(
      body: Center(child: CircularProgressIndicator(),),

  );
  }
}
```

3. Next, we will override the `InitState()` method, which checks the current user status.

4. Inside the method, we'll call an instance of the `Authentication` class and then call the `getUser()` method.

5. If there is a logged-in user available, we'll show the user the `EventScreen`; otherwise, we'll just show the `Login` screen.

6. Notice that, instead of using the `push()` method on the navigator, we're using `pushReplacement()`. This not only pushes the new route to the top of the screen, but it also removes the previous route. This prevents the user from navigating to the `LaunchScreen`. This is illustrated in the following code block:

```
@override
  void initState() {
    super.initState();
    Authentication auth = Authentication();
    auth.getUser().then((user) {
      MaterialPageRoute route;
      if (user != null) {
        route = MaterialPageRoute(builder: (context) =>
        EventScreen());
      }
      else {
        route = MaterialPageRoute(builder: (context) =>
        LoginScreen());
      }
      Navigator.pushReplacement(context, route);
    }).catchError((err)=> print(err));
  }
```

In order to try this out, we'll need to change what happens when the user opens the app for the first time. Currently, as it opens, the app shows the EventScreen, but we want to change that. This is because, if the user is already logged in, they will see the EventScreen; otherwise, we need to show the LoginScreen. Before trying the LaunchScreen, we need to call it from the MyApp class in the main.dart file. So, let's change the home of the MaterialApp,so it calls LaunchScreen, as follows:

```
home: LaunchScreen(),
```

If you try the app right now, after a very short CircularProgressIndicator animation (depending on your device, it might be so fast you won't even see it), you should see the Login screen.

Unfortunately, from there, we can neither log in nor sign in yet, but we are very close. Let's get back to the loginscreen.dart file and add the logic to perform the login and signup tasks, as follows:

1. First, we'll import the authentication.dart file that contains the calls to the Firebase Authentication service, as follows:

   ```
   import '../shared/authentication.dart';
   ```

2. Then, we'll create an Authentication variable called auth, override the initState() method, and create an instance of the Authentication class, as follows:

   ```
   Authentication auth;
     @override
     void initState() {
       auth = Authentication();
       super.initState();
   }
   ```

3. In the submit() method in the _LoginScreenState class, which is called when the user presses the main button, we will reset the _message so that, if there was a previous validation message, it's removed from the screen. We'll also make the method asynchronous, as follows:

   ```
   Future submit() async {
       setState(() {
         _message = "";
       });
   ```

4. Then, in a `try-catch` block, we'll call the `login` or `signup` methods of the `auth` object, based on the value of the `_isLogin` Boolean variable. After each action, we'll also print information about the logged-in or signed-up user in the Debug console, as follows:

```
try {
        if (_isLogin) {
          _userId = await auth.login(txtEmail.text,
           txtPassword.text);
          print('Login for user $_userId');
        }
        else
        {
          _userId = await auth.signUp(txtEmail.text,
           txtPassword.text);
          print('Sign up for user $_userId');
        }
        if (_userId != null) {
          Navigator.push(context, MaterialPageRoute(builder:
          (context)=> EventScreen()));
        }
      } catch (e) {
        print('Error: $e');
        setState(() {
          _message = e.message;
        });
    }
```

If the login or signup tasks were successful, the `_userId` should now contain the ID of the logged-in user. However, if the username or password is wrong, or the call wasn't successful, the Firebase Authentication call should fail, and in this case, we'll print an error message so that the user will be able to see the problem.

In order to try the login procedure, I suggest you try to fail the login a few times, by using a badly formatted email, skipping the password, or entering a wrong email and password, just to see the different messages that the Firebase Authentication service returns when something goes wrong.

After trying the different error messages, you can sign up with your correct data; if the process is successful, you should be redirected to the event screen. Now, if you restart the app, you should skip the login process and be redirected to the event screen immediately, as the app is keeping your login data.

5. We need to add a way for the user to log out. We'll use an `IconButton` widget in the actions of the `AppBar` of the `Scaffold` in the `EventScreen` class to call the logout method of our `Authentication` class, as shown in the following code block:

```
final Authentication auth = new Authentication();
    return Scaffold(
      appBar: AppBar(
        title: Text('Event'),
        actions:[
            IconButton(
              icon: Icon(Icons.exit_to_app),
              onPressed: () {
                auth.signOut().then((result) {
                  Navigator.push(context,
                      MaterialPageRoute(builder: (context) =>
                          LoginScreen())));
                });
              },
            )
        ],
      ),
```

If you try the app now and press the logout `IconButton`, you should be redirected to the login screen again; if you log in, you will be taken back to the `EventScreen`. So now in our app, only logged-in users can access event information.

But the security we've implemented here is only client-side, and any security expert would tell us that this means almost no security at all. The good news is that we can very easily set up server-side security in Firebase. Let's see how, next!

Introducing Firebase rules

In Firebase, and specifically in the Cloud Firestore, you can implement server-side security leveraging the user authentication information and setting **authorization rules**, thus controlling access to data based on user identity. For example, you can decide that only authenticated users can read data, or can write their own data.

You can access the authorization rules in the Cloud Firestore database page, by clicking on the **Rules** pane, as shown in the following screenshot:

From there, we want to allow access to data—with read and write permissions—only to logged-in users. We can achieve this by setting the following rules:

```
// Allow read/write access on all documents to any user signed in to the
application
service cloud.firestore {
  match /databases/{database}/documents {
    match /{document=**} {
      allow read, write: if request.auth.uid != null;
    } } }
```

If you try the app right now, you should still see all the data as before, but now you have the benefit of server-side security.

The only feature we'll add to the app is giving our users the chance to choose their favorite items in the event calendar.

Writing data to Firebase: Adding the favorite feature

We want to give users the ability to choose their favorite parts of the event program. In this way, we'll also see how to write data to the Cloud Firestore database, and to query data based on specific selection criteria.

Just as we did for the EventDetail class, let's create a new model class that will contain the user's favorites, as follows:

1. Let's create a new file in the models directory, called favorite.dart.

2. A favorite object needs to contain an ID, the **user ID (UID)** of the user, and the ID of the selected event detail. We'll mark all the properties as private, and we'll create an unnamed constructor to set a new instance of a favorite, as follows:

```
class Favorite {
  String _id;
  String _eventId;
  String _userId;
  Favourite(this._id, this._eventId, this._userId);
}
```

3. Then, we'll create a named constructor called `map` that will take a `DocumentSnapshot` containing data read from a document in a Cloud Firestore database. In a `DocumentSnapshot` object, you always find a `documentId`, which is the ID of the document, and a `data` object, which contains the key-value pairs that were specified inside the document, as shown in the following code snippet:

```
Favourite.map(DocumentSnapshot document) {
  this._id = document.documentID;
  this._eventId = document.data['eventId'];
  this._userId = document.data['userId'];
}
```

4. We also need to create a method that returns a `Map`, so that it will be easier to write data to the Cloud Firestore database. We can call this method `toMap()`. The keys of the `Map` will be `Strings`, and its values will be `dynamic`. The code of the `toMap()` method is shown in the following code snippet:

```
Map<String, dynamic> toMap() {
  Map map = Map<String, dynamic>();
  if (_id!= null) {
    map['id'] = _id;
  }
  map['eventId'] = _eventId;
  map['userId'] = _userId;
  return map;
}
```

The `Favourite` class is now complete. What we need now is to build the methods that will perform the required reading and writing tasks. As there will be several methods, and it's always a good idea to separate the logic of an app from the UI, we'll create a new file to host those methods, as follows:

1. In the `shared` folder, create a new file called `firestore_helper.dart`. This will contain helper methods to interact with the Cloud Firestore database.

2. In this file, import the two model classes and the Cloud Firestore package.

3. Then, create a static db property, which will be an instance of Firestore and will be used throughout the class, as shown in the following code snippet:

```
import '../models/event_detail.dart';
import '../models/favourite.dart';
import 'package:cloud_firestore/cloud_firestore.dart';
class FirestoreHelper {
  static final Firestore db = Firestore.instance;
}
```

All methods of this class will be static, as we don't actually need to instantiate this class in order to use them.

4. The first method we'll create in this class will add a new favorite into the Firestore database. It's a static method called addFavourite that will take the currently logged-in user uid, and the Event that will be added as a favorite, as follows:

```
static Future addFavourite(EventDetail eventDetail, String uid) {
  Favourite fav = Favourite(null, uid, eventDetail.id);
  var result = db.collection('favourites').add(fav.toMap())
    .then((value) => print(value))
    .catchError((error)=> print (error));
  return result;
}
```

As you can see, inside the method, we create an instance of the Favourite class and call it fav. Then, from the database instance, we add to the collection called favourites the fav object, transformed into a Map.

We print the result in the Debug console if everything works correctly, or print the error if something goes wrong.

Now, we need a way to enable the user to add their favorites from the UI. To make this possible, we can add a star icon in the event calendar list so that, when the user presses the star icon, the favorite will be added. Later on, we'll also change the icon color, so that the favorites will be immediately recognizable.

Before we add the star IconButton, after logging in, let's send to the event screen the UID of the user that was logged in. In this way, it will be easier to read and write the favorites data from the screen itself.

We will proceed as follows:

1. In the EventScreen class, let's add a String uid property and set it in the constructor, as follows:

```
final String uid;
```

2. When we call the EventList class from the body of the Scaffold, let's pass the uid, like this:

```
EventList(uid);
```

3. We'll do the same in the EventList class, adding a uid property and receiving it in the constructor, as follows:

```
final String uid;
EventList(this.uid);
```

4. In this way, we've propagated the uid from the authentication process back to the _EventListState, and now we have all the data we need to read and write the user's favorites.

5. Now, let's create a method called toggleFavourite() that will take the EventDetail that has to become a favorite and call the FirestoreHelper addFavourite() method, as follows:

```
void toggleFavourite(EventDetail ed) {
    FirestoreHelper.addFavourite(ed, widget.uid);
}
```

6. Then, in the build() method of the EventListState class in the event_screen.dart file, let's add a trailing IconButton widget to the ListTile in the ListViewBuilder widget. This will be the widget that will add the favorites from the Cloud Firestore database; later, we'll also use colors to tell the user whether the current item on a list is a favorite or not and whether to remove the favorite from the database. The code for this is illustrated in the following snippet:

```
trailing: IconButton(
        icon: Icon(Icons.star, color: Colors.grey),
        onPressed: () {toggleFavourite(details[position]);},
    ),
```

7. Before trying this new feature, we need to modify the calls to the `EventScreen` class. One is in the `LaunchScreenState` class, in the `launchscreen.dart` file. When we set the route that calls the `EventScreen` class, we need to modify the route, as shown in the following snippet:

```
route = MaterialPageRoute(builder: (context) =>
EventScreen(user.uid));
```

8. Then, in the `login_screen.dart` file, in the `submit()` method of the `_LoginScreenState` class, we need to add the `_userId` variable to the `MaterialPageRoute`, as shown in the following snippet:

```
if (_userId != null) {
        Navigator.push(
          context, MaterialPageRoute(builder: (context)=>
          EventScreen(_userId))
          );
      }
```

9. Let's try the app now. In the **events** screen, press the star IconButton on any item of the List. If everything is working correctly, when you go to your Firebase console and see the database data, you should find a Favorites collection with some data in it, as shown in the following screenshot:

This means that the app is now writing favorites to the Cloud Firestore database.

Next, we need to read the favorites, give some feedback to the user, and delete the favorites from the database.

Showing and deleting favorites

In the `FirestoreHelper` class, we need to add two new features: a method to delete an existing favorite from the database, and a method to retrieve all the favorites for the currently logged-in user.

Let's begin with the `deleteFavourite()` method. This will just take the ID of the Favourite that will be deleted; as usual, it will be `static` and `asynchronous`. In order to actually delete an item from a collection in a Cloud Firestore database, you just need to navigate to the collection, go to the specific document with its ID, and then call the `delete()` method, as follows:

```
static Future deleteFavourite(String favId) async {
    await db.collection('favourites').document(favId).delete();
}
```

The static and asynchronous `getUserFavourites()` method will take the user `id` as a parameter and return a `Future` containing a list of `Favourite` objects.

Inside the function, we have the chance to see an incredibly useful feature of the Cloud Firestore database, which is querying inside a collection with the `where()` method. This takes the field where we want to apply the filter and the type of filter we need to apply—in this case, `isEqualTo`—and the value of the filter itself. We apply the `getDocuments()` method to return an object of type `QuerySnapshot` that we can use to transform the result of the query into a `List` of `Favourite`, and return it to the caller.

Basically, this method will return a list containing all the favorite documents of the user whose ID is passed as a parameter, as follows:

```
static Future<List<Favourite>> getUserFavourites(String uid) async {
    List<Favourite> favs;
    QuerySnapshot docs = await db.collection('favourites')
      .where('userId', isEqualTo: uid).getDocuments();
    if (docs != null) {
      favs = docs.documents.map((data)=> Favourite.map(data)).toList();
    }
    return favs;
}
```

Now we need to show which items in the event calendar are user favorites, and we'll do that by coloring the star icon with a bright amber color, proceeding as follows:

1. Back in the `_EventListState` class in the `eventscreen.dart` file, let's declare a `List` of **Favourite**, called `favourites`:

   ```
   List<Favourite> favourites = [];
   ```

2. Then, in the `initState()` method, we'll call the `FirestoreHelper.getUserFavourites()` method, which will call the `setState()` method to update the favorites array, as follows:

   ```
   FirestoreHelper.getUserFavourites(uid).then((data){
       setState(() {
         favourites = data;
       });
   });
   ```

3. As favorites and details are two separate objects, we need a way to quickly check whether an event detail is actually a favorite or not. Let's create a method that does exactly that. It will return `true` if the event detail is a favorite, and `false` if it's not, as illustrated in the following code snippet:

   ```
   bool isUserFavourite (String eventId) {
       Favourite favourite = favourites
         .firstWhere((Favourite f) => (f.eventId == eventId),
       orElse: () => null  );
       if (favourite==null)
         return false;
       else
         return true;
   }
   ```

   The `firstWhere()` method, called from a `List`, retrieves the first element in the `List` that satisfies the condition that you specify in the test parameter. The **favorite** variable will contain the first `Favorite` whose id is equal to the `Event id` that was passed to the function, if available. Otherwise, it will return `null`.

4. In order for this code to work, we also need to create a getter method in the `Favourite` class in the `favourite.dart` file, as follows:

   ```
   String get eventId => _eventId;
   ```

5. Now we only need to leverage everything we've prepared so far to color the star icon in the list. In the `build()` method of the `_EventListState` class, in the `itemBuilder` parameter of the `ListView.builder` constructor, we'll declare a `Color` widget that will depend on the `EventDetail` being a favorite or not. We'll set amber when the detail is a favorite and grey if it's not, as follows:

```
Color starColor = (isUserFavourite(details[position].id) ?
Colors.amber : Colors.grey);
```

6. For the trailing icon, instead of returning a fixed color, we'll return the `starColor` value, as follows:

```
trailing: IconButton(
            icon: Icon(Icons.star, color: starColor),
```

7. Now, if you restart the app, you should see that the values you clicked previously have an amber star color. This helps the user see which items on the list are their favorites.

8. So far, we can add favorites, but we cannot remove them. We need to add a small tweak to the `toggleFavourite()` method, as shown in the following code block:

```
toggleFavourite(EventDetail ed) async{
    if (isUserFavourite(ed.id)) {
      Favourite favourite = favourites
         .firstWhere((Favourite f) => (f.eventId == ed.id));
      String favId = favourite.id;
      await FirestoreHelper.deleteFavourite(favId);
    }
    else {
      await FirestoreHelper.addFavourite(ed, uid);
    }
    List<Favourite> updatedFavourites =
        await FirestoreHelper.getUserFavourites(uid);
    setState(() {
      favourites = updatedFavourites;
    });
}
```

As you can see now, the method can call `addFavourite()` as before, but also `deleteFavourite()`, depending on the result of the call to the `isUserFavourite` method over the ID of the `EventDetail` that was passed to the method.

After adding or deleting the `Favourite` in the database, the method also calls the `getUserFavourites()` method to update the state. This will update the UI with the changes to the favorites list. Depending on the device connection speed, you might notice a small delay when the user presses the star icon button, but this is normal while the network calls are completed.

If you try the app right now, you'll find that you can add or remove favorites from the list by clicking the star `IconButton`. And with this last feature, the app is now complete. Well done! You now have the skills required to create a full-stack application leveraging Flutter and Firebase!

Summary

In this chapter, you've seen how to build a full-stack app from scratch: server-side, we've used Firebase to create a web service, including database and authentication services; client-side, we've used Flutter to read and write data to the cloud.

In detail, you've seen how to create a new Firebase project, which is the entry point for all Flutter services. Inside the project, you've created a new NoSQL database with the Cloud Firestore database. This database contains collections, which in turn contain documents. Documents are made up of key-value pairs or fields. Then, we saw how to integrate Firebase into a Flutter project, both in iOS and Android. This multi-step process includes downloading a configuration file, different for the two operating systems, and adding it in your projects; of course, it also includes adding the relevant packages to the `pubspec.yaml` file.

We've seen how to add an instance of a Cloud Firestore database, and how to retrieve documents from a collection, with or without filters. We've also seen how to add and delete documents from Flutter code. All read and write methods in Firebase are asynchronous. We've seen how the Authentication service works in Firebase. We have added new users for our app and logged them before letting them retrieve data. In this context, we introduced Firestore authorization rules, and at the same time, how to implement server-side security.

Finally, we seen how to provide personalized content to our users by querying the database, and adding user information when inserting new documents. Adding Firebase to your toolbox gives you the power to create remote services without the need to write server-side code or create databases, and gives you virtually unlimited scaling capabilities.

In the next chapter, we'll use two very important features for your apps: Geo-localisation and maps!

Questions

Please try to answer the following questions (when in doubt, have a look at the content in the chapter itself—you'll find all the answers there!):

1. In a Cloud Firestore database, what's the difference between a document and a collection? And can a document contain a collection?

2. Can you name three of the main differences between a SQL and a NoSQL database?

3. Consider the following code:

```
docs = await db.collection('favourites')
.where('userId', isEqualTo: uid).getDocuments();
```

What does this query perform? And which data type is the `docs` variable?

4. In a Cloud Firestore database, is it possible to allow data access only to authenticated users? If so, how can you achieve that?

5. How can you create an instance of a `FirebaseAuth` class?

6. Consider the following code:

```
var result = db.collection('favourites').add(fav.toMap()
    .then((value) => print(value.documentID))
    .catchError((error)=> print (error));
```

Can you explain what these instructions perform?

7. When would you create a getter method for a property in a class? And how do you write the code to create it?

8. When do you need a `Map` object to interact with a Cloud Firestore database?

9. How do you delete a document from a Cloud Firestore database?

10. How do you pass data from one screen to another?

Further reading

The most comprehensive resource if you want to learn more about Firebase in general, and how to integrate Firebase with the technology of your choice in particular, is the official Firebase documentation, available at the following address: `https://firebase.google.com/docs/guides`.

Still in the official documentation, you'll also find guides on the Firestore database at `https://firebase.google.com/docs/firestore` and Firestore Authentication at `https://firebase.google.com/docs/firestore/security/get-started`, as well as a specific guide on how to install Firebase with Flutter: `https://firebase.google.com/docs/flutter/setup`. For an updated list of available authentication providers, have a look at `https://firebase.google.com/docs/reference/js/firebase.auth.AuthProvider`.

For a detailed explanation about NoSQL database and for the different kinds on the NoSQL database, IBM has provided a very easy-to-read document at `https://www.ibm.com/cloud/learn/nosql-databases`.

A concept that may cause confusion the first time you deal with security is the difference between authentication and authorization. There's a brief but very clear explanation at `https://auth0.com/docs/authorization/concepts/authz-and-authn`.

8
The Treasure Mapp - Integrating Maps and Using Your Device Camera

Let's say you are walking along the street, and you see a new shop that inspires you; or, maybe you've had dinner in a memorable restaurant, and want to remember its location and how it looks; or, you've parked your car, and need to remember where you left it. Wouldn't it be great if you could mark any place, and maybe add a brief description and a picture?

The Treasure Mapp is an app that allows users to mark places on a map, and then add a name and a picture over it. Pictures will be taken by using the device camera. Users will be able to see all the saved places, marked on a map or through a list. They will also be able to edit or delete them.

This project covers two important features of mobile programming: geolocation, and the device camera. It also covers dealing with device permissions.

The following topics will be covered in this chapter:

- Geolocation and camera: a powerful duo
- Integrating Google Maps into Flutter
- Using the device camera

Technical requirements

You'll find the completed app code on the book's GitHub repository at `https://github.com/PacktPublishing/Flutter-Projects`.

To follow along with the code examples in this book, you should have the following software installed on your Windows, Mac, Linux, or Chrome OS device:

- The Flutter **Software Development Kit (SDK)**.
- When developing for Android: the Android SDK, easily installed by Android Studio.
- When developing for iOS: macOS and Xcode.
- An emulator (Android), a simulator (iOS), or a connected iOS or Android device enabled for debugging.
- An editor: **Visual Studio Code (VS Code)**, Android Studio, or IntelliJ IDEA are recommended. All should have the Flutter/Dart extensions installed.
- For this chapter, an iOS or Android device is required to use the hardware camera and geolocation features.

Geolocation and camera – a powerful duo

If you were asked to name some of the most important features of your mobile device, you would probably include in your list the camera and the built-in **Global Positioning System (GPS)**. These two features that we take for granted today are very specific to mobile development and can make your apps stand out from the crowd.

The *geolocation* feature enables you as a developer to identify the coordinates of your app's users—in particular, their *latitude* and *longitude*. It will also potentially save those coordinates for future use. This gives developers a huge potential: think of social networks suggesting nearby events, or travel agents recommending restaurants or hotels, or dating apps suggesting new contacts. There are so many potential scenarios to give your users relevant and personalized information!

The case for pictures is even more obvious: people love shooting and sharing their pictures. The most successful social media contain more pictures than text messages. Even the phone manufacturers base an important part of their marketing on how good their camera is. So, as developers, we should be ready to leverage this opportunity and give our users what they love, which is the ability to use their camera whenever it may add quality to your app.

And what if we put together geolocation and camera in a single app? Welcome to the Treasure Mapp!

Integrating Google Maps into Flutter

For this project, we'll be using the Google Maps API to show the user a map and add markers to it. As with other Google services, Maps is free up to a certain threshold. You, as a developer, should be able to use it for free in most cases. For production purposes, though, this threshold might not be enough.

 For details about pricing and thresholds in Google Maps for a production app, have a look at the following page: `https://cloud.google.com/maps-platform/pricing/`.

Let's begin integrating our maps into Flutter, as follows

1. Create a new Flutter app, and call it `treasure_mapp`.
2. Add the Google Maps plugin as a dependency in the `pubspec.yaml` file. The package is called `google_maps_flutter`, and you can find the latest version on `pub.dartlang.org`. The code can be seen in the following snippet:

```
dependencies:
    google_maps_flutter: ^0.5.24+1
```

3. Then, you need to **obtain an API key** to use Google Maps. You can get one from the **Google Cloud Platform (GCP)** console at the following address: `https://console.cloud.google.com`.

4. After logging in with your Google Account, you should see the console, as shown in the following screenshot:

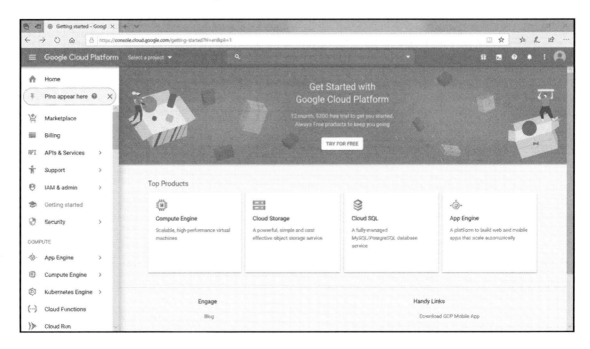

5. Every API key belongs to a project, so you'll need to create one or select an existing one before obtaining your credentials. Let's call the project `Treasure_Mapp`, leave **No organization** for your location, and then click **Create**, as shown in the following screenshot:

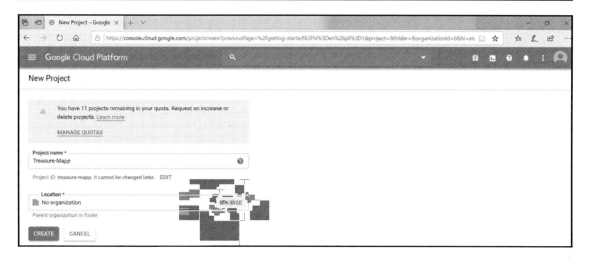

6. Now, click the menu button and select **APIs & Services** | **Credentials**, and, on the **Credentials** page, select **Create credentials** | **API key**.

7. Now that you have the key, we need to add it to our project. **For Android**, you need to add the information into the `android/app/src/main/AndroidManifest.xml` application manifest. Just place the code in the application node, under the icon, as follows:

```
<application
        android:name="io.flutter.app.FlutterApplication"
        android:label="testing"
        android:icon="@mipmap/ic_launcher">
        <meta-data android:name="com.google.android.geo.API_KEY"
            android:value="ADD YOUR KEY HERE"/>
```

You might wonder about the role of this file in your Flutter project. The Android App Manifest, which is a necessary file for any Android build, contains essential information about your app. This information is used for the Android build tools, the Android **operating system (OS)** itself, and the Google Play store when you publish your app.

For example, among several other things, the manifest contains the app's package name, the permissions that the app needs in order to access protected parts of the system (such as the camera, or an internet connection) or other apps, and the hardware and software feature the app requires.

8. For an **iOS** app, the procedure is slightly different. After obtaining the API key, you need to open the `AppDelegate` file at the following location: `ios/Runner/AppDelegate.swift`.

9. At the top of the file, import `GoogleMaps`, as follows:

```
import UIKit
import Flutter
import GoogleMaps
```

10. Then, add the code line in bold in the `AppDelegate` class, as follows:

```
@objc class AppDelegate: FlutterAppDelegate {
    override func application(
        _ application: UIApplication,
        didFinishLaunchingWithOptions launchOptions:
        [UIApplication.LaunchOptionsKey: Any]?
        ) -> Bool {
        GMSServices.provideAPIKey("YOUR API KEY HERE")
        GeneratedPluginRegistrant.register(with: self)
        return super.application(application,
        didFinishLaunchingWithOptions: launchOptions)
    }
}
```

The `AppDelegate.swift` file manages the app's shared behaviors and is the **root object of an iOS app**.

For your iOS project, you also need to opt in to the embedded views preview. Get to this by adding a Boolean property to the app's `Info.plist` file.

11. So, open your project `ios/Runner/Info.plist` file, and add the following code in the `<dict>` node:

```
<key>io.flutter.embedded_views_preview</key>
<true/>
```

Now that Google Maps is correctly set up in your Android or iOS app, let's show a map on the screen.

Showing a map with Google Maps

With everything ready for iOS and Android, we can now add a `GoogleMap` widget to the main screen of our app, as follows:

1. To use a package, as usual, we can import it at the top of the file. So, let's include the required Google Maps dependency in the `main.dart` file, like this:

```
import 'package:flutter/material.dart';
import 'package:google_maps_flutter/google_maps_flutter.dart';
```

 You'll find the entire code for `main.dart` here: https://github.com/
PacktPublishing/Flutter-Projects/blob/master/ch_08/lib/main.dart

2. Then, remove the stateful widget from the default app, and create a new stateful widget called `MainMap`, as follows:

```
class MainMap extends StatefulWidget {
  @override
  _MainMapState createState() => _MainMapState();
}

class _MainMapState extends State<MainMap> {
  @override
  Widget build(BuildContext context) {
    return Container(
    );
}}
```

3. In the `_MainMapState` class, we'll return a `Scaffold` whose title is `'The Treasure Mapp'` (I'm so proud of this app's nerdy title), and the body will contain a `Container` whose child will be a `GoogleMap` widget. `GoogleMap` is the object that shows a map on the screen. In our app, it will take all the available space. This is illustrated in the following block of code:

```
Widget build(BuildContext context) {
  return Scaffold(
    appBar: AppBar(title: Text('The Treasure Mapp'),),
    body: Container(child: GoogleMap(),),
  );
}
```

You may notice that the `GoogleMap` widget requires an `initialCameraPosition` parameter. This is the center of the map when we first show it to our user. Google uses geographic coordinates—latitude and longitude—to position a map or place markers on it.

The latitude/longitude system has been in use, with a few small changes, since the mathematician, astronomer, and geographer Claudius Ptolemy wrote the *Geography* world atlas in the year 150 AD. It's fascinating how two numbers can tell you exactly your position, wherever you are on earth.

Until recently, mariners have been the primary users of this system, but now, with the availability of GPS and easy access to maps, it's important you understand how this system works. If you want to learn more about this, have a look at `https://gisgeography.com/latitude-longitude-coordinates/`.

Let's temporarily create a fixed coordinate for the `initialCameraPosition` of our map. They are the coordinates of Rome, Italy, but feel free to choose your favorite position, possibly near your own location.

4. A `CameraPosition` requires a `target`, which takes a `LatLng` to express the actual position. Optionally, you can also specify a `zoom` level—the bigger the number, the higher the scale of the map. We'll begin with a zoom level of `12`. At the top of the `_MainMapState` class, let's write the following code:

```
final CameraPosition position = CameraPosition(
  target: LatLng(41.9028, 12.4964),
  zoom: 12,
);
```

5. Then, in the `GoogleMap` constructor, we can specify the
`initialCameraPosition`, as follows:

```
body: Container(
  child: GoogleMap(
    initialCameraPosition: position,
),),
```

6. If you try out the app right now, you should see a map similar to the one in the
following screenshot:

This means that everything is working so far. The next step will be adding a **marker** to the
map, which highlights our position.

Using geolocation to find the current position

There's a Flutter plugin called `Geolocator` that provides access to the platform-specific location services. Let's get started, as follows:

1. We need to add the dependency in the `pubspec.yaml` file, like this:

   ```
   geolocator: ^5.3.0
   ```

2. Then, in the `main.dart` file, we'll import the `Geolocator` library, as follows:

   ```
   import 'package:geolocator/geolocator.dart';
   ```

3. In order to find the current location of our user, we'll create a new method called `_getCurrentLocation` that will use the device GPS to find the latitude and longitude of the current location, and return it to the caller, as follows:

   ```
   Future _getCurrentLocation() async {}
   ```

   `Geolocator` methods are all asynchronous, so our method will be asynchronous as well.

4. Not all devices have the geolocation service available, so, inside the `_getCurrentLocation` method, we can check whether the functionality is available or not before finding the current position, by running the following code:

   ```
   bool isGeolocationAvailable = await
   Geolocator().isLocationServiceEnabled();
   ```

5. Then, if the service is available, we'll try to get the current position; otherwise, we'll return the previously set fixed position, as follows:

   ```
   Position _position = Position(latitude:
   this.position.target.latitude, longitude:
   this.position.target.longitude);
       if (isGeolocationAvailable) {
         try {
           _position = await Geolocator().getCurrentPosition(
           desiredAccuracy: LocationAccuracy.best);
         }
         catch (error) {
           return _position;
         }
       }
       return _position;
   ```

The `Geolocator().getCurrentPosition()` method **returns a** `Position` **object**. This not only contains latitude and longitude, but can also contain other data—such as altitude, speed, and heading—that we don't need for this app but which might be useful to you for other apps.

Now that we have the current location of our user, let's see how to place a marker on that position on the map.

Adding a marker to the map

A `Marker` identifies a location on a Map. We'll use markers to show our user their current position, and we'll also add the saved places' markers to our map. Let's look at the steps:

1. Create a `List` of `markers` at the top of the `_MainMapState` class, like this:

   ```
   List<Marker> markers = [];
   ```

2. Then, we'll add a generic method that will add a `Marker` to the `markers` list. It will take a `Position`, a String containing the identifier of the Marker, and another String for the title.
   The way to show information about the Marker itself to the user is the `infoWindow` parameter. In particular, this takes a `title` that contains a text that will appear whenever the user taps on the `Marker` itself.

3. A `Marker` uses a **default image**, but it's also possible to choose custom images for a `Marker`. We'll use the default icon for this app, but we'll change the color for the marker of the current position. The default color for a `Marker` is red. In our app, if the `MarkerId` is `currpos`, we'll choose an azure color to help the user identify their position. For the other markers, we'll choose an orange color.

4. Once the marker is added, we'll call the `setState` method to update the screen. Here is the code for the steps described previously—add it at the bottom of the `_MainMapState` class, like this:

   ```
   void addMarker(Position pos, String markerId, String markerTitle )
   {
       final marker = Marker(
           markerId: MarkerId(markerId),
           position: LatLng(pos.latitude, pos.longitude),
           infoWindow: InfoWindow(title: markerTitle),
           icon: (markerId=='currpos') ?
               BitmapDescriptor.defaultMarkerWithHue
               (BitmapDescriptor.hueAzure) :BitmapDescriptor
               .defaultMarkerWithHue(BitmapDescriptor
   ```

```
                    .hueOrange)
        );
        markers.add(marker);
        setState(() {
          markers = markers;
        });
    }
```

5. Now, we need to call this method after the current position has been found. So, we'll override the `initState` method, and, inside it, we'll call the `_getCurrentLocation()` method. After the result is retrieved, we'll call the `addMarker` method to actually show the marker on the map. In case of an error, we'll just print the error in the debug console. All of this is achieved by running the following code:

```
@override
void initState() {
    _getCurrentLocation().then((pos){
      addMarker(pos, 'currpos', 'You are here!');
    }).catchError(
      (err)=> print(err.toString()));
    super.initState();
}
```

6. The last detail for this part is adding the markers to the map. In the `build()` method, when we call the `GoogleMap` constructor, we'll add the markers as shown in the following code block:

```
child: GoogleMap(
          initialCameraPosition: position,
          markers: Set<Marker>.of(markers),
```

If you try the app right now, you should see your current position, as shown in the following screenshot:

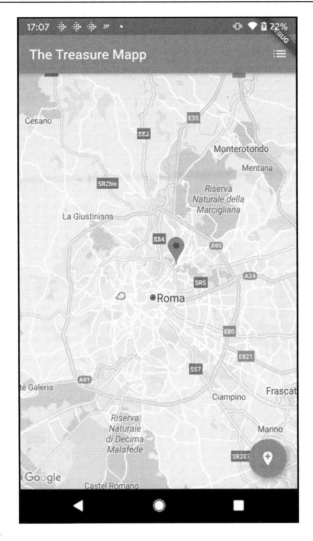

Now, let's give our users the power to save their favorite places and show them on our map!

Creating the place model and helper classes

In order to save the user's favorite places, we will use an SQLite database. As we did for the project in Chapter 6, *Store That Data - Using Sq(F)Lite to Store Data in a Local Database*, we'll use a model to insert the places to the database. So, let's begin, as follows:

1. Create a new file in our project, called place.dart. Inside the file, we'll create a class, called Place, which will contain five properties:

    - The id integer.
    - The name String.
    - Two doubles for the latitude and longitude.
    - A String that will later contain an image.

    The properties under Place will look like the following:

    ```
    class Place {
      int id;
      String name;
      double lat;
      double lon;
      String image;
    }
    ```

2. Next, let's create a constructor that will set all the properties, like this:

    ```
    Place(this.id, this.name, this.lat, this.lon, this.image);
    ```

3. Finally, we'll create a toMap() method that will return a Map of type String, dynamic. As you might recall, a Map is a collection of key/value pairs: the key is a String, and, as we have different types in the table, the value will be dynamic. The code is shown in the following block:

    ```
    Map<String, dynamic> toMap() {
      return {
        'id': (id==0)?null:id,
        'name': name,
        'lat': lat,
        'lon': lon,
        'image': image
      };
    }
    ```

4. Now that we have completed the `Place` class, let's also create a helper file that will interact with the database: let's call it `dbhelper.dart`. This file will contain the methods to create the database and to retrieve and write data.

   As we'll be using the `sqflite` package, we need to add the dependency in the `pubspec.yaml` file, as follows:

   ```
   dependencies:
     [...]
   sqflite: ^1.2.1
   path: ^1.6.4
   ```

 In order to find the latest version of the dependency, please visit `https://pub.dev/packages/sqflite`. We'll also be using the `path` package so that we can access the database with the same code for iOS and Android.

5. In the `dbHelper.dart` file, we'll import `sqflite.dart` and `path.dart`, as follows:

   ```
   import 'package:path/path.dart';
   import 'package:sqflite/sqflite.dart';
   ```

6. Next, let's create the `DbHelper` class, like this:

   ```
   class DbHelper {}
   ```

7. Inside the class, we'll create two variables. One is an integer with the `version` of the database, which at the beginning is 1; then, we will create the variable that will contain the database itself, called `db`, as follows:

   ```
   final int version = 1;
   Database db;
   ```

8. Next, we'll create the `openDb()` method: this will open the database if it exists, or create it if it doesn't. All database operations are asynchronous, so the `openDb()` function will be asynchronous and will return a `Future` of type `Database`, as illustrated in the following code snippet:

   ```
   Future<Database> openDb() async {   }
   ```

9. Inside the function, we'll first check whether the `db` object is `null` by running the following code:

   ```
   if (db == null) {}
   ```

If db is null, we need to open the database. We'll call the sqflite opendatabase() method, passing the path and version of the database, and the onCreate parameter that will be called if the database at the path specified is not found. We'll call this database mapp.db, and it will only contain a single table that has the same schema as the Place class.

10. After opening or creating the database, we'll return it to the caller, like this:

```
Future<Database> openDb() async {
    if (db == null) {
        db = await openDatabase(join(await getDatabasesPath(),
        'mapp.db'),
           onCreate: (database, version) {
        database.execute(
            'CREATE TABLE places(id INTEGER PRIMARY KEY, name TEXT,
                lat DOUBLE, lon DOUBLE, image TEXT)');
        }, version: version);
    }
    return db;
}
```

11. We don't need to have multiple instances of the DbHelper class throughout the app, so we'll create a Factory constructor that, instead of creating a new instance each time it's called, only returns a single instance of the class, as follows:

```
static final DbHelper _dbHelper = DbHelper._internal();
DbHelper._internal();

factory DbHelper() {
    return _dbHelper;
}
```

Now, let's insert some fake data so that we can see the markers on our map and test if everything is working correctly.

12. We'll create a new method, called insertMockData(), whose purpose is to insert some default data into our database. We'll insert three records in the places table (feel free to change the coordinates so that they are closer to where you are right now), and, as usual, this method will be asynchronous, as illustrated in the following code block:

```
Future insertMockData() async {
    db = await openDb();
    await db.execute('INSERT INTO places VALUES (1,
    "Beautiful park", 41.9294115, 12.5380785, "")');
```

```
        await db.execute('INSERT INTO places VALUES (2,
        "Best Pizza in the world", 41.9294115, 12.5268947, "")');
        await db.execute('INSERT INTO places VALUES (3,
        "The best icecream on earth", 41.9349061, 12.5339831, "")');
        List places = await db.rawQuery('select * from places');
        print(places[0].toString());
    }
```

13. At the top of the `DbHelper` class, declare a `List` of the `Place` object that will contain the result of the query, as follows:

```
    List<Place> places = List<Place>();
```

14. Then, let's create a method that will retrieve all records from the `places` table. Here, we will use the `query()` helper method to retrieve all records from the `places` table. The `query()` method returns a `List` of Map, and we will use it to transform each `Map` into a `Place`. We'll call the method `getPlaces()`, as illustrated in the following code block:

```
    Future<List<Place>> getPlaces() async {
        final List<Map<String, dynamic>> maps = await
        db.query('places');
        this.places = List.generate(maps.length, (i) {
            return Place(
                maps[i]['id'],
                maps[i]['name'],
                maps[i]['lat'],
                maps[i]['lon'],
                maps[i]['image'],
            );
        });
        return places;
    }
```

15. Now, in the `main.dart` file, let's import the `dbhelper.dart` and `place.dart` files, like this:

```
    import 'dbhelper.dart';
    import 'place.dart';
```

16. Then, in the `_MainMapState` class, we'll declare a `DbHelper` object, as follows:

```
DbHelper helper;
```

17. In the `initState()` method, we'll call the object instance, like this:

```
helper = DbHelper();
```

18. Still in the `_MainMapState` class, let's create a new method that will retrieve the places from the database. We'll call it `_getData()`, as shown in the following code snippet:

```
Future _getData() async {}
```

Inside the method, we'll call the helper `openDb()` method, then the `insertMockData()` method to add the first markers to our app, and then, we'll read them with the `getPlaces()` method. The `_places` list will contain the places that were retrieved.

19. Next, for each `Place` in the `_places` list, we'll call the `addMarker()` method that we've created previously, as follows:

```
await helper.openDb();
// await helper.testDb();
List <Place> _places =  await helper.getPlaces();
for (Place p in _places) {
  addMarker(Position(latitude: p.lat, longitude: p.lon),
    p.id.toString(), p.name) ;
}
setState(() {
  markers = markers;
});}
```

20. Finally, at the end of the `initState()` method, let's also call `insertMockData()` (**only the first time the app executes**) and `_getData()`, as follows:

```
helper.insertMockData();
_getData();
```

From the second execution of our app, we'll comment out the `helper.insertMockData()` instruction.

Now that we can retrieve our current position and all the saved places we've saved, let's try out the app. You should see a screen similar to the one in the following screenshot:

If you tap on any of the markers on the map, you should also be able to see its title.

To sum up, our app is now showing all the data to our user. When they first enter the app, they immediately see their current position and the saved places on the map.

At the moment, users cannot insert, edit, or delete any data relative to the saved places. This is what we will cover next.

Inserting new places on the map

We now need to allow our users to insert new data and edit or delete existing records in the database.

The first step is creating the asynchronous method that will add a new record to the places table. This will take an instance of Place, and call the insert() database helper method to add the new place. Add the following code in the DbHelper class in the dbhelper.dart file:

```
Future<int> insertPlace(Place place) async {
    int id = await this.db.insert( 'places',
        place.toMap(),
        conflictAlgorithm: ConflictAlgorithm.replace,
    );
    return id;
}
```

Both the insert and edit functions require some **user interface** (UI) that can contain the text that the user types. We'll use another dialog box for the add and edit features, and proceed as follows:

1. Let's create a new file, called place_dialog.dart, in the lib folder of our app. Here, we want to show our user a dialog window that allows them to insert or edit a Place, including its coordinates. This dialog will be called from the main screen when the user wants to add a new Place.

2. At the top of the new file, we'll import the required dependencies—material.dart, our dbHelper, and the places.dart file, as follows:

   ```
   import 'package:flutter/material.dart';
   import './dbhelper.dart';
   import './place.dart';
   ```

3. Then, create the class that will contain the UI for the dialog, as follows:

   ```
   class PlaceDialog{}
   ```

4. For this class, we want to show the user some text boxes. So, at the top of the PlaceDialog class, let's first create three TextEditingControllers that will contain the name and coordinates of the Place, as follows:

   ```
   final txtName = TextEditingController();
   final txtLat = TextEditingController();
   final txtLon = TextEditingController();
   ```

5. Next, we'll create two other fields for this class: a Boolean telling whether this is a new place, and a `Place` object, as follows:

```
final bool isNew;
final Place place;
```

6. When `PlaceDialog` gets called, we want it to always receive a `Place` and a Boolean telling whether the `Place` is new, so we'll create a constructor that takes both parameters, like this:

```
PlaceDialog(this.place, this.isNew);
```

7. Then, we'll create a method called `buildDialog()` that will take the current `BuildContext`, which, in Flutter is required to show a dialog window. The `buildDialog` method will return a generic `Widget`, as follows:

```
Widget buildAlert(BuildContext context) {}
```

8. Inside the `buildDialog()` method, first, we'll call the `DbHelper` class. Here, we don't need to call the `openDb()` method, as, from this window, we already know that it's been called previously, and we are receiving an existing instance of the class, as shown in the following code snippet:

```
DbHelper helper = DbHelper();
```

9. Then, we'll set the text of the `TextEditingController` widgets to the values of the `Place` that was passed, as follows:

```
txtName.text = place.name;
txtLat.text = place.lat.toString();
txtLon.text = place.lon.toString();
```

10. Finally, we can return the `AlertDialog` that will contain the UI that our users will see, as follows:

```
return AlertDialog();
```

11. The title of the `AlertDialog` will simply be a `Text` widget containing `'Place'`, as illustrated in the following code snippet:

```
title: Text('Place'),
```

12. For the content, we'll place all the widgets into a `SingleChildScrollView`, to make scrolling available in case the widgets do not fit into the screen, as follows:

```
content: SingleChildScrollView()
```

13. Inside the `SingleChildScrollView`, we'll place a `Column`, as we want the widget in this dialog to be placed vertically, as follows:

```
child: Column(children: <Widget>[]),
```

14. The first element inside the `Column` will be three `TextField` widgets—one for the name, one for the latitude, and one for the longitude. After setting the relevant controller, for all the `TextFields`, we'll set the `hintText` of an `InputDecoration` object to guide the user in using the UI, as follows:

```
TextField(
    controller: txtName,
    decoration: InputDecoration(
        hintText: 'Name'
    ),
),
TextField(
    controller: txtLat,
    decoration: InputDecoration(
        hintText: 'Latitude'
    ),
),
TextField(
    controller: txtLon,
    decoration: InputDecoration(
        hintText: 'Longitude'
    ),
),
```

15. Later on, we'll also add an image here, but for now, let's place a `RaisedButton` as the last widget of the `Column`. When pressed, all changes will be saved. The child of the button will be a `Text` with an `'OK'` String. In the `onPressed` property, we will update the `Place` object with the new data coming from the `TextFields`, and then we'll call `insertPlace()` on the `helper` object, passing the `Place` containing the data in the `TextFields`.

16. Finally, we'll call the `pop()` method of the `Navigator` to close the dialog and return to the caller, which at the moment is the map screen, as follows:

```
RaisedButton(
    child: Text('OK'),
    onPressed: () {
        place.name = txtName.text;
        place.lat = double.tryParse(txtLat.text);
        place.lon = double.tryParse(txtLon.text);
        helper.insertPlace(place);
        Navigator.pop(context);
```

```
        },
    )
```

The next step is calling the dialog from the map. I'd say that adding a new place from the map is the main action of the screen, so we can add a `FloatingActionButton` widget to the `Scaffold` of the `_MainMapState` class.

Back in the `main.dart` file, in the `build()` method of the `_MainMapState`, when we call the `Scaffold`, let's add a `floatingActionButton` parameter that will contain a `FloatingActionButton` widget. There's an icon called `add_location` that's perfect for our purpose, and we'll use this as a `child`.

When the user presses the `FloatingActionButton`, first, we'll find the marker whose `markerId` contains the String `currpos` that contains the current position that we found previously. If this marker isn't found, we just create a `LatLng` object with 0 as latitude and longitude.

In case the `Marker` containing the current position is found, we'll get the coordinates on a `LatLng` object, and we'll create a `Place` object with the current position.

Next, we create a `PlaceDialog` instance, passing the place and a `true` value, as this is a new `Place`. Finally, we'll call the `showDialog()` method, passing the current context, as shown in the following code block:

```
floatingActionButton: FloatingActionButton(
        child: Icon(Icons.add_location),
        onPressed: () {
          int here = markers.indexWhere((p)=> p.markerId ==
          MarkerId('currpos'));
          Place place;
          if (here == -1) {
            //the current position is not available
              place = Place(0, '', 0, 0, '');
          }
          else {
          LatLng pos = markers[here].position;
            place = Place(0, '', pos.latitude, pos.longitude, '');
          }
          PlaceDialog dialog = PlaceDialog(place, true);
          showDialog(
            context: context,
            builder: (context) =>
                dialog.buildAlert(context));
      },
  )
```

If you try the app right now, you should see a new `FloatingActionButton`, and, when you press it, you should see the dialog with the current coordinates, as shown in the following screenshot:

And if you insert a name and press the **OK** button, the new place will be saved into the database. Now that we can add a new `Place` to our list, we also need a way to edit and delete saved items from the database. Let's do that next!

Editing and deleting existing places

The easiest way to add the features to edit and delete items from the database is probably by creating a new screen with a `ListView` widget, containing all the items that were saved. In order to achieve this, we'll create a new screen in our app, as follows:

1. In the `lib` folder, create a new file called `manage_places.dart`.

2. After importing the `material.dart` library, we'll also import the `place_dialog.dart` file and our `dbhelper.dart`, as follows:

```
import 'package:flutter/material.dart';
import 'place_dialog.dart';
import 'dbhelper.dart';
```

3. Inside this file, we'll create a new stateless widget, calling it `ManagePlaces`. This will contain a `Scaffold` whose `AppBar` title is `'Manage Places'`, and, in the body, we'll call a new widget, called `PlacesList`, that we'll create next, as follows:

```
class ManagePlaces extends StatelessWidget {
  @override
  Widget build(BuildContext context) {
    return Scaffold(
      appBar: AppBar(title: Text('Manage Places'),),
      body: PlacesList(),
    );
  }
}
```

4. Now, we need to create the `PlacesList` class. It will be a stateful widget. At the top of the class, we'll call an instance of `DbHelper`, calling it `helper`, which includes the methods to interact with the database, and, in the `build()` method, we'll return a `ListView.builder()` constructor, as shown in the following code block:

```
class PlacesList extends StatefulWidget {
  @override
  _PlacesListState createState() => _PlacesListState();
}

class _PlacesListState extends State<PlacesList> {
  DbHelper helper = DbHelper();
  @override
  Widget build(BuildContext context) {
    return ListView.builder()
```

```
    }
  }
```

The `itemCount` parameter contains the length of the `placesList` of the `helper` object. For the `itemBuilder`, we'll return a `Dismissible` to make it easy for the user to delete an item through a gesture. As you may remember, a `Dismissible` requires a `key`, which, in this case will be the name of the item in the `places` list, at the current position.

5. In the `DbHelper` class in the `dbhelper.dart` file, let's add the method that will delete a record from the `places` table. We'll use the `delete()` helper method of the database to remove the `Place`, as illustrated in the following code block:

```
Future<int> deletePlace(Place place) async {
  int result = await db.delete("places", where: "id = ?", whereArgs:
  [place.id]);
  return result;
}
```

For the `onDismissed` function, we can call the `deletePlace()` method of the `helper` object, passing the place at the current position. Then, we call the `setState()` method to update the UI, and we show a message using a `SnackBar`, informing the user that the `Place` has been removed, as illustrated in the following code block:

```
Widget build(BuildContext context) {
  return ListView.builder(
    itemCount: helper.places.length,
    itemBuilder: (BuildContext context, int index) {
      return Dismissible(
          key: Key(helper.places[index].name),
          onDismissed: (direction) {
            String strName = helper.places[index].name;
            helper.deletePlace(helper.places[index]);
            setState(() {
              helper.places.removeAt(index);
            });
            Scaffold.of(context)
                .showSnackBar(SnackBar(content: Text("$strName
                deleted")));
          },
      ));
    },
  );
```

6. For the child of the `Dismissible`, we can use a `ListTile`, whose title is the name of the `Place` at the current position. For the `trailing` parameter, we'll use an `IconButton`, whose icon is the `edit` icon.

When the user presses the `IconButton`, we want to call an instance of `PlaceDialog` to allow the user to edit an existing `Place`. Note that when we create the instance of `PlaceDialog`, we are passing `false` as the second parameter, as this is NOT a new `Place`, but an existing one. This is illustrated in the following code block:

```
child:ListTile(
    title: Text(helper.places[index].name),
    trailing: IconButton(
        icon: Icon(Icons.edit),
        onPressed: () {
            PlaceDialog dialog = PlaceDialog(helper.places[index],
             false);
            showDialog(
                context: context,
                builder: (context) =>
                    dialog.buildAlert(context));
                },
    ),
```

7. Now, we need a way to call this screen from the main screen of the app. From the `main.dart` file, in the `build()` method of the `_MainMapState` class, we can add an `actions` parameter to the `Scaffold`.

Here, we can add an `IconButton`, with a `list` icon, which, when pressed, will create a `MaterialPageRoute` that builds an instance of `ManagePlaces` and calls the `Navigator.push()` method, to change the screen and show the `ListView` with the saved places, instead of showing the map, as follows:

```
return Scaffold(
    appBar: AppBar(title: Text('The Treasure Mapp'),
    actions: <Widget>[
        IconButton(
            icon: Icon(Icons.list),
            onPressed: () {
                MaterialPageRoute route =
                MaterialPageRoute(builder: (context)=>
                ManagePlaces());
                Navigator.push(context, route);

            },
```

```
            ),
        ],
    ),
```

8. If you try the app right now, when you click the `IconButton` list, you should see your list of saved places, as shown in the following screenshot:

If you swipe any of the places in the list, the place will be deleted, and you'll see the `SnackBar` confirmation message. If you press the edit `IconButton`, you'll see the dialog with the name and coordinates of the place you've selected, and you'll be able to change the place data.

Now, there's one last feature that we need to introduce in our app, and it's the ability to shoot pictures and add them to the places: let's do that next.

Using the device camera

Being able to use the camera functionality is an important part of any mobile development framework, and Flutter provides the camera plugin for this purpose. **The camera plugin allows you to get a list of the available cameras in the device, show previews, and take photos and videos**.

The first step in order to use the camera is to set up the app. To do so, we'll proceed as follows:

1. In the pubspec.yaml file, let's add the dependencies. We'll—of course—need camera, but also path (which we already added at the beginning of this project) and path_provider, to save and retrieve the photos we take from the app, as shown in the following code block:

   ```
   camera: ^0.5.7
   path_provider: ^1.4.4
   ```

   For Android, you'll need to change the minimum Android SDK version to 21 (or higher) in your android/app/build.gradle file, as follows:

   ```
   minSdkVersion 21
   ```

   If you're using **iOS**, you'll need to add two rows to the ios/Runner/Info.plist file, as follows:

   ```
   <key>NSCameraUsageDescription</key>
   <string>Enable TreasureMapp to access your camera to capture your photo</string>
   <key>NSMicrophoneUsageDescription</key>
   <string>Enable TreasureMapp to access mic to record your voice</string>
   ```

   Now that the app is configured, we can actually write the code to use the camera. We'll be able to take a picture when the user clicks an IconButton from the PlaceDialog screen. In order to save the picture to the right place, we'll always need to pass the place Id.

2. In our app, we'll create a new file, called camera_screen.dart. This will contain the UI to take a new picture. At the top of the file, let's import all the required libraries, as follows:

   ```
   import 'package:flutter/material.dart';
   import 'package:camera/camera.dart';
   import 'package:path/path.dart';
   ```

```
import 'package:path_provider/path_provider.dart';
import 'place.dart';
```

3. Next, we'll create a stateful widget called `CameraScreen`, like this:

```
class CameraScreen extends StatefulWidget {
  @override
  _CameraScreenState createState() => _CameraScreenState();
}

class _CameraScreenState extends State<CameraScreen> {
  @override
  Widget build(BuildContext context) {
    return Container(
    ); } }
```

4. At the top of the `_CameraScreenState` class, we'll declare a few fields—a `Place` called `place`, and a `CameraController` called `_controller`. **A** `CameraController` **establishes a connection to the device's camera, and you can use it to actually take the pictures**. The code for this is shown in the following snippet:

```
Place place;
CameraController _controller;
```

5. Let's fix the `CameraScreen` as well so that it can receive a `Place` from its caller, like this:

```
class CameraScreen extends StatefulWidget {
  final Place place;
  CameraScreen(this.place);
  @override
  _CameraScreenState createState() => _CameraScreenState();
}
```

 Most devices have two cameras, one on the front and the other on the back, but depending on the user's device, there may be only one—or even more than two—if they connect an external camera. In this project, we'll only use the first camera, but it's very easy to switch from one camera to another. If you want to learn more about switching cameras, have a look at the following link: `https://pub.dev/packages/camera`.

6. Still in the `_CameraScreenState` class, at the top of it, we'll declare a few other variables— a list of the available cameras, the selected camera, a generic widget for the preview, and an image. The widget that contains a camera is `CameraDescription`, as shown in the following code snippet:

```
List<CameraDescription> cameras;
CameraDescription camera;
Widget cameraPreview;
Image image;
```

The first method we'll create in the `_CameraScreenState` class will set the camera on our device.

The method that returns all the available cameras is, predictably, called `availableCameras()`, and it returns a `Future` of type `List<CameraDescription>`. So, the `setCamera()` method will be asynchronous as well and will set the `camera` to be the first camera on the device (which is generally the main one), on the back of the device.

7. To avoid raising an error if there is no camera, we will also check if the `List` is empty, as follows:

```
Future setCamera() async {
    cameras = await availableCameras();
    if (cameras.length != 0) {
        camera = cameras.first;
    }
}
```

8. Next, we'll override the `initState()` method. Inside the method, we'll call `setCamera()`, and when the asynchronous method returns, we'll create a new `CameraController`, passing the specific camera we will use for this controller and defining the resolution to use—in this case, `ResolutionPreset.medium`.

9. Then, we'll call the asynchronous `initialize()` method for the `CameraController`, and when in the `then()` function, we'll call the `setState()` method to set the `cameraPreview` widget to a `CameraPreview` widget of the controller, as follows:

```
@override
  void initState() {
    setCamera().then((_) {
      _controller = CameraController(
        // Get a specific camera from the list of available
        // cameras.
```

```
    camera,
    // Define the resolution to use.
    ResolutionPreset.medium,
  );
  _controller.initialize().then((snapshot) {
    cameraPreview = Center(child: CameraPreview(_controller));
    setState(() {
      cameraPreview = cameraPreview;
    });
  });
});
super.initState();
}
```

 A `CameraPreview` widget displays a preview of the camera's feed.

10. Next, we'll override the `dispose()` method for the `_CameraScreenState` class—this will dispose of the controller when the widget itself is disposed of, as follows:

```
@override
void dispose() {
    _controller.dispose();
    super.dispose();
}
```

Now, this screen is ready to show a camera preview to our user. Let's build the UI to test this functionality, as follows:

1. In the `build()` method, we'll return a `Scaffold`. In the `appBar` of the `Scaffold`, we'll show a `Text` with `'Take Picture'`. Later, we'll use the `appBar` to take the picture as well, but for now, we'll just show the preview.

2. In the body of the `Scaffold`, we'll place a `Container` whose child is the `cameraPreview` we've set in the `initState()` method, as follows:

```
@override
  Widget build(BuildContext context) {
    return Scaffold(
        appBar: AppBar(
          title: Text('Take Picture'),
        ),
        body: Container(
          child: cameraPreview,
        ));
  }
```

3. To check whether the camera is working, we need to call this screen from the `PlaceDialog` class. So, in the `place_dialog.dart` file, in the `buildAlert()` method, let's add an `IconButton` under the longitude `TextField`.

   The icon will be a `camera_front` icon, and, when the user presses the `IconButton`, if the `Place` is a new place, first we insert it into the database by calling the `insertPlace()` method over the `DbHelper` instance.

4. Then, we create a new `MaterialPageRoute` to call the `CameraScreen` route.

The full code is shown here:

```
IconButton(
    icon: Icon(Icons.camera_front),
    onPressed: () {
        if (isNew) {
            helper.insertPlace(place).then((data){
                place.id = data;
                MaterialPageRoute route = MaterialPageRoute(builder:
                (context)=>
                CameraScreen(place));
                Navigator.push(context, route);
                });
            }
        else {
                MaterialPageRoute route = MaterialPageRoute(builder:
                (context)=>
                CameraScreen(place));
                Navigator.push(context, route);
            }
        }),
```

In order to try the camera preview, from the `PlaceList` screen, tap on any place. In the dialog, you should see the camera IconButton—click on it, and the camera preview should be visible. An example that will probably be very close to what you can see right now (if you are following along and building the app, as you should be!) is shown in the following screenshot:

 If you are using an iOS emulator, you cannot use the camera—you should use a real device to test the camera functionality for this app.

What we need to do now is take the picture itself.

Saving and retrieving pictures as local files

Still in the `_CameraScreenState` class, in the `AppBar` in the `build()` method, we'll set the `actions` parameter so that it contains an `IconButton`. When pressed, this will store the picture in the temp directory, which can be found using the `path_provider` plugin. The name of the file will just be the current date and time.

Next, we can finally call the `takePicture()` method of the `CameraController`. This will save the picture into the provided path, as shown in the following code block:

```
actions: <Widget>[
    IconButton(
        icon: Icon(Icons.camera_alt),
        onPressed: () async {
            final path = join(
                (await getTemporaryDirectory()).path,
                '${DateTime.now()}.png',
            );
            // Attempt to take a picture and log where it's been saved.
            await _controller.takePicture(path);
        },
    )
],
```

After we take the picture, we want to show it to our users. We'll create another screen, called `PictureScreen`.

Let's add the code that will change the screen, calling the new one that we'll create next, after the `await _controller.takePicture(path);` instruction, as follows:

```
MaterialPageRoute route = MaterialPageRoute(
    builder: (context) => PictureScreen(path, place)
);
Navigator.push(context, route);
```

For your apps, you may want to choose a different place for your pictures, and probably interact with the gallery itself. If you want to learn more about how to save an image to the device gallery with Flutter, have a look at the `image_gallery_saver` plugin, available at this link: https://pub.dev/packages/image_gallery_saver.

We'll now create the `PictureScreen` widget. The purpose of this screen is to show the picture that was taken and save its path in the database, in the relevant `Place` record.

So, in the `lib` folder, let's create a new file, called `picture_screen.dart`. Into that file, we will import the required dependencies and create a stateless widget, as follows:

```
import 'dart:io';
import 'package:flutter/material.dart';
import './main.dart';
import 'place.dart';
import 'dbhelper.dart';

class PictureScreen extends StatelessWidget {
  @override
  Widget build(BuildContext context) {
    return Container(
    );
  }
}
```

This widget will receive two variables: one is the path of the image that has been taken from the calling screen, and the other is the place whose picture has been taken. So, let's create the fields and the constructor **at the top of the** `PictureScreen` **class**, as follows:

```
final String imagePath;
final Place place;
PictureScreen(this.imagePath, this.place);
```

In the `build()` method, we'll call the instance of `DbHelper`; then, we'll return a `Scaffold`. In the body of the `Scaffold`, we will place a `Container` whose child will be an `Image`.

The `Image.file()` constructor creates a widget that displays an image obtained from a file in your device.

In the `appBar` of the `Scaffold`, in the `actions` property, we'll place an `IconButton` whose icon will be the `save` icon. In the `onPressed` property, we'll save the path of the image to the database, calling the `insertPlace()` method.

Note that even if the `Place` already exists in the database, we can still call `insertPlace()` because the conflict algorithm we chose is `replace`.

After saving the path, we return to the main screen of the app, as follows:

```
DbHelper helper = DbHelper();
    return Scaffold(
        appBar: AppBar(
            title: Text('Save picture'),
            actions: <Widget>[
                IconButton(
                    icon: Icon(Icons.save),
                    onPressed: () {
                        place.image = imagePath;
                        //save image
                        helper.insertPlace(place);
                        MaterialPageRoute route = MaterialPageRoute(
                            builder:(context)=> MainMap());
                        Navigator.push(context, route);
                    },
                )
            ],
        ),
        body:Container(
            child: Image.file(File(imagePath)),
        )
    );
```

At the moment, we have no way of knowing whether the picture has been correctly saved or not. In the `PlaceDialog` screen, we want to show the picture we've taken, if it's available.

So, in the `buildAlert()` method of the `PlaceDialog` class, let's add an image—if available—under the latitude `TextField`, just before the `IconButton`, as follows:

```
(place.image!= '')?Container(child:
Image.file(File(place.image))):Container(),
```

Let's try the app now, to see if we can add a new picture to an existing place. Here are the steps:

1. From the `PlaceList` screen, choose an item from the `List`.
2. From the dialog screen, press the camera `IconButton`.
3. From the preview, take a picture using the appbar `IconButton`.
4. From the `pictureScreen`, press the **Save** `IconButton` on the `AppBar`.

5. Open the list again, and press on the item you chose before. You should now see the picture, as illustrated in the following screenshot:

And with that, we have completed all the functions for this app.

Let's recap on what we've accomplished, and see what you can do to make this app better.

Summary

Geolocation is a technology that allows you to identify the physical location of a device, and this is a very useful tool for a mobile developer because today, location-enabled smartphones are in almost everyone's pocket, and it's incredibly important for an app to give relevant messages that meet users' needs. In this chapter, you've learned how to find your users' coordinates by using `Geolocator`, the library that provides access to platform-specific location services.

Another very interesting feature of this project has been integrating the Google Maps API into the app, using the `google_maps_flutter` package. You've seen how to show a map, and how to add `Markers` into it. This was a rare opportunity to use information stored in an `SQLite` database and show it in a different way—instead of using the usual `ListViews` or forms, all data was placed in a `Map`.

You've also seen how to leverage the `camera` plugin to use your device's camera. You've used camera previews, taken pictures, and saved the pictures in a temporary directory of the device, using the `path` and `path_provider` libraries.

At this time, the app is still a prototype: the files should probably be saved in a different place; pictures and data could be shared and saved over the web; the interaction with the camera could be smoother, and the app itself could be made more secure and reliable. However, the main functions we've used here can serve as a starting point to create personalized and engaging experiences for your users.

The next chapter will be fun: you'll create a dice game using animations with Flare!

Questions

At the end of each project, you'll find a few questions to help you remember and review the contents covered in the chapter. Please try to answer the following questions (when in doubt, have a look at the content in the chapter itself—you'll find all the answers there!):

1. What is the purpose of adding the `path` and `path_provider` libraries into your app?
2. In which files do you add the API key for Google Maps in your project for Android and/or iOS?
3. When you pass the `initialCameraPosition` to a `GoogleMap` widget, which type of widget do you need to pass?
4. How can you get the current position of a device?

5. What is a Marker and when do you use it?
6. When do you need to use a `LatLng` widget in a Marker?
7. Which is the method that returns a List of the available cameras on a device?
8. How can you show the camera preview to your users?
9. What's the purpose of a `CameraController`, and how do you create one?
10. How do you take a picture in Flutter?

Further reading

Google Codelabs provide guided tutorials that show how to build small applications that use a specific technology: there's one very clear and easy-to-follow tutorial that uses a web service to retrieve data and show it on a map. This could be a perfect tutorial to follow to add new features to the project you've built in this chapter. You can access the codelab at the following link: `https://codelabs.developers.google.com/codelabs/google-maps-in-flutter`.

Similar to Google Codelabs, but specific to Flutter, are the Flutter cookbooks: there is one that shows ways to use the camera. You can find it at this address: `https://flutter.dev/docs/cookbook/plugins/picture-using-camera`.

You can find an example of an app using the `camera` plugin extensively at `https://flutterawesome.com/a-simple-camera-app-built-with-flutter-and-using-sqlfite-for-sqlite-storage/`.

There are several ways you could make the project of this chapter better: one is dealing with files and folders in your app in a more solid way. If you want to learn more about that, have a look at the following cookbook about reading and writing files with Flutter: `https://flutter.dev/docs/cookbook/persistence/reading-writing-files`.

Apps using geolocation and the device camera need permissions when you create a production app: there's a great tool in Flutter called `permission_handler`. For more information, visit the package page at `https://pub.dev/packages/permission_handler`.

9
Let's Play Dice: Knockout - Creating an Animation with Flare

An important part of what makes an app special for its users is how engaging and smooth the animations in the **user interface** (UI) are. Flutter has several ways to include animations in your apps, and you've already seen some of those in Chapter 4, *Pong Game - 2D Animations and Gestures*. In this chapter, we'll introduce another powerful software to bring your animation skills to the next level: Flare.

The following topics will be covered in this chapter:

- What's Flare?
- Creating objects with Flare
- Animating objects with Flare
- Integrating Flare into a Flutter app

Technical requirements

You'll find the completed app code on the book's GitHub repository at `https://github.com/PacktPublishing/Flutter-Projects`.

To follow along with the code examples in this book, you should have the following software installed on your Windows, Mac, Linux, or Chrome OS device:

- The Flutter **software development kit (SDK)**.
- When developing for Android: the Android SDK, easily installed by Android Studio.
- When developing for iOS: macOS and Xcode.
- An emulator (Android), a simulator (iOS), or a connected iOS or Android device enabled for debugging.
- An editor: **Visual Studio Code (VS Code)**, Android Studio, or IntelliJ IDEA are recommended. All should have the Flutter/Dart extensions installed.

Project overview

The app we will build in this chapter is the second (and last) game of this book, after the Pong game we built in Chapter 4, *Pong Game - 2D Animations and Gestures*. This time, we'll deal with dice, and create a revisited version of the Knockout dice game.

The app will contain two screens: the first one will only contain a single dice that the user will be able to roll. This will show the animation that you'll create with Flare.

The screen will look similar to the following screenshot:

The second screen will contain the Knockout game. The rules are very simple:

- The player plays against the device (which we will call **AI** in the app).
- The player clicks the **Play** button. This will animate two dice (with six faces, from 1 to 6), and, after a few seconds, a random result will be generated.
- The sum of the two dice will be added to the player's score unless the sum of the dice is 7 (knockout number).
- If the sum of the two dice is 7, nothing will be added to the score.
- The same rules apply to the **AI**, but the animation will be performed only for the human player. For the **AI**, only the score will change.
- The game stops when the player or the **AI** reaches at least 50 points. When that happens, the player wins if their score is higher than the **AI**'s score, and loses if the opposite is true. In the case of a draw, nobody wins.
- At any time, the game can be reset by clicking the **Restart** button.

You can see an example of the layout of the **Knockout Game** screen in the following screenshot:

Completing this project should require about 3 hours, including the creation of the Flare animation.

What's Flare?

Flare is a vector design and animation tool that exports directly to Flutter. It was presented at Flutter Live 2018, and one of the greatest features about it is that you get to work exactly on the same assets that will be used in your Flutter app. The animations you create with Flare can be changed from your Flutter code at runtime, making it great for apps that need user interaction.

This means that you have a designer's tool whereby you can create assets and animate them, and then enclose the final results of your design work straight into Flutter.

> Flare supports not only Flutter, but also JavaScript, React, Swift, and Framer. For an updated list of the runtimes, have a look at the following link: `https://rive.app/runtimes`.

In larger workgroups, with Flare, designers can create, animate, and share their files with developers, and that's exactly how the end users will see them in the finished app.

Even developers can easily import assets to Flare and animate them with a smooth learning curve. Flare itself can be used directly from your browser, so you won't need to install anything on your PC or Mac. Flare is completely free to use, as long as you share your work with the community.

Creating objects with Flare

In order to use Flare, you just need to sign in into the `rive.app` website (formerly 2dimensions.com), and then you'll be able to use it for free from your browser.

Here are the steps involved:

1. In your browser, navigate to the `rive.app` site, and choose the **Register** button.
2. You'll be asked to create a free account. Just follow the instructions provided by the service itself.

3. Once registered, you'll be able to navigate through several projects: have a look at them if you want to get an idea of what other designers have created. You'll also find a **Your Files** button at the top right of the screen. You should see a page like the following:

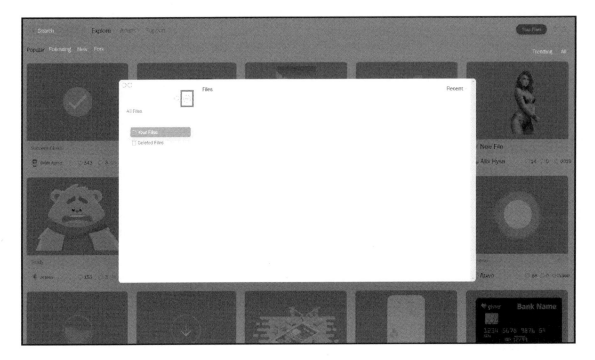

4. Create a new project by clicking on the **+** button, and choose **Flare** as project type. Call this new project **Dice**.

5. From there, you can open your new project. You are now ready to start building your objects and animations with Flare.

Flare is part of the Open Design movement. You can use Flare for free, but you will be sharing your files with the community. This means that other designers can open the source of your creations directly in their browser. This is great when experimenting and learning, but, in some cases, you may want to protect your work, especially if it is for commercial purposes. In this case, Rive offers a paid plan, at a reasonable price. For more information about this, have a look at their pricing page: `https://rive.app/pricing`.

Next, let's start designing the dice that we'll later use in Flutter.

Creating new objects in Flare

When you enter a new project in Flare, you see your **Stage**. The Stage is the working area where you create all your designs, and where you place **Artboards**.

An Artboard is the top-level node of a Flare hierarchy, and this is where you place all your objects and animations. The **Hierarchy** is a tree view that shows the parent/child relationships between the items on the stage. So, you have an Artboard, and everything you put into it is its child. You can add items to the hierarchy by adding other objects and making them children of their ancestors.

Each Flare project requires at least one Artboard, but you can create as many as you like.

Flare has two modes of operations: **Design** and **Animate.** In Design mode, you create graphic objects, and in Animate mode, you animate the objects that you have designed. Flare's interface and tools will change based on the mode in which you are working.

In the following screenshot, you can see the interface, as follows:

- On the left Current View mode, the hierarchy, and the assets
- In the center, the **Create** tool button and the Artboard
- On the right, the properties and **Options** pane

In order to rename the artboard, just double-click on its name in the **Hierarchy** pane, as shown in the following screenshot:

We will now design the dice surface, as follows:

1. From the Design mode, click on the **Create tool** button, and add a **Rectangle** to the Artboard, as you can see in the following screenshot:

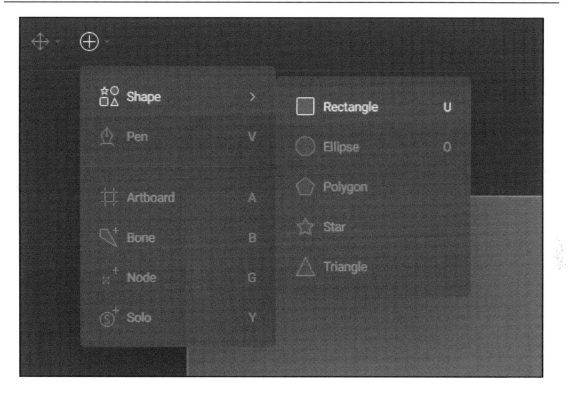

2. After drawing the rectangle on the Artboard, you can select it, so that its properties appear on the right.

3. Change the position to **500** for **X** and **400** for **Y**.

4. Change the size to **600** both for **Width** and **Height**.

5. Set the **Corner Radius** to **25**. This will smooth the angles of our dice.

6. Change the **Fill** color to be white (Hex #FFFFFF).

7. Remove the **Stroke**. The **Stroke** is the border of the shape.

The shape should now look like the one in the following screenshot. Note that, when an object is selected, it's light blue, even if the selected **Fill** color is white:

Now the surface of our dice is complete, we need to add the numbers for each side of the dice. We'll use the classic six-sided dice, and we'll design the numbers with the shapes, as you can see in the following image:

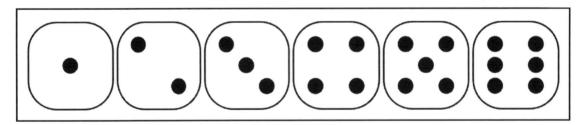

In order to achieve this, we'll design seven black circles that will cover all the possible combinations of values for the dice, as follows:

1. Add a new shape to the Artboard, of type `Ellipse`. It will be the first circle for the dice.
2. Place the shape at the top-left corner of the dice.
3. Make the **Ellipse** shape a child of the **Rectangle** shape, by dragging it under the rectangle in the hierarchy pane.
4. Double-click the **Ellipse** shape and rename the shape as **TopLeft**.
5. Change the properties of the **TopLeft** shape.
6. Position: **-180** for **X** and **Y**.
7. Size: **80** for **Width** and **Height**.
8. **Fill**: Black color (Hex: #000000).
9. Remove the **Stroke**.

The final result is shown in the following screenshot:

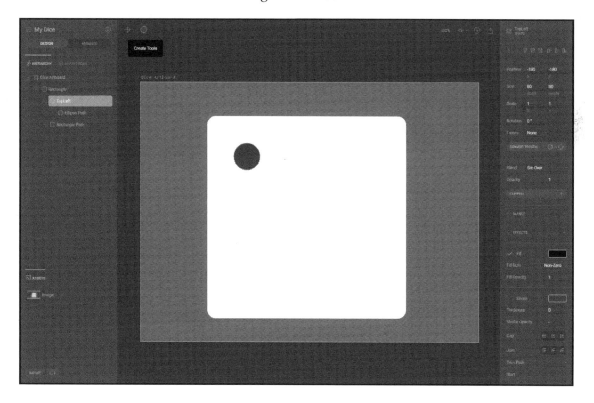

Now, let's copy **TopLeft** six times. All the **Ellipse** shapes should be children of the rectangle. This is because, in that way, we are grouping all the objects together, and when moving the rectangle, we'll be able to also move all its content.

For each of the circles, we'll change name and position, based on the following values:

Name	Position
CenterLeft	-180 0
BottomLeft	-180 180
TopRight	180 -180
CenterRight	180 0
BottomRight	180 180
CenterCenter	0 0

The final result is shown in the following screenshot:

This completes the design process of our dice. Next, the fun part: we will create animations that will make our app more interesting to use.

Animating objects with Flare

Let's switch from Design mode to Animate mode. You'll notice that a **timeline** appears at the bottom of the page. You'll probably find the timeline familiar if you've used other animation tools, or you've produced video or audio content. **A timeline is where you control the progression of your animation**. In Flare, you can also specify the duration of the animation and the number of **frames per second** (**FPS**).

In the following screenshot, you can see the animation page for our project. Notice the timeline and the duration, and the FPS settings:

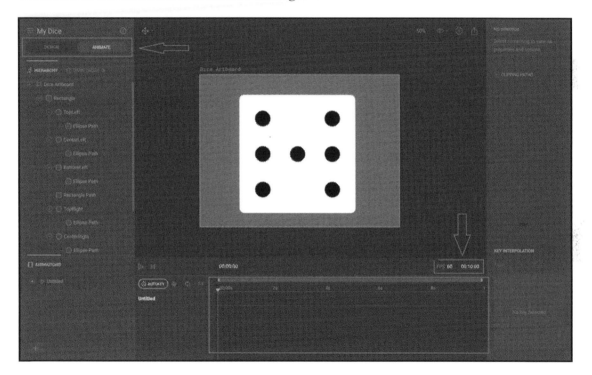

FPS, or frame rate, tells how many images will be displayed for every second of animation. The default value of **60** is generally considered extremely high and creates very smooth animations. Flutter aims to provide 60 FPS performance, and this is one of its strengths. Of course, if you want to save some resources in your device, you can try to see how the animation behaves at 30 FPS. In the example in this chapter, we'll leave the default value of 60 FPS.

Now, we'll see how to create our first animation so that we can get familiar with the timeline.

If you select the rectangle, in the **Properties** pane on the right of the page, you will see all the settings that can be changed in order to perform the animation. For example, you could change the **Size/Position** of the rectangle. Let's look at the steps, as follows:

1. Let's say we want to rotate the square 90 degrees. Select the square in the **Dice Artboard**.
2. Check that the playhead is positioned at the beginning of the animation (**00.00.00** seconds).
3. The timeline displays objects and properties that have been "keyed". **Keying in Flare means adding an object to the animation sequence.** Press the diamond shape near the **Rotation** property of the square—this will key the rotation in the timeline at the beginning of the animation. The diamond changes color and the rectangle appears on the timeline. In the following screenshot, you can see a detail of the result in the Properties pane:

4. Move the playhead in the timeline to 2 seconds, as shown in the following screenshot:

5. Set the rotation of the square to **45°** and key the square again, as shown in the following screenshot:

6. If you press the spacebar, you will see that the square is rotating from the initial position to 45 degrees, and it's taking 2 seconds to do that. Flare is "magically" filling all the frames to get there in the 2 seconds that we specified as the duration from the first to the second key.

7. Repeat the process according to the following table:

0:00	0°
2:00	45°
4:00	90°
6:00	135°
8:00	180°

8. Set the duration of the animation to 8 seconds.

9. Rename the animation by double-clicking on its name (untitled). Let's call it **Rotate**.

10. Press the **Loop** button so that the animation will automatically restart as soon as it finishes, and try the animation: you should see the dice rotating endlessly.

You may have noticed that all the circles that you designed on the surface of the square are rotating with the square itself. This happens because the circles are children of the square.

You have now created your first animation and, hopefully, familiarized yourself with the Flare interface. Unfortunately, we won't be using this specific animation in our app, but we can keep it here for reference. Next, we'll create the real animations that will be needed in our app.

Creating the Roll animation

In our app, there will be several animations. The first one we will create is to simulate the dice "rolling". We won't create a 3D animation as this goes far beyond the scope of this project, so we'll just change the numbers that are shown to the user, from 1 to 6. We'll reach this result by changing the **Fill Opacity** of each of the circles that we have placed on the surface of our Rectangle. Perform the following steps:

1. Create a new animation by clicking the + button in the animations pane, and call it `Roll`.
2. Set the duration of the animation to **1** second.
3. Select all the circles on the dice surface except the central one, by pressing the *Ctrl* button (*cmd* on a Mac) on your keyboard and clicking on each circle except **CenterCenter.**
4. Set the **Fill Opacity** to be **0**, and press the **Key** button near the **Fill Opacity** value.
5. Change the **KEY INTERPOLATION** value to **Hold.**
6. Select the **CenterCenter** circle while pressing the *Ctrl/cmd* key, then set the **Fill Opacity** value to **1**, the **KEY INTERPOLATION** type value to **Hold**, and key the object.

The result of this task should look like the following screenshot:

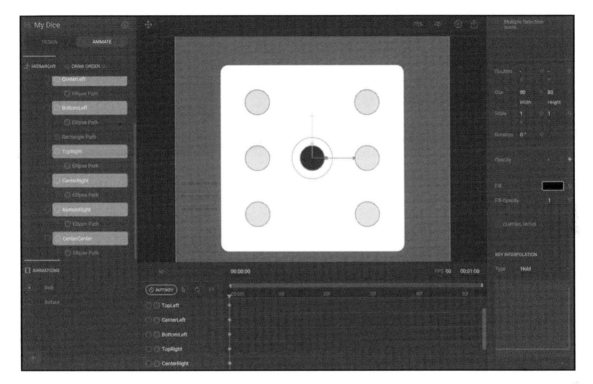

7. Move the playhead in the timeline to **00.00.10** seconds.
8. Select the central circle, called **CenterCenter** in the hierarchy pane; set the **Fill Opacity** value to **0**, the **KEY INTERPOLATION** value to **Hold**, and key the object.
9. Select the **TopLeft** and **BottomRight** circles, and set the **Fill Opacity** value to **1**, the **KEY INTERPOLATION** value to **Hold**, and key the object. We have now completed the animation to circle 2.
10. Move the playhead in the timeline to **00.00.20** seconds.
11. Select the **CentralCentral** circle in the hierarchy pane, set the **Fill Opacity** value to **1**, the **KEY INTERPOLATION** value to **Hold**, and key the object. We have now completed the animation to circle 3.
12. Move the playhead in the timeline to **00.00.30** seconds.
13. Select the **CentralCentral** circle in the hierarchy pane, set the **Fill Opacity** value to **0**, the **KEY INTERPOLATION** value to **Hold**, and key the object.

14. Select the **TopRight** and **BottomLeft** circles, and set the **Fill Opacity** value to **1**, the **KEY INTERPOLATION** value to **Hold,** and key the object. We have now completed the animation to circle 4.

15. Move the playhead in the timeline to **00.00.40** seconds.

16. Select the **CentralCentral** circle in the hierarchy pane, set the **Fill Opacity** value to **1**, the **KEY INTERPOLATION** value to **Hold,** and key the object. We have now completed the animation to circle 5.

17. Move the playhead in the timeline to **00.00.50** seconds.

18. Select the **CentralCentral** circle in the hierarchy pane, set the **Fill Opacity** value to **0**, the **KEY INTERPOLATION** value to **Hold,** and key the object.

19. Select the **CenterLeft** and **CenterRight** circles, and set the **Fill Opacity** value to **1**, the **KEY INTERPOLATION** value to **Hold,** and key the object. We have now completed the animation to circle 6 and have thus completed this animation.

20. Press the **Loop** button, so that the animation will loop whenever it completes.

Try the animation by pressing the spacebar on your keyboard. You should see the dice changing its values from 1 to 6 in a single second, as shown in the following screenshot:

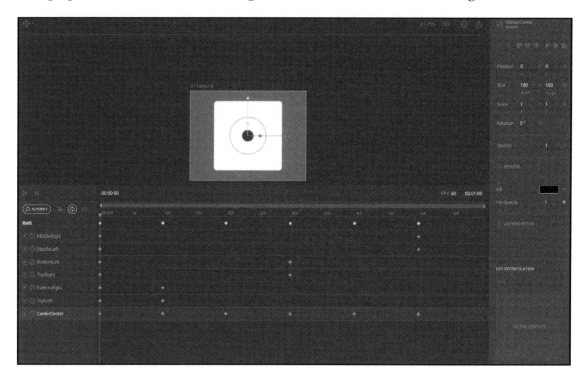

Now, the **Roll** animation is complete. This animation will be called from the app whenever the user plays and throws the dice. After rolling, the result of any of the numbers will be between 1 and 6. Therefore, we now need to create an animation for each of the possible results.

We'll keep things simple here: we'll just rotate the dice surface left and right, and show the number of the result. Let's begin with 1, then we'll repeat from 2 to 6, as follows:

1. Create a new animation by clicking the + button in the animations pane, and call it Set1.
2. Set the duration of the animation to **1** second.
3. Set the **Fill Opacity** property of the **CenterCenter** circle to **1**, and all the other circles to **0**, and key the objects.
4. Move the playhead to **00:00:06**.
5. Select the surface of the dice.
6. Set the **Rotation** property to **5°** and key the object. The result is shown in the following screenshot:

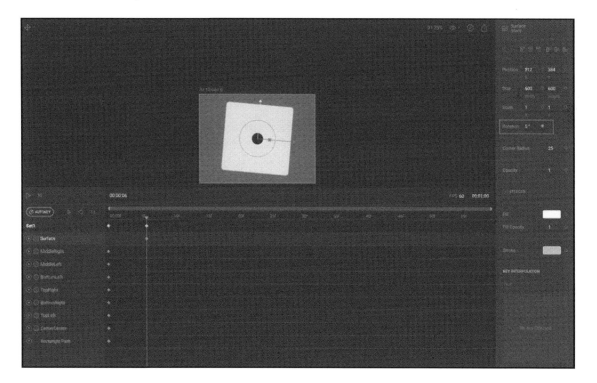

7. Move the playhead to **00:00:11**.

8. Set the **Rotation** property to **-5°** and key the object, as shown in the following screenshot:

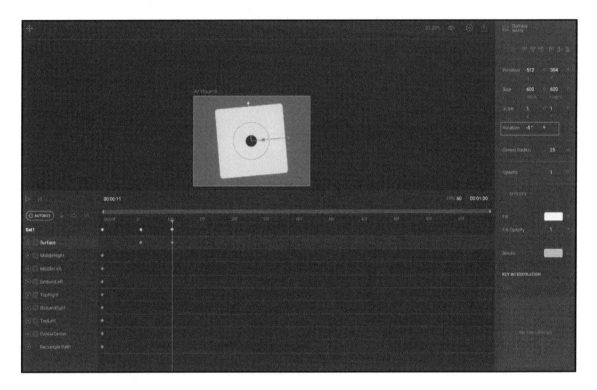

9. Move the playhead to **00:00:15**.

10. Set the **Rotation** property to **0°** and key the object, as shown in the following screenshot:

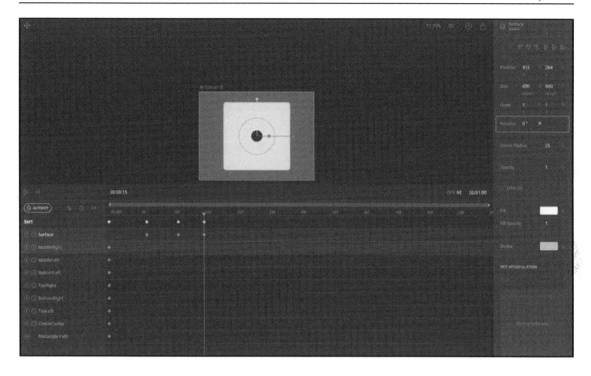

Try the animation—you should see the surface of the dice going left and right very quickly, and then stopping and showing **1** as a result.

Now, repeat the preceding steps for the remaining possible results, calling the animations **Set2**, **Set3**, up to **Set6**.

There is only one small animation we have to create before getting to Flutter: the animation that will be shown at the beginning before the user plays. Actually, it won't even be an animation, but just a static image of number 6 on the surface of the dice. To do this, perform the following steps:

1. Create a new animation by clicking the + button in the animations pane, and call it Start.
2. Set the duration of the animation to **1** second.
3. Set the **Fill Opacity** property of the **CenterCenter** circle to **0**, and all the other circles to **1**, and key the objects.

The result of these tasks is shown in the following screenshot:

That's it. We have completed everything we need for the app in Flare. Feel free to experiment with some animations if you want to move the dice when the screen of the app is built.

Just to recap, in Flare, you should have built the following animations that we'll call from our app:

- **Start**
- **Roll**
- **Set1**
- **Set2**
- **Set3**
- **Set4**
- **Set5**
- **Set6**

Next, we'll create the app and see how to integrate Flare animations in Flutter.

Integrating Flare into a Flutter app

As you have seen, Flare is a great tool to build animations, but it would be completely useless for our purposes if we couldn't use them in a Flutter app. These are a few easy steps to help us do so:

1. Adding the `flare_flutter` package
2. Exporting the Flare animation as a file
3. Including the exported file into the app assets
4. Declaring the assets into the `pubspec.yaml` file

Once the setup is complete, we'll also need to integrate Flare in our Dart code so that we can interact with our users and show them the relevant animation. Let's begin, as follows:

1. Create a new Flutter project, calling it `'Dice'`, and update the `main.dart` file so that it contains the following code:

```
import 'package:flutter/material.dart';
void main() => runApp(MyApp());
class MyApp extends StatelessWidget {
@override
Widget build(BuildContext context) {
 return MaterialApp(
  title: 'Dice',
  theme: ThemeData(
   primarySwatch: Colors.orange,
  ),
  home: Scaffold(),
 );
}
}
```

2. Create a new folder in the root of your app, called `assets`.

3. We need to get back briefly to our Flare files, only to export the files that we will add to the `assets` folder. Let's go to the `rive.app` website, and from the `dice` file, press the **Export** button at the top right of the screen, and select the **Export** menu, choosing the **Binary** option.

4. Depending on your system, the file that should be called `dice.flr` will be downloaded locally. Move the downloaded file to the `assets` folder that you created in *Step 2*.

5. Open the `pubspec.yaml` file and add the `flare_flutter` dependency (please check the right version in the library page), as follows:

```
dependencies:
    flutter:
        sdk: flutter
    flare_flutter: ^1.8.0
```

6. Still in the `pubspec.yaml` file, also add the animation in the `assets` section, like this:

```
assets:
- assets/dice.flr
```

Now, the setup is complete. Let's add the animations to our code next!

Creating the Dice class

The first screen we will create in the app will show a single dice. When opening the screen, our users will see the dice at the Start position, and a button to play. When they press the button, they will be able to roll the dice, see the **Roll** animation, and get a random result from 1 to 6. You can see an example of the **Single Dice** screen in the following screenshot:

Before adding the first screen, let's create a new service class that will contain the methods necessary to get a random number and the names of the animations for the result, as follows:

1. Create a new file in the `lib` folder of your project, called `dice.dart`.

2. At the top of the new file, import the `math` library that is needed to generate a random number, as follows:

```
import 'dart:math';
```

3. Create a new class called `Dice`, as follows:

```
class Dice {}
```

4. In the class, add a static list of animations, called `animations`. This contains the animations that will be called from the app when the result must be shown, and the code can be seen in the following block:

```
static List<String> animations = [
    'Set1',
    'Set2',
    'Set3',
    'Set4',
    'Set5',
    'Set6',
];
```

5. Create a static method called `getRandomNumber()` that returns a random number between 1 and 6, as follows:

```
static getRandomNumber() {
    var random = Random();
    int num = random.nextInt(5) + 1;
    return num;
}
```

6. Create another static method, returning a `Map` of type `int` and a `String` called `getRandomAnimation`. The purpose of the method is to generate a random number between 0 and 5 and return a `Map` containing the number and the name of the animation in the `animations` list at the position of the number itself. You can see the necessary code in the following snippet:

```
static Map<int, String> getRandomAnimation() {
    var random = Random();
    int num = random.nextInt(5);
    Map<int, String> result = {num: animations[num]};
    return result;
}
```

7. The last method of this class, still static, is called `wait3seconds()`. The purpose of the function, as you might guess, is just waiting 3 seconds. This is the duration we want to give the rolling animation of the dice. You might recall that the original duration of the rolling animation is only 1 second. By waiting for 3 seconds, we will repeat the animation three times, as each one only lasts 1 second.

Add the following code in the class:

```
static Future wait3seconds() {
    return new Future.delayed(const Duration(seconds: 3), () {});
}
```

That completes the `Dice` class. Now, we'll create the `single.dart` screen!

Creating the Single Dice screen

The first screen that we will create in the app is a screen that will allow the user to "throw" a single dice: no rules, no play. We'll just give the user a random value between 1 and 6. This will give us the opportunity to see a Flare animation in action in a Flutter screen. To do this, perform the following steps:

1. Create a new file in the `lib` folder of the project, called `single.dart`.
2. At the top of the file, import three files—the usual `material.dart`, our `dice.dart` file, and the library that will allow us to use Flare, which is `flare_actor.dart`, as follows:

```
import 'dice.dart';
import 'package:flutter/material.dart';
import 'package:flare_flutter/flare_actor.dart';
```

3. Create a stateful widget, using the `stful` shortcut, and call this class `Single`.
4. Declare a `String` called `currentAnimation` at the top of the `_SingleState` class, as follows:

```
class _SingleState extends State<Single> {
String currentAnimation;
```

5. Override the `initState()` method, and inside it, set the `currentAnimation` String so that it contains `Start`. This is the name of the Flare animation that we want to show at the beginning when the screen is loaded for the first time, and the necessary code can be seen in the following snippet:

```
@override
void initState() {
    currentAnimation = 'Start';
    super.initState();
}
```

6. At the top of the `build()` method, find the available height and width for the app, calling the `MediaQuery.of(context)` size properties.

7. Still in the `build()` method, return a `Scaffold`, whose `appBar` contains a title of `Single Dice`.

8. The `body` of the `Scaffold` contains a `Center` widget, whose child is a `Column`.

9. The first widget of the `Column` is a `Container`. Set the `height` of the `Container` to be `height / 1.7`, and the width to be `width * 0.8`. You may adjust this setting according to your preferences.

10. The `child` of the `Container` widget is, finally, the Flare animation. In order to show it, call the `FlareActor` constructor, which, as a first parameter, takes the name of the asset that we want to show—in this case, it's `assets/dice.flr`.

11. The second parameter is the `fit` property. Set it to `BoxFit.contain` so that the Flare content is included within the bounds of the widget. The last parameter is the name of the animation that will be shown. Here, we'll place the `currentAnimation` String.

12. Under the animation, insert a button that will allow the user to play. As we want to make this button rather large, based on the available width and height of the screen, use a `SizedBox` as a parent of the `MaterialButton`. The text of the button will be just **Play**.

13. When the button is pressed, we want to show the **Roll** animation.

14. After 3 seconds, we want to show the animation containing the result, and in order to achieve this, we will create a function called `callResult()`.

At the end of this process, your code should look like the following:

```
@override
Widget build(BuildContext context) {
    double width = MediaQuery.of(context).size.width;
    double height = MediaQuery.of(context).size.height ;
    return Scaffold(appBar: AppBar(
```

```
                title: Text('Single Dice'),
            ),
        body: Center(
            child: Column(
            children: <Widget>[
                Container(
                    height: height / 1.7,
                    width: width * 0.8,
                    child: FlareActor(
                        'assets/dice.flr',
                        fit: BoxFit.contain,
                        animation: currentAnimation,
                    )),
                SizedBox(
                    width: width/2.5,
                    height: height / 10,
                    child:RaisedButton(
                        child: Text('Play'),
                        shape: RoundedRectangleBorder(
                            borderRadius: BorderRadius.circular(24)
                        ),
                        onPressed: () {
                            setState(() {
                                currentAnimation = 'Roll';
                            });
                            Dice.wait3seconds().then((_){
                            callResult();
}) ;},))],)),);}
```

15. Now, in order to complete the screen, add the `callResult()` method, which will be asynchronous.

16. Inside the method, declare a `Map` of type `int, String` called `animation`, which will call the `getRandomAnimation()` static method from the `Dice` class.

17. Once the animation is ready, just call the `setState()` method to set the `currentAnimation` to be the one that was randomly returned. You may remember that the `getRandomAnimation()` method returns **Set1**, **Set2**, and so on. The necessary code can be seen in the following snippet:

```
void callResult() async {
    Map<int, String> animation = Dice.getRandomAnimation();
        setState(() {
            currentAnimation = animation.values.first;
        });
}
```

18. The last step before trying the animation in our app is calling the screen from the MyApp class in the `main.dart` file: we'll need to import `single.dart` and set the `Single` class as the home of the `MaterialApp`, like this:

```
import 'single.dart';
import 'package:flutter/material.dart';

void main() => runApp(MyApp());

class MyApp extends StatelessWidget {
  @override
  Widget build(BuildContext context) {
    return MaterialApp(
      title: 'Flutter Demo',
      theme: ThemeData(
        brightness: Brightness.dark,
        primarySwatch: Colors.blue,
      ),
      home: Single(),
    );
  }
}
```

Now, just try the app. When you open the app, you should see the dice at the top of the screen. When you press the **Play** button, the rolling animation is shown for 3 seconds, and after that, you get a random number.

To sum everything up, on this screen, you added a Flare animation and interacted with it. You are now ready to create the screen and logic for the **Knockout** game.

Creating the Knockout game

The final screen for this project contains the **Knockout** game. In this screen, the player will play against the device. Instead of having a single dice, there will be two dice that will use the same animations that you've already used in the `single` screen class.

When the user plays, the sum of the two dice will be added to their score, unless the sum of the dice is 7. In this case, nothing will be added to the score. When the player or the **AI** reaches at least 50 points, the player with the highest score wins. So, let's begin, as follows:

1. Start by adding a new screen to the app: we'll call it `knockout.dart`.

2. At the top of the file, add the required imports: we'll need the `flare_actor.dart` library for the animations, the `dice.dart` for the dice logic, the usual `material.dart`, and the other screen of the app, `single.dart`, which we'll use to be able to navigate from the **Knockout** screen to the **Single Dice** screen. All of this can be achieved by running the following code:

```
import 'single.dart';
import 'package:flare_flutter/flare_actor.dart';
import 'package:flutter/material.dart';
import 'dice.dart';
```

3. Then, create a stateful widget using the `stful` shortcut, and call it KnockOutScreen, as follows:

```
class KnockOutScreen extends StatefulWidget {
    @override
    _KnockOutScreenState createState() => _KnockOutScreenState();
}
class _KnockOutScreenState extends State<KnockOutScreen> {
    @override
    Widget build(BuildContext context) {
        return Container();
    }
}
```

4. At the top of the _KnockOutScreenState class, we'll create a few variables: two integers for the player's and AI's score, two strings for the animations of the two dice, and a String called _message that we'll use to give the player a message when the game ends. We'll also create a GlobalKey that we'll later use to retrieve the correct context to use a SnackBar for the message at the end of the game. The necessary code can be seen in the following snippet:

```
int _playerScore = 0;
int _aiScore = 0;
String _animation1;
String _animation2;
String _message;
var _scaffoldKey = new GlobalKey<ScaffoldState>();
```

Global keys are used to uniquely identify elements. Global keys give access to other objects related to those elements, including the `BuildContext`.

5. Next, override the `InitState` method, to set the initial animations to the `'Start'` animation that you've already created in Flare, as follows:

```
@override
void initState() {
    _animation1='Start';
    _animation2='Start';
    super.initState();
}
```

6. In the `build()` method, retrieve the current screen width and height using the `MediaQuery.of(context)` size values, then return a `Scaffold`.

7. In the `appBar` of the `Scaffold`, we'll just place the `Knockout Game` title, in a `Text` widget. For the body, in a `SingleChildScrollView`, insert a `Column` widget that will contain the UI widgets for this screen, as follows:

```
@override
Widget build(BuildContext context) {
    double width = MediaQuery.of(context).size.width;
    double height = MediaQuery.of(context).size.height;
    return Scaffold(
        key: _scaffoldKey,
        appBar: AppBar(
        title: Text('Knockout Game'),
        ),
        body: SingleChildScrollView(
            child: Container(
                alignment: Alignment.center,
                padding: EdgeInsets.all(24),
                child: Column(
                    children: []
                )
            )
    )))};
```

8. The first widgets inside the `Column` will be two dice containing the Flare animations. The two dice will be positioned next to each other, in the same row.

9. Inside the `Column`, create a `Row` widget whose children will be two `Containers`. Each `Container` will have a height of one-third of the screen, and a width of the available screen width divided by 2.5.

10. Each `Container` will include a `FlareActor` that will load our `dice.flr` asset: the animation for the first dice will be _animation1, and the second—quite predictably—_animation2, as shown in the following code block:

```
child: Column(
    children: [
        Row(
            mainAxisAlignment: MainAxisAlignment.spaceEvenly,
            children: <Widget>[
                Container(
                    height: height / 3,
                    width: width / 2.5,
                    child: FlareActor(
                        'assets/dice.flr',
                        fit: BoxFit.contain,
                        animation: _animation1,
                )),
                Container(
                    height: height / 3,
                    width: width / 2.5,
                    child: FlareActor(
                        'assets/dice.flr',
                        fit: BoxFit.contain,
                        animation: _animation2,
                )),
        ],),
```

Under the `Row` containing the two dice, we'll place a few `Text` widgets for the scores of the player and the AI. As these widgets need to be repeated several times, we'll create a new widget specifically for that, as follows:

1. At the bottom of the file, let's create a new stateless widget using the `stless` shortcut. Let's call this `GameText`.

2. Inside the class, create two final properties: a `String` called `text` and a `Color` called `color`. Both will be set in the constructor.

3. In the `build()` method, return a `Container` whose child will be a `Text` widget, containing the text that was passed to the widget, and whose style will set the font size to `24` and the color to the color that was passed.

Here is the code after you have executed the preceding steps:

```
class GameText extends StatelessWidget {
    final String text;
    final Color color;
    GameText(this.text, this.color);
    @override
    Widget build(BuildContext context) {
        return Container(
            child: Text(text,
            style: TextStyle(
                fontSize: 24,
                color: color
    ),),);}
}
```

4. Back to the `Column` in the body of the `Scaffold` in the `build()` method of the `_KnockOutScreenState` class, add two new rows that will show the player's and the AI's scores. Each row will contain a label **Player** or **AI**, and the score itself, and the two widgets will be spaced evenly, using the `mainAxisAlignment` property of the `Row` widget.

5. Between the two rows and after the second row, add a `Padding` widget, taking the screen height divided by `24`. This will create some space between the rows, and the code for this can be seen in the following block:

```
Row(
    mainAxisAlignment: MainAxisAlignment.spaceEvenly,
    children: <Widget>[
        GameText('Player: ', Colors.deepOrange, false),
        GameText(_playerScore.toString(), Colors.white, true),
    ],),
    Padding(padding: EdgeInsets.all(height / 24),),
    Row(
        mainAxisAlignment: MainAxisAlignment.spaceEvenly,
        children: <Widget>[
            GameText('AI: ', Colors.lightBlue, false),
            GameText(_aiScore.toString(), Colors.white, true),
        ],),
    Padding(
```

```
                padding: EdgeInsets.all(height / 12),
        ),
```

The last row of the column will contain two buttons: one to play, and one to reset the game. This time, instead of using a `Container`, we'll use a `SizedBox`.

There is very little difference between a `Container` and a `SizedBox` in this case. When you use a `SizedBox`, you should specify the width or height, or both. To learn more about the `SizedBox`, have a look at the following clip: `https://www.youtube.com/watch?v=EHPu_DzRfqAvl=it`.

6. In each of the `SizedBox` widgets, insert a `RaisedButton`. The first one's child has a `'play'` text, and its color is `green`; the second has a `'Restart'` text, and its color is `grey`. Both will have rounded corners, so the shape contains a `RoundedRectangleBorder` with a circular `borderRadius`, with a radius of `24`.

7. When pressed, the first button will call a `play()` method, and the second, a `reset()` method. We'll create the methods next.

You can see the code for the described steps here:

```
Row(
    mainAxisAlignment: MainAxisAlignment.spaceEvenly,
    children: <Widget>[
        SizedBox(
            width: width / 3,
            height: height / 10,
            child:RaisedButton(
                child: Text('Play'),
                color: Colors.green,
                shape: RoundedRectangleBorder(
                    borderRadius: BorderRadius.circular(24)
                ),
                onPressed: () {
                    play(context);
                },
        )),
        SizedBox(
            width: width / 3,
            height: height / 10,
            child:RaisedButton(
                color: Colors.gray,
                child: Text('Restart'),
                shape: RoundedRectangleBorder(
                borderRadius: BorderRadius.circular(24)
                ),
                onPressed: () {
```

```
                            reset();
                        },
                )),
            ],),
```

8. The `reset()` method is rather simple. It just needs to call the `setState()` method to set the animation strings to the `'Start'` value, and the scores for the player and the **AI** to 0.

    Add the following code to the `_KnockOutScreenState` class:

```
void reset() {
    setState(() {
        _animation1 = 'Start';
        _animation2 = 'Start';
        _aiScore = 0;
        _playerScore = 0;
    });
}
```

The `play()` method contains the logic of the game. This method will be responsible for throwing the dice, calling the relevant animations for the result, adding the score to the player and the AI, and updating the screen with the result. This will also call a method that will show a message to the user at the end of the game.

9. Add a new method called `play()` in the `_KnockOutScreenState` class. As this will call an animation lasting a few seconds, the `play()` method will be asynchronous. It will also take a `BuildContext` parameter to show the `SnackBar` to the user, as shown in the following code snippet:

```
Future play(BuildContext context) async {}
```

10. Inside the `play()` method, create a `String`, called `message`, and set its initial value to be an empty String, as follows:

```
String message = '';
```

11. Next, call the `setState()` method, to set the animations to be the `'Roll'` animation that you've already created in Flare, as follows:

```
setState(() {
    _animation1 = 'Roll';
    _animation2 = 'Roll';
});
```

12. Keep the rolling animation going for 3 seconds to add some suspense to the game by calling the static `wait3seconds()` method in the `Dice` class. After the 3 seconds have passed, using the `then` function we can generate a random number (and animation) by calling the `getRandomAnimation()` method of the `Dice` class: we will call this for both `animation1` and `animation2`, as follows:

```
Dice.wait3seconds().then((_) {
    Map<int, String> animation1 = Dice.getRandomAnimation();
    Map<int, String> animation2 = Dice.getRandomAnimation();
}
```

13. Still in the `then()` function, add the two dice results (as the `List` is zero-based, we need to add 1 to the position in the `List`) and put the sum into a new variable called `result`, as follows:

```
int result = animation1.keys.first +1 + animation2.keys.first+1;
```

14. Next, still in the `then()` function, the **AI** will play as well: we just need to call the `getRandomNumber()` of the `Dice` class twice and sum the results. The variable we'll declare here is called `aiResult`, as shown in the following code snippet:

```
int aiResult = Dice.getRandomNumber() + Dice.getRandomNumber();
```

15. The knockout number is 7: so, if the sum of the two dice equals 7, nothing will be added to the total score of the player or the **AI**. Add the code under the previous instruction, still in the `then()` method, as follows:

```
if (result == 7) result = 0;
if (aiResult == 7) aiResult = 0;
```

The probability of throwing a 7 with two dice is 16.67%, or 1 out of 6, which is the highest probability of all the possible outcomes. The lowest probability is throwing 2 or 12: each of them has a probability of 2.78%, or 1 out of 36.

16. Next, still in the `then()` method, call the `setState()` method to update the player and **AI** scores, and the dice animations, as follows:

```
setState(() {
    _playerScore += result;
    _aiScore += aiResult;
    _animation1 = animation1.values.first;
    _animation2 = animation2.values.first;
});
```

17. After updating the scores, we need to check whether the player or the **AI** has reached 50 points. When they do, the message gets updated, and a new method, showMessage(), gets called. We'll create that method next. Meanwhile, add the following code at the bottom of the play() method:

```
if (_playerScore >= 50 || _aiScore >= 50) {
    if (_playerScore > _aiScore) {message = 'You win!';}
    else if (_playerScore == _aiScore) {message = 'Draw!'; }
    else {message = 'You lose!';}
    showMessage(message);
}
```

18. The last method of our app is the showMessage() method. It just creates a SnackBar telling the player whether they won, lost, or got a draw. Please note that we are using the _scaffoldKey as the context for the SnackBar. Add the following code in the _KnockOutScreenState class:

```
void showMessage (String message) {
    SnackBar snackBar = SnackBar(content: Text(message),);
    _scaffoldKey.currentState.showSnackBar(snackBar);
}
```

In order to complete our app, we only need to add the navigation that will allow the user to navigate from the **Single Dice** screen to the Knockout game and vice versa. Let's do that:

1. So, in the single.dart file, add the required import, as follows:

```
import 'knockout.dart';
```

2. In the build() method, add to the Appbar the IconButton that, when pressed, will call the Navigator.push() method to open the Knockout screen, as follows:

```
appBar: AppBar(
    actions: <Widget>[
        IconButton(
            icon: Icon(Icons.fitness_center),
            onPressed: () {
                MaterialPageRoute route =
                MaterialPageRoute(builder:
                (context)=>
                 KnockOutScreen());
                Navigator.push(context, route);
            },
        )
    ],
```

3. Then, do the same in the `knockout.dart` file, but this time, we need to call the `single.dart` screen instead, as follows:

```
appBar: AppBar(
    actions: <Widget>[
        IconButton(
            icon: Icon(Icons.repeat_one),
            onPressed: () {
                MaterialPageRoute route =
                MaterialPageRoute(builder: (context)=>
                        Single());
                Navigator.push(context, route);
            },
        )
    ],
```

And with that, the app is now complete! Just play Knockout a few times to check whether everything is working as expected, but don't spend too much time on it. You still have a couple of projects to complete in this book!

Summary

Flare is a vector design and animation tool that exports directly to Flutter. There are several advantages to using Flare for your Flutter apps, one being that the animations you create with Flare can be changed from your Flutter code at runtime. You can create assets and animate them, and then enclose the objects straight into Flutter. Flare can be used from a browser and does not require any installation. Flare is free to use, as long as you agree to share your work.

You've seen how to interact with the **Stage**, the working area where you create your designs, and where you place **Artboards,** which, in turn, are the top-level nodes of a Flare hierarchy. We've used both the **Design** and **Animate** modes. In the Design mode, we've created the dice for our app, and in the Animate mode, you have created the dice animations that we've used in our app.

After exporting and downloading the `.flr` file in the `rive.app` website, we've followed the steps required to use a Flare asset into a Flutter project.

Once we completed the integration of our dice into the app, we've started interacting with them from the app: in particular, we've leveraged the `FlareActor` widget, which allows you to specify the asset you wish to use, the animation you wish to show, and how the animation should fit into the screen.

We've interacted with the Flare animations by adding some logic to our app. We've seen how to use random numbers to change the dice result and programmatically set the animations based on the dice results. Finally, we've added the Knockout game logic to the app.

In the next chapter, we'll see a design pattern that Google developers recommend for your Flutter apps: the **Business Logic Component (BLoC)** pattern.

Questions

At the end of each project, you'll find a few questions to help you remember and review the contents covered in the chapter. Please try to answer the following questions (when in doubt, have a look at the content in the chapter itself: you'll find all the answers there!):

1. In the `pubspec.yaml` file, where should you place the `.flr` file you have exported from Flare?
2. In Flare, what is the difference between the **Design** and **Animate** modes?
3. How many Artboards are required in a Flare project?
4. What is the purpose of the timeline in Flare?
5. What is a hierarchy in Flare?
6. When using a Flare asset in a Flutter project, when and why do you use the animation name?
7. Which widget can you use to show a Flare animation in Flutter?
8. How do you generate a random number between 1 and 6 in a Flutter app?
9. When would you use a Flare animation in an app, instead of built-in animations?
10. In the following code, what would you put as the first parameter?

```
FlareActor([YOUR ANSWER HERE],
    fit: BoxFit.contain,
    animation: _animation1,
)
```

Further reading

The fastest way to learn a new technology is using it, but a not-so-distant second is looking at projects that experienced developers and designers have already created: for a few great samples in Flare, have a look at `https://github.com/2d-inc/Flare-Flutter/tree/master/example`.

In this chapter, you've built a simple game using Flare. If you are interested in developing games with Flutter, you'll probably be glad to know that there's also a gaming engine that can make your life easier: have a look at Flame (`https://flame-engine.org`) for more info about that!

For a refresher on using built-in animations into your apps, have a look at the official Flutter guide, which you can find at the following link: `https://flutter.dev/docs/development/ui/animations`.

If you are really serious about developing games, there's a great free resource that will give you general principles on which you can rely, whichever language or platform you are using—have a look at `https://www.freecodecamp.org/news/learn-game-development-from-harvard/` for more info.

10
ToDo App - Leveraging the BLoC Pattern and Sembast

Designing the structure or architecture of an app is often one of the most important problems that developers need to solve when creating or upgrading an app, especially when the complexity and size of the project grows.

Each language has a 'favorite' pattern, such as **model–view–controller** (**MVC**), or **model–view–viewmodel** (**MVVM**). Flutter is no exception, and the pattern that Google developers are suggesting at this time is the **BLoC** (**business logic components**) pattern. There are many advantages of using BLoCs, and one of them is that they don't require any plugin, as they're already integrated into Flutter.

In previous chapters, you've seen the different ways to persist data in an app, such as SQFlite and the Firebase Firestore database. For this project, we'll introduce another tool so that you can choose the best solution in different contexts—the **simple embedded application store database** (short for *sembast)*. Using this tool is far easier than remembering its name.

Also, instead of using `setState()` to deal with the state of our app, we will use the BLoC pattern. This leverages the streams functionality to manage state changes in Flutter. Using the BLoC pattern helps to separate the business logic from the UI.

By the end of this project, you'll be able to use the simple embedded application store database with the BLoC pattern to persist the data and states in your apps. In this chapter's project, we'll use a BLoC pattern as the interface between the UI and the data.

The following topics will be covered in this chapter:

- Using the simple embedded application store database, or sembast
- Introducing the BLoC pattern
- Using BLoCs and streams to update the UI

Technical requirements

You'll find the completed app code in the book's Github repository at `https://github.com/PacktPublishing/Flutter-Projects`.

To follow along with the code examples in this book, you should have the following software installed on your Windows, Mac, Linux, or Chrome OS device:

- The Flutter SDK.
- If you are developing for Android, you should have the Android SDK, which is easily installed by Android Studio.
- If you are developing for iOS, you should have MacOS and Xcode.
- An emulator (Android), simulator (iOS), or a connected iOS or Android device enabled for debugging.
- An editor: Visual Studio Code, Android Studio, and IntelliJ Idea are recommended. All should have the Flutter/Dart extensions installed.

Project overview

The app we'll build in this chapter is a simple 'to do' management application. It consists of two screens: the first one contains a list of todos that need to be completed: from here, the user will be able to delete any item on the list by swiping left or right, and add a new todo item or edit an existing one by calling the second screen of the app. The following is a screenshot of the first page of the app:

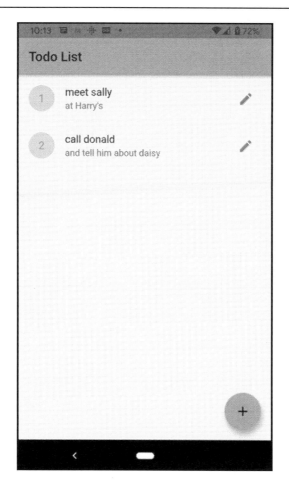

The second screen of the app is the detail of a single todo: here the user will be able to insert the details of the todo and save them to the **sembast** database. The fields required for a todo are the name of the todo, its description, priority, and date.

By clicking the **Save** button, all changes will be persisted; by clicking the 'back' button, the changes will be discarded. The following is a picture of the second screen:

The project in this chapter is particularly code intensive, as there are several steps required to implement the BLoC pattern in an app, but once this chapter is completed, you'll be able to easily reuse the code in other projects.

The total time required to complete this project is approximately three hours.

Using sembast to store data

In many cases, when you need to persist structured data in your app, you will likely choose an SQL database, such as SQFLite, which we've used in Chapter 6, *Store That Data - Using Sq(F)Lite To Store Data in a Local Database*. But, there are cases where your data is not structured, or it's so simple that you don't need an SQL database. For those cases, there is a very efficient solution for Flutter—the simple embedded application store database.

Sembast is a document-based database that resides in a single file. It is loaded in memory when you open it from the app, and it's very efficient, as the file is automatically compacted when needed. Data is stored in JSON format, with key–value pairs. You can even encrypt data if your app requires it.

The library is written in Dart and the only requirement that you need in order to use Sembast is the addition of the dependency in your pubspec.yaml file:

Create a new app with your editor and open the pubspec.yaml file. In the dependencies node, add the code to add the sembast and path_provider libraries. As usual, I recommend checking out the latest versions in the Dart packages website at https://pub.dev/:

```
sembast: ^2.3.0
path_provider: ^1.6.5
```

The reason why path_provider is included here is that each device saves into the file system in a different way; by using path_provider, you make sure that the app is compatible with both iOS and Android.

As usual, everything begins with a class. The first step in our project is the creation of the class for the todo itself:

1. In the lib folder of your app, create a data folder.
2. In the data folder, create a new file called todo.dart.

3. In the file, add a class called `Todo` with the fields that we'll use in the database: `id`, `name`, `description`, a `completeBy` string that will contain the date that the task should be completed by, and an integer for the `priority`:

```
class Todo {
    int id;
    String name;
    String description;
    String completeBy;
    int priority;
}
```

4. To simplify the creation of a todo, create a constructor that will take all the fields (except the ID) of a todo object:

```
Todo(this.name, this.description, this.completeBy, this.priority);
```

In sembast, the ID is automatically generated from the database and is unique for each store/document, similar to what happens with SQLite.

As data is stored as JSON in sembast, we need a method to convert a `Todo` object into a `Map`; the sembast engine will then automatically convert the `Map` to JSON.

5. In the `Todo` class, create a function called `toMap()` that will return a `Map` of the `String, dynamic` type containing the fields of the `Todo`. Add the following code to create the `toMap()` method:

```
Map<String, dynamic> toMap() {
  return {
     'name': name,
     'description': description,
     'completeBy': completeBy,
     'priority': priority,
  };
}
```

6. The last method of the `Todo` class will do exactly the opposite: when a `Map` is passed, the function will return a new `Todo`. This method is static, as it does not require an object to return a `Todo`. Add the following code to create the `fromMap()` function:

```
static Todo fromMap(Map<String, dynamic> map) {
  return Todo(map['name'], map['description'],
map['completeBy'],map['priority']);
  }
```

This completes the `Todo` class. Next, let's deal with the data.

Sembast: dealing with data

In this section, we'll create the class to create the database, open it, and then add the methods to perform the CRUD operations over it:

1. In the data folder of the app, create a new file called `todo_db.dart`.

2. Place the following required imports at the top of the `todo_db.dart` file:

```
import 'dart:async';
import 'package:path_provider/path_provider.dart';
import 'package:path/path.dart';
import 'package:sembast/sembast.dart';
import 'package:sembast/sembast_io.dart';
import 'todo.dart';
```

3. The `TodoDb` class needs to be a singleton, as it wouldn't make sense to open the database more than once. So, after creating the `TodoDb` class, add a named constructor called `_internal`, then create a static private `TodoDb` object called `_singleton` that we will return whenever a new `TodoDb` instance is called:

```
class TodoDb {
  //this needs to be a singleton
  static final TodoDb _singleton = TodoDb._internal();
  //private internal constructor
  TodoDb._internal();
}
```

4. Finally, create a `factory` constructor that will return the `_singleton` object:

```
factory TodoDb() {
return _singleton;
}
```

A normal constructor returns a new instance of the current class. A factory constructor can only return a single instance of the current class: that's why factory constructors are often used when you need to implement the singleton pattern.

Next, we will add the objects and methods that are needed to interact with the database.

Opening a sembast database

The first object we'll use is a `DatabaseFactory`. A database factory allows us to open a sembast database. Each database is a file. Let's look at the steps:

1. Add the following code under the constructors to create a `DatabaseFactory`:

   ```
   DatabaseFactory dbFactory = databaseFactoryIo;
   ```

2. After opening the database, you need to specify the location in which you want to save files. **Stores** could be considered 'folders' inside the database: they are **persistent maps,** and their values are the `Todo` objects. Add the following code to specify the store for our read/write operations:

   ```
   final store = intMapStoreFactory.store('todos');
   ```

3. Next, we'll open the database itself: first declare a `Database` object, called `_database`:

   ```
   Database _database;
   ```

4. Then add a getter that will check whether the `_database` has already been set: if it has, the getter will return the existing `_database`. If it hasn't, it will call the `_openDb()` asynchronous method, which we will create in the next step. This is a pattern that you can use whenever you need a singleton in your code:

   ```
   Future<Database> get database async {
       if (_database == null) {
         await _openDb().then((db) {
           _database = db;
         });
       }
       return _database;
     }
   ```

5. Now we are ready to write the _openDb() asynchronous method, which will open the sembast database:

```
Future _openDb() async {}
```

6. Inside the openDb() method, we'll get the specific directory where data will be stored: this is platform specific, but as we are using the path library, there's no need to worry about the way the operating system is storing data. Add the following code to retrieve the document directory for your system:

```
final docsPath = await getApplicationDocumentsDirectory();
```

7. Next, call the join() method to join the docsPath and the name of the database, which we will predictably call todos.db, into a single path using the current platform's separator. The .db extension is optional:

```
final dbPath = join(docsPath.path, 'todos.db');
```

8. Finally, using the dbFactory, call the openDatabase() method to actually open the sembast database and return it:

```
final db = await dbFactory.openDatabase(dbPath);
    return db;
```

Now that the database is open, we need to write the methods for the create, read, update, and delete tasks. Let's do that next:

Creating CRUD methods with sembast

CRUD methods in sembast are similar to those in other databases that we have seen in previous projects in this book: the syntax is shown in the following table:

Task	Method
Insert a new document	add()
Update an existing document	update()
Delete a document	delete()
Retrieve one or more documents	find()

Let's see these methods in action in our project:

1. To insert a new item in a sembast database, you just need to call the `add()` method over the `Store`, passing the database and the `Map` of the object you want to insert. As you can expect, read and write operations in a sembast database are asynchronous.

2. Add the following code to implement the `insertTodo()` method:

```
Future insertTodo(Todo todo) async {
    await store.add(_database, todo.toMap());
}
```

3. Similarly, to update an existing item in the database, you can call the `update()` method of the store. The difference here is that you also need another object: a `Finder`. A `Finder` is a helper that you can use to search inside a store. With the `update()` method, you need to retrieve a `Todo` before updating it, so you need the `Finder` before you update the document.

   A `Finder` takes a parameter named `filter`, which you can use to specify how to filter the documents. In this case, we'll search for the `Todo` using its ID, so we'll use the `byKey()` method of the filter.

4. Add the following code to implement the `updateTodo()` method:

```
Future updateTodo(Todo todo) async {
    //Finder is a helper for searching a given store
    final finder = Finder(filter: Filter.byKey(todo.id));
    await store.update(_database, todo.toMap(), finder: finder);
}
```

   We also need the finder to delete an existing item. This time, the method to call over the store is `delete()`, which takes only the database and a finder.

5. Add the following code to implement the `deleteTodo()` method:

```
Future deleteTodo(Todo todo) async {
    final finder = Finder(filter: Filter.byKey(todo.id));
    await store.delete(_database, finder: finder);
}
```

6. It might also be useful to create a method that can delete all records from the store. Add the following code to implement the `deleteAll()` method:

```
Future deleteAll() async {
    // Clear all records from the store
```

```
await store.delete(_database);
}
```

We also need a method to retrieve the available `Todos`. In this case, we can still use a finder, but instead of filtering data, we can specify a sort order for the list. We'll sort the items by `priority` and `id`.

The function returns a `List` of `Todo`, and, as usual, is asynchronous.

7. Add the following code to create the `getTodos()` function:

```
Future<List<Todo>> getTodos() async {
    await database;
    final finder = Finder(sortOrders: [
      SortOrder('priority'),
      SortOrder('id'),
    ]);
}
```

Now the `Finder` is set. The method to retrieve data from a sembast store is the `find()` method, which again takes a database and a `Finder`.

> The `find()` method returns a `Future<List<RecordSnapshot>>` and not a `List<Todo>`.

8. Add the following code inside the `getTodos()` function after setting the finder:

```
final todosSnapshot = await store.find(_database, finder: finder);
```

9. As the `find` method returns a `Snapshot`, we need to use the `map()` method to convert the snapshot into a `Todo`. We can call the `map()` function on any list to convert the values of the list from one type to another. Add the following code to call the `map()` method on the `todosSnapshot` object and transform the snapshot into a `List` of `Todo` objects:

```
return todosSnapshot.map((snapshot){
    final todo = Todo.fromMap(snapshot.value);
    //the id is automatically generated
    todo.id = snapshot.key;
    return todo;
}).toList();
```

The data part of our `Todo` app is complete. Let's test whether everything's working as expected.

Using sembast

We can now test the methods to check that everything is working and add a few sample data before moving to the next part of our project:

1. Open the `main.dart` file, delete the existing code, and add the required imports:

```
import 'package:flutter/material.dart';
import 'data/todo_db.dart';
import 'data/todo.dart';
```

2. Add the `main()` method, which will call a stateless widget that we can call `MyApp`. Also remove the debug sign at the top of the screen by adding `debugShowCheckedModeBanner: false` to the `MaterialApp`:

```
void main() => runApp(MyApp());

class MyApp extends StatelessWidget {
  @override
  Widget build(BuildContext context) {
    return MaterialApp(
      title: 'Todos BLoC',
      debugShowCheckedModeBanner: false,
      theme: ThemeData(
        primarySwatch: Colors.orange,
      ),
      home: HomePage(),
    );
  }
}
```

3. Now create a stateful widget called `HomePage()`. This is the main screen of our app that will contain the list of todos. At this time, we'll only use it for testing purposes:

```
class HomePage extends StatefulWidget {
  @override
  _HomePageState createState() => _HomePageState();
}

class _HomePageState extends State<HomePage> {
  @override
  Widget build(BuildContext context) {
    return Container();
  }
}
```

4. In the `_HomePageState` class, add an asynchronous method called `_testData()`, that will call and test the CRUD methods that we've written in the `todo_db.dart` file.

5. Inside the `_testData()` method, create an instance of the `TodoDb` class.

6. Call the `getTodos()` method once; this will also open the database.

7. Call the `deleteAll()` method to delete all the records from the database. This will make sure that we do not have data remaining from previous tests if we need to call `_testData()` more than once.

The code for steps 4 to 7 is shown as follows:

```
Future _testData() async {
    TodoDb db = TodoDb();
    await db.database;
    List<Todo> todos = await db.getTodos();
    await db.deleteAll();
    todos = await db.getTodos();
}
```

8. After the initial setup, while we're still in the `_testData()` method, let's test the `insertTodo()` method. We'll create three simple `Todo` objects and we'll call the `insertTodo()` method on each of them.

9. Next, update the `todos` list again, calling the `getTodos()` method:

```
await db.insertTodo(Todo('Call Donald', 'And tell him about Daisy',
'02/02/2020', 1));
await db.insertTodo(Todo('Buy Sugar', '1 Kg, brown', '02/02/2020',
2));
await db.insertTodo(Todo('Go Running', '@12.00, with neighbours',
'02/02/2020', 3));
todos = await db.getTodos();
```

10. After inserting the three documents into the database, we can use the debug console to check whether everything worked as expected:

```
debugPrint('First insert');
todos.forEach((Todo todo){
    debugPrint(todo.name);
});
```

11. Next, we can test the `updateTodo()` method by changing the first document from `'Call Donald'` to `'Call Tim'`, as shown in the following code block:

```
Todo todoToUpdate = todos[0];
todoToUpdate.name = 'Call Tim';
await db.updateTodo(todoToUpdate);
```

12. Now test the `deleteTodo()` method by removing the `'Buy sugar'` todo: after all, sugar isn't good for your health!

```
Todo todoToDelete = todos[1];
await db.deleteTodo(todoToDelete);
```

13. Now read the data again. We expect to have only two documents instead of the initial three, and the first one should be `'Call Tim'`:

```
debugPrint('After Updates');
  todos = await db.getTodos();
   todos.forEach((Todo todo){
     debugPrint(todo.name);
   });
```

14. In the `build()` method of the `_HomePageState` class, call the `_testData()` method:

```
@override
  Widget build(BuildContext context) {
    _testData();
    return Container();
  }
```

15. Run the app. After a few seconds, you should see a result in the Debug Console that looks like the following image:

```
PROBLEMS    OUTPUT    TERMINAL    DEBUG CONSOLE
-------------------------------------------------
I/flutter ( 9024): First insert
I/flutter ( 9024): Call Donald
I/flutter ( 9024): Buy Sugar
I/flutter ( 9024): Go Running
I/flutter ( 9024): After Updates
I/flutter ( 9024): Call Tim
I/flutter ( 9024): Go Running
```

If the debug console shows the data correctly, then that means you can read and write data in the sembast database. In the next section, we'll use a BLoC pattern to interact with the database.

The BLoC pattern

In most of the projects we have built so far, we've dealt with the state using stateful widgets. While this approach is great for prototyping or simple apps, it is not ideal when your app grows.

There are several reasons for this. Arguably, the most important reason is that you would put at least part of the logic of your app in the same class as your layout. You should avoid mixing layout and code, as it's hard to maintain and reuse the same code in different circumstances. It also makes it easier for developers in a group to work on the same code base if you keep the logic and UI clearly separated.

Also, if you have data that changes in your app, and you need to update several widgets on different screens, then you also risk unnecessarily duplicating your code. Maintaining your app may become extremely costly, and keeping the quality of your software might become challenging.

The BLoC pattern is a state management system for Flutter recommended by Google developers. BLoC helps in managing the state and accessing data from a shared class in your project.

There are several ways to manage the state in Flutter. BloC is the recommended one at this time, but it's also worth mentioning the **inherited widget** method, which allows the propagation of data to its child widgets, and the **scoped model method**, which is an external package built on top of Inherited Widget, and **Redux**, which may be familiar to you if you've used React. For more information about the different options for maintaining a state, have a look at `https://flutter.dev/docs/development/data-and-backend/state-mgmt/options`.

Using the BLoC pattern

When using the BLoC pattern, everything is a **stream** of events.

A BLoC is a layer between a source of data in your app and the widgets that need the data—for example, the source might be an HTTP response from a web API or a query result from a database, and the widget might be a ListView that receives the data.

The BLoC receives streams of **events** or data from your source, deals with the business logic, and returns or **publishes** one or more streams of data to widgets that **listen** or **subscribe** to them.

A simple diagram of the role of a BLoC is shown in the following image:

 Futures and streams are two ways to deal with asynchronous programming in Dart. The difference is that futures have a single request and response, whereas streams are a continuous series of responses to a single request.

A BLoC has two components, **sinks** and **streams**, both of which are part of a `StreamController`.

You could think of a stream as a pipe. This pipe has two ends: a way in and a way out. It's a 'one-way only' pipe. When you insert something into the pipe, it enters by the `Sink`, possibly being transformed inside (if you want it to be), and then exits from the `Stream`.

You should bear in mind the following facts when using the BLoC pattern in Flutter:

- The pipe is called a `Stream`.
- To control the stream, you use a `StreamController`.
- The way into the stream is the `sink` property of the `StreamController`.
- The
- way out of the stream is the `stream` property of the `StreamController`.

For a strange choice of properties and class names, Stream (uppercase S) is the class that provides an asynchronous sequence of data, and stream (lowercase s) is the property of the StreamController where data comes out.

In order to use the Stream and be notified when something comes out of it, you need to **listen** to the Stream. You define a listener with a StreamSubscription object.

The StreamSubscription is notified every time an event related to the Stream is triggered—for example, whenever some data flows out from the stream or when there is an error.

You can also transform the data inside a Stream through an object called StreamTransformer—for example, to filter or modify the data.

The BLoC guideline step by step

There are several steps involved in implementing a BLoC in your app: I'll highlight them here so that we have a map for the next few steps:

1. Create a class that will serve as the BLoC.
2. In the class, declare the data that needs to be updated in the app (in this case, the list of Todo objects).
3. Set the StreamControllers.
4. Create the getters for streams and sinks.
5. Add the logic of the BLoC.
6. Add a constructor in which you'll set data

1. and listen to changes.
2. Set the dispose() method.
3. From the UI, create an instance of the BLoC.
4. Use a StreamBuilder to build the widgets that will use the BLoC data.
5. Add events to the sink for any changes to the data.
6. Call the dispose() method.

I'll use this list as a map for the steps that we will perform in the remainder of this chapter.

1. Creating the BLoC class

In order to implement the BLoC pattern in the app, create a new folder in the `lib` folder of our app called `bloc`.

Inside the `bloc` folder, create a new file called `todo_bloc.dart`.

The `StreamControllers` can be accessed via the `'dart:async'` library, so, in our imports, we'll add the `dart:async`, our `todo.dart` file, and the `todo_db.dart` to connect to the database.

Add the code for the required imports:

```
import 'dart:async';
import '../data/todo.dart';
import '../data/todo_db.dart';
```

This file will contain a class called `TodoBloc`, which will serve as an interface between the UI and the data of the app:

```
class TodoBloc {}
```

2. Declaring the data that will change

Inside the class, declare a `TodoDb` class and a `List` of `Todo` items:

```
TodoDb db;
List<Todo> todoList;
```

3. Setting the StreamControllers

Create the `StreamControllers`: one for the `List` of `Todo` items and three more for the insert, update, and delete tasks. The `StreamControllers` are generics, so we also need to specify the type of data that the `StreamController` will manage: a single `todo` for the updates and a `List` of the `Todo` type for the `_todosStreamController`.

There are two kinds of Streams: **single-subscription** Streams and **broadcast** Streams. Single-subscription Streams only allow a single listener during the whole lifetime of the Stream. Broadcast Streams, on the other hand, allow multiple listeners that can be added at any time: each listener will receive data from the moment it begins listening to the Stream. In our project, we will use a broadcast stream, allowing multiple listeners:

```
final _todosStreamController = StreamController<List<Todo>>.broadcast();
//for updates
final _todoInsertController = StreamController<Todo>();
```

```
final _todoUpdateController = StreamController<Todo>();
final _todoDeleteController = StreamController<Todo>();
```

4. Creating the getters for streams and sinks

Now, let's create the Stream getters. In our data flow, we'll use the sink property to add data and the stream property to get data:

```
Stream<List<Todo>> get todos => _todosStreamController.stream;
StreamSink<List<Todo>> get todosSink => _todosStreamController.sink;
StreamSink<Todo> get todoInsertSink => _todoInsertController.sink;
StreamSink<Todo> get todoUpdateSink => _todoUpdateController.sink;
StreamSink<Todo> get todoDeleteSink => _todoDeleteController.sink;
```

5. Adding the logic of the BLoC

Next, still in the TodoBloc class, create the functions needed to implement the stream of data, starting with the method that will get the todos from the sembast database. The getTodos() returns a Future, and will await the result of db.Todos before updating the todos list:

```
Future getTodos() async {
    List<Todo> todos =  await db.getTodos();
    todoList = todos;
    todosSink.add(todos);
}
```

Also, create a function that just returns the todos list, calling it returnTodos:

```
List<Todo> returnTodos (todos) {
return todos;
}
```

Finally, create the three methods needed to call the database methods to delete, update, and add a Todo. After calling each database function, call the getTodos() method to update the stream of data:

```
void _deleteTodo(Todo todo) {
    db.deleteTodo(todo).then((result){
        getTodos();
    });
}
void _updateTodo(Todo todo) {
    db.updateTodo(todo).then((result){
      getTodos();
    });
```

```
}
void _addTodo(Todo todo)  {
    db.insertTodo(todo).then((result) {
        getTodos();
});
});
```

6. Creating the constructor

The next step is to add a constructor to the `TodoBloc` class:

```
TodoBloc() {}
```

In the constructor, call the instance of the `TodoDb` class and then call the `getTodos()` method:

```
db = TodoDb();
getTodos();
```

Next, still in the constructor, listen to the changes for each of the methods that we have created:

```
//listen to changes:
_todosStreamController.stream.listen(returnTodos);
_todoInsertController.stream.listen(_addTodo);
_todoUpdateController.stream.listen(_updateTodo);
_todoDeleteController.stream.listen(_deleteTodo);
```

7. Setting the dispose() method

As the last step for this class, add a `dispose()` method, in which you'll close the four `StreamController` objects. This may prevent memory leaks and errors that are difficult to debug:

```
//in the dispose method we need to close the stream controllers.
void dispose() {
_todosStreamController.close();
_todoInsertController.close();
_todoUpdateController.close();
_todoDeleteController.close();
}
```

The BLoC is now complete. The last step required is to implement the user interface in a way that will use the BLoC pattern to deal with the state in our app.

Using BLoCs and Streams to update the UI

All of the plumbing of the app is now complete. We just need to add the user interface in order to interact with the BLoC and show data to the user.

The main screen of the app will contain the list of `todos` in a ListView. The screen will look similar to the following image:

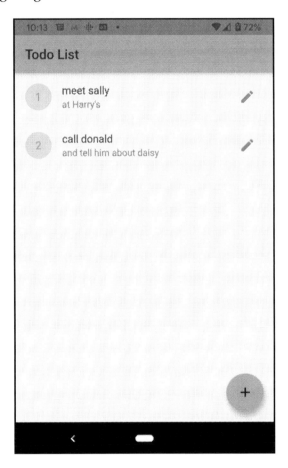

In this section, we will complete the remaining steps required to interact with a BLoC from the user interface:

1. We'll create an instance of the BLoC.
2. Then we'll include the UI in the `StreamBuilder`, which is the object you use when showing a stream.
3. Next, we'll add events to the `sink` for the changes to the data.
4. Finally, we'll override the `dispose()` method and, from there, call the `dispose()` method of the BLoC in order to prevent memory leaks, which are very difficult to debug; that's also why a Stateful widget is recommended, even though you don't need to use the `setState()` method.

The HomePage screen user interface

The HomePage screen will read data from the BLoC and show a `ListView` containing the `Todo` objects to the user. From this screen, the user will also write to the BLoC by deleting an object when they swipe an element from the `ListView`:

1. In the `main.dart` file, edit the imports so that they contain a reference to the `todo_bloc.dart` file and a file that we will add shortly called `todo_screen.dart`. Remove all other imports:

   ```
   import 'package:flutter/material.dart';
   import 'todo_screen.dart';
   import 'data/todo.dart';
   import 'bloc/todo_bloc.dart';
   ```

2. At the beginning of the `_HomePageState` class, create a field for the `TodoBloc` and one for the `List` of `Todo` that will be shown on the screen, and remove the preexisting code:

   ```
   class HomePage extends StatefulWidget {
     @override
     _HomePageState createState() => _HomePageState();
   }

   class _HomePageState extends State<HomePage> {
     TodoBloc todoBloc;
     List<Todo> todos;
   }
   ```

3. Override the `initState()` method and inside the function, let's set the `todoBloc` field to be an instance of the `TodoBLoc` class. *This creates an instance of the BLoC:*

```
@override
  void initState() {
    todoBloc = TodoBloc();
    super.initState();
  }
```

4. Also override the `dispose()` method so we don't forget to do it later. Here, we'll just call the `dispose()` method of the `todoBloc` object:

```
@override
void dispose() {
    todoBloc.dispose();
    super.dispose();
}
```

5. In the `build()` method, add the code to create a new empty `todo` and to populate the list of `Todo` objects that we called todos. The `todoList` property of the BLoC contains the objects retrieved from the database:

```
@override
Widget build(BuildContext context) {
  Todo todo = Todo('', '', '', 0);
  todos = todoBloc.todoList;
}
```

6. Then, still in the `build()` method, return a `Scaffold` whose `AppBar` will have a title of `'Todo List'`, and a body with a `Container`:

```
return Scaffold(
    appBar: AppBar(
        title: Text('Todo List'),
    ),
    body: Container()
);
```

Finally, after building all the plumbing for our app, we can use the `Streambuilder` widget. This will listen to the events from the `Stream` and will rebuild all its descendants, using the latest data in the Stream. You can connect it to the Streams through the `stream` property and a `builder` that contains the UI that needs to be updated. We can also set the `initialData` property to make sure we control what is shown at the beginning before we receive any event.

7. In the `Container`, add a `Streambuilder` as a child that connects to the `todos` Stream of the `todoBloc` instance, and has the `todos` list as the initial data: as you might remember, you *use a StreamBuilder to build the widgets that will use the BLoC data*:

```
child: StreamBuilder<List<Todo>>(
  stream: todoBloc.todos,
  initialData: todos,
)
```

8. Then set the `builder` method, which takes the context, and the snapshot, which contains the data received from the Stream:

```
builder: (BuildContext context, AsyncSnapshot snapshot) {}
```

9. Inside the `builder` method of the `StreamBuilder`, add a `ListView.builder`. For the `itemCount` parameter, we'll use a ternary operator. If the `snapshot.hasData` property is `true`, we'll use the length of the data contained in the snapshot; otherwise, we'll use 0. Then we'll set an empty `itembuilder` for the `ListView`:

```
return ListView.builder(
    itemCount: (snapshot.hasData) ? snapshot.data.length :  0,
    itemBuilder: (context, index) {}
);
```

10. In the `builder` function of the `ListView`, return a `Dismissible` so that the user will be able to swipe on the item and delete the `Todo` from the sembast database. This will happen by the app calling the `todoDeleteSink` and adding the `Todo` at the `index` position. This is step 10 of the BLoC guideline in the previous section:

```
return Dismissible(
    key: Key(snapshot.data[index].id.toString()),
    onDismissed: (_) =>
    todoBloc.todoDeleteSink.add(snapshot.data[index])
);
```

11. The child of the `Dismissible` widget is a `ListTile` that shows the priority in a `CircleAvatar`, then the name of the `Todo` as `title`, and the description as `subtitle`. Add the following code to set the `ListTile` in the `Dismissible` widget:

```
child: ListTile(
    leading: CircleAvatar(
        backgroundColor: Theme.of(context).highlightColor,
        child: Text("${snapshot.data[index].priority}"),
    ),
    title: Text("${snapshot.data[index].name}"),
    subtitle: Text("${snapshot.data[index].description}"),
)
```

Still inside the `ListTile`, we'll add a `trailing` icon. When the user presses the icon, the app will bring them to the second screen of the app, which shows the todo detail and allows the user to edit and save the todo that they selected. As this is for editing, we'll choose the `Icons.edit` icon, and in the `onPressed` function, we'll use the `Navigator.push()` method to navigate to the `TodoScreen` that we'll create right after completing this screen. We'll pass to the to-be-created screen the todo that was selected and a Boolean (`false`) that tells the screen that this is not a new todo, but an existing one.

12. Add the following code to create a trailing `IconButton` and navigate to the second screen of the app:

```
trailing: IconButton(
    icon: Icon(Icons.edit),
    onPressed: () {
        Navigator.push(
            context,
            MaterialPageRoute(
                builder: (context) => TodoScreen(
                    snapshot.data[index], false)),
        );
    },
),
```

13. In the `Scaffold`, under the `appBar`, set a `FloatingActionButton` that the user will press to create a new `Todo`. This will also navigate to the second screen of the app, but this time the boolean value that is passed is `true`, as this is a new todo.

14. Add the following code in the `Scaffold` to add the `FloatingActionButon`:

```
floatingActionButton: FloatingActionButton(
    child: Icon(Icons.add),
    onPressed: () {
        Navigator.push(
            context,
            MaterialPageRoute(builder: (context) =>
            TodoScreen(todo, true)),
        );
    },
),
```

Now that the HomePage screen is ready, let's add the TodoScreen next.

The TodoScreen user interface

The last part of the app we need to create is the todo detail screen, which will allow the user to view, edit, or add a todo in the sembast database:

1. In the `Lib` folder, add a new file called `todo_screen.dart`. At the top of the file, add the required imports:

```
import 'package:flutter/material.dart';
import 'bloc/todo_bloc.dart';
import 'data/todo.dart';
import 'main.dart';
```

2. Next, add a stateless widget and call it `TodoScreen`:

```
class TodoScreen extends StatelessWidget {
  @override
  Widget build(BuildContext context) {
    return Container(
    );
  }
}
```

3. At the top of the class, declare a few final variables: one for the `Todo` object that will be shown and edited by the user, a Boolean that will tell whether the todo is a new or existing one, and the `TextEditingController` for the `TextField` widgets we'll put in the screen:

```
final Todo todo;
final bool isNew;
```

```
final TextEditingController txtName = TextEditingController();
final TextEditingController txtDescription =
TextEditingController();
final TextEditingController txtCompleteBy =
TextEditingController();
final TextEditingController txtPriority = TextEditingController();
```

4. Add a `TodoBloc`, called `bloc`, and create a constructor that will set the `Todo` with the one that is passed and the boolean variable to decide whether the `Todo` is new.

5. Inside the constructor, create an instance of the `TodoBloc` class:

```
final TodoBloc bloc;
TodoScreen(this.todo, this.isNew) : bloc = TodoBloc();
```

The part after the colon in the TodoScreen constructor is an initializer list, a comma-separated list that you can use to initialize final fields with calculated expressions.

Inside this screen, we only need one method—`save()`—that will be called when the user presses the **Save** button on the screen. The purpose of this method is to read the data in the form and use the BLoC to update the events of the stream. If the `Todo` object is new, it will call the `add()` method of the `todoInsertSink` in the BLoC; otherwise, it will call the same method in the `todoUpdateSink`.

6. Add the following code to create the `save()` method:

```
Future save() async {
    todo.name=txtName.text;
    todo.description = txtDescription.text;
    todo.completeBy = txtCompleteBy.text;
    todo.priority = int.tryParse(txtPriority.text);
    if (isNew) {
      bloc.todoInsertSink.add(todo);
    }
    else {
        bloc.todoUpdateSink.add(todo);
    }
  }
```

7. At the top of the `build()` method, we'll set the content of the `TextField` widgets based on the value of the `Todo` object that was passed, and create a constant to add some spacing between the widgets:

```
final double padding = 20.0;
txtName.text = todo.name;
txtDescription.text = todo.description;
txtCompleteBy.text = todo.completeBy;
txtPriority.text = todo.priority.toString();
```

8. Return a `Scaffold` whose `appBar` contains a `Text` with `'Todo Details'` and whose `body` contains a `SingleChildScrollView` to prevent the widget from taking up more than the available space:

```
return Scaffold(
      appBar: AppBar(
        title: Text('Todo Details'),
      ),
      body: SingleChildScrollView()
  )
```

9. As a child of the `SingleChildScrollView`, place a `Column` whose children will contain the `TextFields` for the `Todo`: in order to create some space between the form widgets, each `TextField` will be included in a `Padding` widget. The first `TextField` will be for the name property of the todo, and, to help the user, we'll also add a `hintText` of `'Name'`:

```
body: SingleChildScrollView(
        child: Column(
          children: <Widget>[
            Padding(
              padding: EdgeInsets.all(padding),
              child: TextField(
                controller: txtName,
                decoration: InputDecoration(
                  border: InputBorder.none,
                  hintText: 'Name'
                ),
            )),
```

10. The second `TextField` widget in the `Column` is for the description of the `Todo`, with a `hintText` of `'Description'`:

```
Padding(
    padding: EdgeInsets.all(padding),
    child: TextField(
      controller: txtDescription,
      decoration: InputDecoration(
        border: InputBorder.none,
          hintText: 'Description'
      ),
)),
```

11. Under the description, put another `TextField`, this time for the `'Complete by'` field, setting the `hintText` accordingly:

```
Padding(
      padding: EdgeInsets.all(padding),
      child: TextField(
        controller: txtCompleteBy,
        decoration: InputDecoration(
          border: InputBorder.none,
          hintText: 'Complete by'
        ),
    )),
```

12. The last `TextField` is for the priority. As this is a number, we can set the `keyboardType` to `numeric`:

```
Padding(
    padding: EdgeInsets.all(padding),
    child: TextField(
      controller: txtPriority,
      keyboardType: TextInputType.number,
      decoration: InputDecoration(
        border: InputBorder.none,
        hintText: 'Priority',
      ),
)),
```

13. The last widget of this screen is the **Save** MaterialButton. When pressed, it will call the save() asynchronous method, and, when this completes its execution, the user will get back to the home screen. In this case, instead of using a simple push() method on the navigator, we can use a pushAndRemoveUntil() that will delete the navigation stack, which means it doesn't have to show the back button from the home screen:

```
Padding(
    padding: EdgeInsets.all(padding),
    child: MaterialButton(
        color: Colors.green,
        child: Text('Save'),
        onPressed: () {
            save().then((_)=> Navigator.pushAndRemoveUntil(
                context,
                MaterialPageRoute(builder: (context) => HomePage()),
                    (Route<dynamic> route) => false,
                ));
        },
    )),
```

This completes this chapter's project. You are now ready to try the app and start adding, editing, and deleting items from the sembast database using the BLoC pattern.

Summary

The main point of working on the project that you've built in this chapter isn't the app features themselves—you could create a todo app in much simpler ways. The focus here is the architecture that you've seen in action: using an asynchronous stream of data to update the state of an app is a pattern that can help you scale your projects to enterprise levels.

At the beginning of this chapter, you saw how to use the simple embedded application store database, or sembast, a document-based database that resides in a single file where data is stored in JSON format.

In sembast, a DatabaseFactory allows you to open a database where each database is a file and stores are locations in the database where you can save and retrieve data.

To insert a new item in a sembast database, you need to call the add() method over the store, passing the database and the map of the object you want to insert. A finder is a helper for filtering and ordering data into a given store.

To delete an existing item, you call the `delete()` method on the store: this takes the database and a finder as parameters.

To update an existing item, you call the `update()` method on the store: this takes the database, a map of the updated object, and the finder. To retrieve data, you use a finder and the `find()` method.

Next, you saw how to leverage the BLoC pattern to manage the state of your apps.

When using a BLoC, everything is a stream of events: the BLoC receives streams of events/data from the source, handles any required business logic, and publishes streams of data. A BLoC has two components: Sinks and Streams, both of which are part of a StreamController.

In order to use the Stream and be notified when something comes out of it, you need to listen to the Stream. Therefore, you define a listener with a `StreamSubscription` object that is notified every time an event related to the Stream is triggered.

The `StreamBuilder` widget listens to the events from the Stream and rebuilds its descendants, using the latest data in the Stream.

In the next chapter, you'll see how you can create responsive web apps with Flutter.

Questions

Please try to answer the following questions. When in doubt, have a look at the content in the chapter itself: you'll find all the answers there!

1. When would you prefer to use sembast over SQLite in an app?
2. How can you retrieve all the documents from a store in a sembast database?
3. How can you delete all the documents from a store in a sembast database?
4. How would you complete the following method to update an existing object in a sembast database?

```
Future updateTodo(Todo todo) async {
    //add your code here
}
```

5. What are the main differences between Futures and Streams?
6. When would you use the BLoC pattern in an app?
7. In a StreamController, what are the purposes of `stream` and `sink`?
8. Which is the object that allows you to listen to the events from the Stream and rebuild all its descendants?
9. How do you listen to changes in a Stream?
10. Why would you use a stateful widget when dealing with BLoCs, even though you never called the `setState()` method?

Further reading

The BLoC pattern is the recommended state-management pattern at this time, but you have other choices when using Flutter: the different options for maintaining a state in Flutter are explained in the official documentation at `https://flutter.dev/docs/development/data-and-backend/state-mgmt/options`.

In particular, you should be aware of the following :

- **Inherited Widget**: This propagates data to its child widgets: `https://api.flutter.dev/flutter/widgets/InheritedWidget-class.html`.
- **Scoped Model**: A package to simplify state management: `https://pub.dev/packages/scoped_model`.
- **Redux:** Another package that is great if you've used React: `https://pub.dev/packages/flutter_redux`.

As with state management, there are several tools to choose from when persisting data in Flutter. For a list of your options, have a look at the official documentation at `https://flutter.dev/docs/cookbook/persistence`.

Working with Streams may be challenging at first: to fully understand the main concepts of using Streams in Dart, check out the great tutorial at `https://dart.dev/tutorials/language/streams`.

11
Building a Flutter Web App

The dream of being able to create universal apps is not new, but today, the challenge of creating an app that can run on several form factors is even more urgent. Just think of the many devices people use every day: smartphones, tablets, smartwatches, notebooks, smart TVs, gaming consoles, and desktop PCs. These are all clients where we, as developers, could potentially install our software.

Flutter has been supporting iOS and Android since the beginning, which already solves a huge need for developers, but it's taking huge steps in the direction of the dream of every developer: having a truly universal platform to develop apps that can run anywhere.

The Flutter implementation for the web was presented at Flutter Interact 2019 and is called **Flutter for Web**.

At the time I'm writing this, Flutter supports web development in the **beta channel** of Flutter and desktop development for macOS in its **alpha channel**. In this chapter, we'll be focusing on web development with Flutter, but the same design principles apply to desktops as well.

The following topics will be covered in this chapter:

- Building a Flutter app that runs on a browser
- Creating a responsive **user interface** (UI)
- Using `shared_preferences` to save data in Android, iOS, and the web
- Publishing a Flutter app to a web server

Technical requirements

You'll find the complete app code on the book's GitHub repository at `https://github.com/PacktPublishing/Flutter-Projects`.

To follow along with the code examples in this book, you should have the following software installed on your Windows, Mac, Linux, or Chrome OS device:

- The Flutter **software development kit (SDK)**.
- When developing for Android: the Android SDK, easily installed by Android Studio.
- When developing for iOS: macOS and Xcode.
- An emulator (Android), a simulator (iOS), or a connected iOS or Android device enabled for debugging.
- An editor: **Visual Studio Code (VS Code)**, Android Studio, or IntelliJ IDEA are recommended. All should have the Flutter/Dart extensions installed.
- For this chapter, you should also have a Chrome browser installed on your computer.

Essential theory and context

You already know how to build mobile apps with Flutter, and, therefore, you also already know how to build beautiful, engaging, interactive web sites, as the principles for developing web apps with Flutter for the web are mostly the same. You still use Dart, widgets, libraries, and manage the state of your apps in the same way. There are some features still missing, such as hot reload, and some web-specific limitations, such as writing files on a disk, but you'll find that most of the great reasons for using Flutter are also valid for the web.

Using **Flutter for Web** actually has several advantages: it's easy to deploy, it allows you to quickly iterate on your applications, and—most important—it allows you to use the same code base for both mobile and web platforms.

Browsers today only support HTML, JavaScript, and CSS. With Flutter for Web, your code gets compiled in those languages, and therefore you don't need any browser plugin, nor any specific web server.

On Flutter version 1.14, web support is available on the beta channel, and the **Chrome** browser is required to debug your Flutter apps.

Another great addition to Flutter for Web is the use of plugins. There are already several libraries that also support Flutter for Web. The updated list is available on the following page: `https://pub.dev/flutter/packages?platform=web`.

In the project in this chapter, we will be using the `shared_preferences` library that works on iOS, Android, and the web.

Project overview

The app we will build in this chapter contains two pages. On the home page, the user will see a text field to search for books. After pressing the search button, if books are found, they will see a list of books, with their title and description. For each list, there will be a button that will allow the user to add a book to their favorites. The favorite books will be saved locally.

One of the challenges in having to deal with different form factors is the way you use the space on the screen. So, we will add a small tweak to the app. If the screen is "small", such as in a smartphone, the user will see ListView; otherwise, they will see a table.

Here, you can see a screenshot of the first page for larger screens, containing a table:

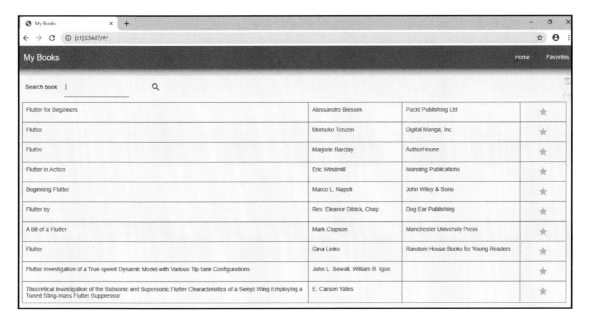

Here, you can see a screenshot of the first page for smaller screens. This is a `ListView` with `ListTiles`. Notice that the `appBar` shows icons to change the routes, instead of full text:

The second screen of the app will be the **Favorite Books** page. This will list all the books marked as favorites. Here, the user will be able to remove a book from their favorites.

Again, the controls used for the app will change based on the size of the screen. Here, you can see a screenshot of the larger screen:

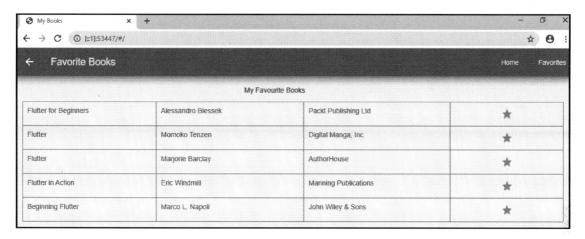

And here is, a screenshot of the smaller version of the same screen:

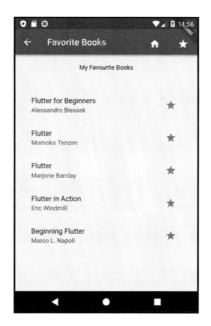

The build time for this project is approximately 2.5 hours.

Building a Flutter app that runs on a browser

Let's summarize the requirements for this app, as follows:

1. The app must work for iOS, Android, and the web.
2. The favorite books need to be saved locally.
3. Depending on the screen size, we will show the user a different layout.

As of Flutter version 1.14, web development for Flutter is available in the beta channel, and you need to set up the environment to explicitly enable web support. However, please check if this is still true when you read this information on the official documentation page at `https://flutter.dev/web`.

The `cli` commands required to add web support to your environment are detailed as follows:

1. Open your Terminal/command prompt and type the following commands to enable the beta channel and web development:

   ```
   flutter channel beta
   flutter config --enable-web
   ```

2. Run the `flutter devices` command, as follows:

   ```
   flutter devices
   ```

   If the web is enabled, you should see a Chrome device, as shown here:

```
Select Command Prompt

C:\>flutter devices
2 connected devices:

Chrome      • chrome      • web-javascript • Google Chrome 79.0.3945.130
Web Server  • web-server  • web-javascript • Flutter Tools

C:\>_
```

3. Create a new Flutter app with your favorite editor, and then move to the folder where you saved the new project.

4. Next, run the app specifying the Chrome browser as a device, as follows:

```
flutter run -d chrome
```

This will open the Chrome browser with your Flutter app, and a local web server serving the app. Maybe for the first time since you started reading this book, you'll see the Flutter example app running in Chrome, as shown here:

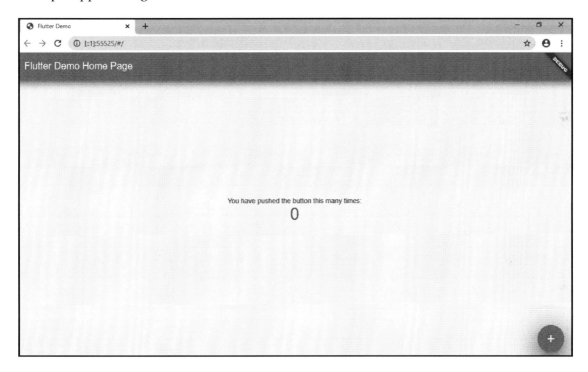

The thing that should be obvious the first time you see the example app in your browser is the impressive amount of space you have to deal with. This is one of the challenges you must consider when you design an app that can run both on mobile devices and on the web (or desktop). In this chapter, we'll see a few suggestions that may help you make responsive apps that allow different form factors.

Connecting to the Google Books API web service

In order to enable searching for books in our app, we'll connect to the Google Books API. This is an incredible web service. Its purpose is to share information about most of the books ever published, anywhere in the world. By leveraging the Google Books API service, the web app you'll build in this chapter will contain the data of millions of books.

In order to get the information we need, we have to reach the Google API through a **Uniform Resource Locator** (**URL**). This URL is made of several parts, described here:

- The scheme: HTTPS, in this case.
- The authority: www.googleapis.com.
- The path that is specific for the books API: books/v1/volumes.
- The query string: a question mark, "q", an equals sign, and the title we are looking for—for example, ?q=flutter.

The full URL would be https://www.googleapis.com/books/v1/volumes?q=flutter.

If you put this URL in a browser, you'll see that indeed, we are connecting to the Google Books API and receiving data in the JSON format. Here, you can see a screenshot of the JSON data retrieved from the service:

As with most web services, the Google Books API takes a key to connect to the web service. To obtain a key to be added to the service, have a look at the `https://developers.google.com/books/docs/v1/using#APIKey` page.

> When you get the API key, make sure you enable the API key for the **Books API**.

The data you see in the browser is what we are going to put into the first page of our web app. From the `items` node that contains an array of volumes, we'll only get the fields we need: the ID, the title from the `volumeInfo` node, the authors, and the description.

> We won't get into the details of parsing JSON data here. For a refresher on connecting to a web service and using JSON, have a look at Chapter 5, *Let's Go to the Movies - Getting Data from the Web*.

In the next section, we'll create the model class from the parsed JSON.

Creating the Book model class

Let's create a model class, with a selection of the JSON data retrieved from the Google Books API that will serve as the content for our app, as follows:

1. In the `lib` folder of the app, create a new directory called `data`.
2. Inside the directory, add a new file called `book.dart`. This will contain the `Book` class that we will use as a model in our app, as shown in the following code snippet:

   ```
   class Book {}
   ```

3. Add to the `Book` class the properties that we will need in our app: `id`, `title`, `authors`, `description`, and `publisher`, as follows:

   ```
   String id;
   String title;
   String authors;
   String description;
   String publisher;
   ```

   The authors are returned as an array in the JSON retrieved from the Google Books API, but we'll treat them as a simple string.

4. Create the constructor that will set all the fields upon creating the class, like this:

```
Book(this.id, this.title, this.authors, this.description, this.publis
her);
```

We also need a named constructor that takes a map and returns a Book. This will be useful when parsing the JSON data and transforming it into a list of Book objects.

5. Add the following code to create the `fromJson` named constructor:

```
factory Book.fromJson(Map<String, dynamic> parsedJson) {
  final String id = parsedJson['id'];
  final String title = parsedJson['volumeInfo']['title'];
  String authors = (parsedJson['volumeInfo']
    ['authors'] == null) ? '' : parsedJson[
    'volumeInfo']['authors'].toString();
  authors = authors.replaceAll('[', '');
  authors = authors.replaceAll(']', '');
  final String description = (parsedJson['volumeInfo']['description']
    ==null) ? '' : parsedJson['volumeInfo']['description'];
  final String publisher = (parsedJson['volumeInfo']
    ['publisher'] == null) ? '':
    parsedJson['volumeInfo']['publisher'];
  return Book(
   id,
   title,
   authors,
   description,
   publisher,
  );
}
```

In the code, note that, for the `authors`, we transform the JSON array into a String using the `toString()` method, and then we remove the square brackets using the `replaceAll()` method. We use the ternary operator several times to prevent errors, by checking whether a value is `null`. At the end of the constructor, we return a Book by calling the default constructor.

In order to complete the `Book` class, we need to create the `toJson()` method that returns the values of the class instance in JSON format, as shown in the following code block:

```
Map <String, dynamic> toJson() {
  return {
    'id': id,
    'title': title,
    'authors': authors,
```

```
'description': description,
'publisher': publisher
};
}
```

Now that we have created a model class, let's understand how we can retrieve books using the HTTP service.

Using the HTTP service to retrieve books

Our app will need to connect to the service through HTTP, so the first step we need to perform is adding the latest version of the `http` package in the `pubspec.yaml` file. As we are editing this file, let's also add support for `shared_preferences`, which we'll use later in the chapter. As usual, please make sure you check the latest version on the `https://pub.dev` website.

In the `dependencies` node of `pubspec.yaml`, add the support for HTTP and `shared_preferences`, as follows:

```
http: ^0.12.0+4
shared_preferences: ^0.5.6+1
```

In the `lib/data` folder of our app, let's create a new file called `books_helper.dart` that will contain the class that builds the queries to the Google Books API.

> For a refresher on how to connect to a web service and work with JSON, have a look at `Chapter 5`, *Let's Go to the Movies - Getting Data from the Web* in the *Connecting to a web service and retrieving data with HTTP* section.

In the file, we'll need the `http` package for the connection, the `dart:convert` package, to decode the JSON data, the `dart:async` library to use asynchronous methods, `material.dart` for the navigation, `shared_preferences` to save data locally (more on that later), and, of course, the `Book` class.

Let's start building the `books_helper.dart` file, as follows:

1. Add the following code to add the required imports:

   ```
   import 'package:http/http.dart' as http;
   import 'package:flutter/material.dart';
   import 'dart:convert';
   import 'dart:async';
   import 'package:http/http.dart';
   ```

```
import 'package:shared_preferences/shared_preferences.dart';
import 'book.dart';
```

2. Still in the `bookshelper.dart` file, create a class called `BooksHelper`, like this:

```
class BooksHelper { }
```

3. Inside the `BooksHelper` class, create a few constants to build the URL of the query. `urlKey` will contain your Google Books API key, `urlQuery` contains the user query, and `urlBase` is the fixed part to retrieve information from the web service, as shown in the following code snippet:

```
final String urlKey = '&key=[ADD YOUR KEY HERE]';
final String urlQuery = 'volumes?q=';
final String urlBase = 'https://www.googleapis.com/books/v1/';
```

4. Now, create a new method called `getBooks()`. This will take a String containing the books the user is looking for and will return a `Future` for a `List` of dynamic items, as follows:

```
Future<List<dynamic>> getBooks(String query) async { }
```

5. In the `getBooks()` method, create the full `url` containing the query and the key, like this:

```
final String url = urlBase + urlQuery + query + urlKey;
```

6. Once the `url` String is ready, we can leverage the `http` library to call the `get()` method that will retrieve the `books` data. This is asynchronous and returns a `Response` object, so here, we'll use the `await` statement to get the result, like this:

```
Response result = await http.get(url);
```

7. If the status of the response is successful (`statusCode` 200), we'll decode the body of the result into a variable called `jsonResponse`. In particular, we need a node called `items` from the body, which contains the volume's information.

Once the `items` node is retrieved, just call the `map()` method over it, and for each volume in the `items` node, create a `Book` from the `json` object and then return a `List` of the books that were created.

8. If the status of the `Response` is not successful, then this method returns `null`. Add the following code in the `getBooks()` method to retrieve the data from the Google Books API:

```
    if (result.statusCode == 200) {
     final jsonResponse = json.decode(result.body);
     final booksMap = jsonResponse['items'];
     List<dynamic> books = booksMap.map((i) => Book.fromJson(i)).toList(
);
      return books;
    }
    else {
      return null;
    }
```

Now that we have written the method to search books from the Google Books API, let's add a **user interface** (**UI**) so that we can show some results to our user!

Creating a responsive UI

On the home page of our app, we want to show the user a text field to search for any book from the Google Books API library. The results will be shown under the search box, and the appearance of the results will depend on the screen. From here, the user will be able to add a book to their favorites. Let's look at the steps, as follows:

1. Replace the default example code in the main.dart file with the following:

```
import 'package:flutter/material.dart';
import './data/bookshelper.dart';

void main() => runApp(MyApp());

class MyApp extends StatelessWidget {
 @override
 Widget build(BuildContext context) {
  return MaterialApp(
   title: 'My Books',
   theme: ThemeData(
    primarySwatch: Colors.blueGrey,
   ),
   home: MyHomePage(),
  ); } }
```

Please note that in the preceding code, we have imported the `bookshelper.dart` file and changed the theme colors and the title for the `MateriaLApp`.

2. Next, create a `StatefulWidget` called `MyHomePage`, using the `stful` shortcut. It will generate the following code:

```
class MyHomePage extends StatefulWidget {
  @override
  _MyHomePageState createState() => _MyHomePageState();
}

class _MyHomePageState extends State<MyHomePage> {
 @override
 Widget build(BuildContext context) {
  return Container( );
} }
```

3. In the `_MyHomePageState` class, create a few fields. The first one is an instance of the `BooksHelper` class, then one for the `List` of books that will be shown on the screen, an `integer` for the number of books retrieved, and a `TextEditingController` for the search text field, as shown in the following code block:

```
BooksHelper helper;
List<dynamic> books = List<dynamic>();
int booksCount;
TextEditingController txtSearchController;
```

4. When this screen loads, we want to set the `BooksHelper` instance and the `txtSearchController` object, and then retrieve a `List` of books. For this last action, we'll create a new method called `initialize()`, as follows:

```
@override
 void initState() {
  helper = BooksHelper();
  txtSearchController = TextEditingController();
  initialize();
  super.initState();
 }
```

The `initialize()` method will be asynchronous and will return a `Future`. Inside the method, we'll call the `getBooks()` method from our `BooksHelper`.

For this example, we'll just retrieve the books containing "Flutter". In a real-world app, you would probably choose a smoother first screen, maybe guiding to a new search, but, for this project, this is totally adequate.

5. After retrieving the books, call the `setState()` method to update the `books` list and the `booksCount` fields. Add the following code at the end of the `_MyHomePageState` class:

```
Future initialize() async {
  books = await helper.getBooks('Flutter');
  setState(() {
   booksCount = books.length;
   books = books;
  });
}
```

Next, we'll update the `build()` method, and here, we'll add the first piece of code that will help us build a responsive app.

6. In the `build()` method, create a Boolean called `isSmall` and set it to `false`, as follows:

```
bool isSmall = false;
```

We'll consider a "small" screen to be every screen that has a width of less than 600 units. In order to retrieve the screen size, we'll use the `MediaQuery` widget.

 Flutter measures size with "logical pixels", which are basically the same as **device-independent pixels (dips)** for Android. This allows your apps to look roughly the same size on every device. For more information on the way logical pixels relate to physical pixels, have a look at the following page: `https://api.flutter.dev/flutter/dart-ui/Window/devicePixelRatio.html`.

7. Add the code to check whether the device is "small", as follows:

```
if (MediaQuery.of(context).size.width < 600) {
  isSmall = true;
}
```

As usual, we'll return a `Scaffold` here. The `Scaffold` will contain an `AppBar`, with the title of "`My Books`". Let's also add an `actions` array. From the actions of our user, we'll be able to change the page, and here, we'll add the first responsive widgets for this app.

8. Add the following code to return a `Scaffold` in the `build()` method:

```
return Scaffold(
    appBar: AppBar(
      title: Text('My Books'),
      actions: <Widget>[]
) );
```

In the actions of the `AppBar`, we'll add two `InkWell` widgets, which are simply rectangular areas that respond to touch (or click on desktops).

9. For the first `InkWell` widget child, add a `Padding`, with a `padding` of 20 on every side. The child of the `Padding` widget will depend on the size of the screen. On smaller screens, the user will see the home icon from the `Icons` enumerator. For larger screens, they will see a text with Home, as follows:

```
InkWell(
    child: Padding(
        padding: EdgeInsets.all(20.0),
        child: (isSmall) ? Icon(Icons.home) : Text('Home')),
),
```

10. The second `InkWell` will follow the same logic, but instead of showing the home icon, we'll show the star icon, and the text will be `'Favorites'`, as shown in the following code block:

```
InkWell(
    child: Padding(
        padding: EdgeInsets.all(20.0),
        child: (isSmall) ? Icon(Icons.star) : Text('Favorites')),
),
```

11. In the body of the `Scaffold`, place a `SingleChildScrollView` to prevent the content of the screen overflowing the available space. Its child will be a `Column`, as shown in the following code snippet:

```
body: SingleChildScrollView(
    child: Column(children: [ ]),
```

12. The first widget in the `Column` is a `Padding` so that the small form allowing the user to search for a book will have 20 logical pixels of space in all directions. The child of the `Padding` will be a `Row`, as shown in the following code snippet:

```
Padding(
    padding: EdgeInsets.all(20),
    child: Row(children: []),
)
```

13. In the `Row`, put a `Text` containing a `'Search book'` string, as follows:

```
Text('Search book'),
```

14. Still in the `Row`, add a `Container` with the same 20 logical pixels `padding` and a width of 200. Its child will be a `TextField`, as shown in the following code snippet:

```
Container(
    padding: EdgeInsets.all(20),
    width: 200,
    child: TextField()
)
```

15. Now, we need to set the `TextField`. Its controller will be the `txtSearchController` that we created at the top of the class. For mobile devices that have a virtual keyboard, the `keyboardType` will be of type `text`, and the `textInputAction` will be of type `search`, as shown in the following code snippet:

```
controller: txtSearchController,
keyboardType: TextInputType.text,
textInputAction: TextInputAction.search,
```

Still, only for virtual keyboards, we want to submit the search query when the user clicks on the search button.

16. Add an `onSubmitted()` method that will call the helper `getBooks()` asynchronous method, and when the value of the query returns, call the `setState()` method to update the `books List`, as follows:

```
onSubmitted: (text) {
    helper.getBooks(text).then((value) {
        setState(() {
            books = value;
        });
    });
},
```

17. The last widget in the `Row` will be a search icon button, necessary for all devices that have no virtual keyboards, but visible in all devices. Enclose it into another `Padding` of 20, like this:

```
Container(
    padding: EdgeInsets.all(20),
    child: IconButton(
        icon: Icon(Icons.search),
            onPressed: () =>
                helper.getBooks(txtSearchController.text)
)),
```

18. Now, the `Row` contains the `Search Text`, `TextField`, and `IconButton`. Under this `Row`, we'll need to place the actual result of the query. For now, just add a `Padding` in the column, with a child that will be an empty `Container`, as follows:

```
Padding(
    padding: EdgeInsets.all(20),
    child: Container(),
),
```

The child of the padding should contain the list of `Books` that we retrieved using the `helper.getBooks()` method. And that's exactly what we'll do in the next section.

Responsive widgets: ListView or Table?

The home page (or main screen) of our app will contain a list of volumes. In previous projects in this book, whenever we had a list of data to show to our users, we used the `ListView` widget with vertical scrolling. This is ideal on smartphones, where the height of the device is usually larger than its width, and the user takes for granted scrolling as the default way to view data.

On a notebook or a desktop, the width of the screen is generally larger than its height, and large amounts of data are generally placed in tables that leverage the available space, dividing several pieces of data into rows and columns. Things can only get more complicated when you think about tablets, with their various sizes, resolutions, and orientations.

So, the question is, where should we put our data: in a scrolling `ListView` or in a `Table`?

The answer is… both: if the screen is small, we'll show a `ListView`; otherwise, we'll show a `Table`.

Before we design the UI, there's also another issue. In our app, there are two pages: one to look for books, and another to show the favorites. If you think about it, both pages share the same kind of content: a list of books. What's different is the source of data (web or internal storage) and the actions the user can perform. On the home page, the user will be able to add a book to their favorites; on the favorites page, the opposite is true: they will be able to remove books from the favorites list. The origin of the books does not change the layout, but the action does.

What might work for us is trying to use the same layout for both pages, and only changing the action button in the table or list, and we'll do that next.

Creating the Table for larger devices

Let's begin by designing the table for larger devices, as follows:

1. Create a new file called `ui.dart`, and add two imports at the top of the file—one for the `material.dart` library and another for our `bookshelper.dart` file, as follows:

   ```
   import 'package:flutter/material.dart';
   import 'data/bookshelper.dart';
   ```

2. Next, create a stateless widget called `BooksTable`. When called, this class will take the list of books and a Boolean value specifying whether the caller is the home page or the favorites page (which we still have to create). It will also create an instance of the `BooksHelper` class. Add the following code to create the `BooksTable` stateless widget:

   ```
   class BooksTable extends StatelessWidget {
       final List<dynamic> books;
       final bool isFavorite;
   ```

```
BooksTable(this.books, this.isFavorite);
final BooksHelper helper = BooksHelper();

@override
Widget build(BuildContext context) {
    return Container( );
}
}
```

3. In the `build()` method, instead of returning a `Container`, we will return a `Table` that allows you to place your widgets in a grid. Using a `Table` is rather easy; you simply need to create a `Table` widget and add `TableRow` widgets to it.

   You can also decide the width for each `Column`. In this case, we will use the `FlexColumnWidth` widget to make sure each column takes a relative space in the `Table`. For example, if we create a `Table` with two columns, one with a width of `FlexColumnWidth(1)` and the second with a width of `FlexColumnWidth(2)`, the second column will take twice the space of the first one.

    You can also specify the width of table columns with absolute values. For more information, have a look at the official guide at `https://api.flutter.dev/flutter/widgets/Table-class.html`.

4. In our table, we want four columns: title, authors, publisher, and the action icon button. Add the following code to specify the relative size of each column:

```
return Table(
    columnWidths: {
        0: FlexColumnWidth(3),
        1: FlexColumnWidth(2),
        2: FlexColumnWidth(2),
        3: FlexColumnWidth(1),
    },
```

5. Another great feature of a `Table` widget is being able to specify a `border`. Add the following code to set the `border` for our Table:

```
border: TableBorder.all(color: Colors.blueGrey),
```

6. We are finally ready to put the contents of the table. We can do this using its `children` property. In this case, just call the `map()` method over the `books` list to iterate through the books, like this:

```
children:  books.map((book) {}
```

7. As we want to add some style to the text in the table, we'll create a stateless widget called `TableText` that will take the string we want to show to the user, and will add some style and padding to each value of the book we'll show in the table. Add the following code at the bottom of the `ui.dart` file:

```
class TableText extends StatelessWidget {
    final String text;
    TableText(this.text);

    @override
    Widget build(BuildContext context) {
        return Container(
            padding: EdgeInsets.all(10),
            child: Text(text,
              style: TextStyle(color:
                Theme.of(context).primaryColorDark),),
            );
        }
    }
```

In the `build()` method in the `BooksTable` class, in the `map()` method, we'll return a `TableRow`. Each row in a table must have the same number of children.

A `TableRow` contains one or more `TableCell` widgets, which are the single cells of the table. In each cell, we will place the values of the book passed in the `map()` method: title, authors, and publisher. The last column will contain an `IconButton`, which, depending on the `isFavourite` value, will allow the user to add or remove a book from their favorites. We haven't written the methods to save values locally, but we'll add them in the *Using shared_preferences to save data in Android, iOS, and the web* section, later in this chapter.

8. Add the following code to complete the `BooksTable` class:

```
books.map((book) {
    return TableRow(
        children: [
            TableCell(child:TableText(book.title)),
            TableCell(child:TableText(book.authors)),
            TableCell(child:TableText(book.publisher)),
            TableCell(
```

```
                    child: IconButton(
                        color: (isFavorite) ? Colors.red : Colors.amber,
                        tooltip: (isFavorite) ? 'Remove from favorites' :
                        'Add to favorites',
                        icon: Icon(Icons.star),
                        onPressed: () {}))
            ]);
        }).toList(),
```

The last step before trying the table layout is calling this class from the home page of our app.

9. Get back to the `main.dart` file, and in the last `Padding` in the `build()` method of the `_MyHomePageState` class, add the call to the `BooksTable` class, as follows:

```
Padding(
    padding: EdgeInsets.all(20),
    child:  BooksTable(books, false)
),
```

We are now ready to try the table in our Chrome browser. The final result should look similar to the following screenshot:

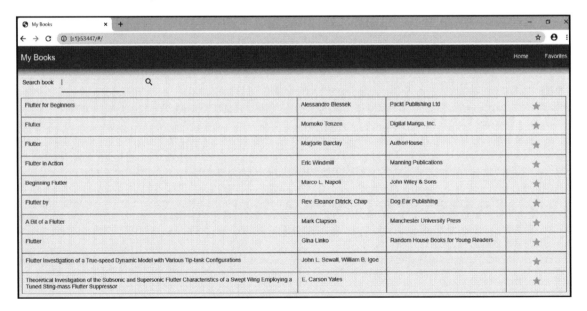

Next, let's design the layout for smaller devices.

Creating the ListView for smaller devices

While the `Table` layout is perfect for larger screens, the `ListView` is what we need for smaller devices. The logic of building a UI is very similar to that for a table. We'll just need to iterate through the list of books and show the values to our user, but instead of using `Table`, `TableRow`, and `TableCell` widgets, we'll use `ListView` and `ListTile` widgets. Let's look at the steps here:

1. In the `ui.dart` file, add another stateless widget called `BooksList`, and create a constructor that takes the `books` list and the `isFavorite` Boolean value. When called, this class will also create an instance of the `BooksHelper` class, as shown in the following code snippet:

```
class BooksList extends StatelessWidget {
    final List<dynamic> books;
    final bool isFavorite;
    BooksList(this.books, this.isFavorite);
    final BooksHelper helper = BooksHelper();

    @override
    Widget build(BuildContext context) {
        return Container(
    ); } }
```

2. In the `build()` method of the `BooksList`, create an integer variable that will contain the number of books, and in the `Container`, set the height to be the height of the screen divided by 1.4 (this will be approximately 60% of the screen height).

3. The child of the `Container` widget is a `ListView`. Call the `ListView.builder` constructor to create an instance of the `ListView`. For the `itemCount` parameter, use a ternary operator. If the `booksCount` variable is null, the `itemCount` will be 0; otherwise, it will take the value of `booksCount`, as shown in the following code block:

```
@override
Widget build(BuildContext context) {
    final int booksCount = books.length;
    return Container(
        height: MediaQuery.of(context).size.height /1.4,
        child: ListView.builder(
            itemCount: (booksCount==null) ? 0: booksCount,
            itemBuilder: (BuildContext context, int position) {}
} ));
```

4. In the `itemBuilder` parameter, return a `ListTile`. The title will take the book title, the subtitle, and the authors. Here, we'll skip the publisher, but, as trailing, add the add/remove favorite action, as shown in the following code block:

```
return ListTile(
    title: Text(books[position].title),
    subtitle: Text(books[position].authors),
    trailing: IconButton(
        color: (isFavorite) ? Colors.red : Colors.amber,
        tooltip: (isFavorite) ? 'Remove from favorites' :
          'Add to favorites',
        icon: Icon(Icons.star),
        onPressed: () {}
));
```

5. When the app is running on a smaller screen, we want to show the `BooksList` instead of the `BooksTable` widget. Get back to the `main.dart` file, in the last `Padding` in the `build()` method of the `_MyHomePageState` class, and edit the code, as shown here:

```
Padding(
    padding: EdgeInsets.all(20),
    child: (isSmall) ? BooksList(books, false) : BooksTable(books,
      false)),
```

You can now try the app on smaller screens. If you are using a browser, just reduce the width of the browser until you see the `ListView` appearing instead of the table. If you are trying it on a smartphone or simulator/emulator, you should already see the `ListView`.

And, with our first responsive layout in place, let's now get into locally saving the favorites data on our device... universally.

Using shared_preferences to save data in Android, iOS, and the web

The `shared_preferences` plugin allows simple data (key-value pairs) to be asynchronously persisted locally and is currently available for Android, iOS, and Flutter for Web.

This is possible because `shared_preferences` wraps different technologies based on the system on which it's run. In iOS, it leverages `NSUserDefaults`; in Android, it leverages `SharedPreferences`, and in the browser, it leverages the `window.localStorage` object. Basically, you have a universal way to save data and don't have to worry about duplicating any code for the different devices on which your app will be running.

> `shared_preferences` should not be used for critical data as data stored there is not encrypted, and writes are not always guaranteed. For sensitive or critical data, other technologies that we've used in previous chapters, such as `sembast` and the `Firestore` database, are already compatible with Flutter for Web.

At this time, there are already several libraries that also support Flutter for Web, but many of them don't. Things are changing very fast, and I wouldn't be surprised if, by the time you read this, most of the libraries that are not totally device-specific become available for the web (and for desktop).

> For an updated list of the libraries that currently support Flutter for Web, have a look at the following page: `https://pub.dev/flutter/packages?platform=web`.

Now, let's add the code to persist data into our app.

We'll use the existing `bookshelper.dart` file to add the methods to read and write to `shared_preferences`. We'll need three methods: one to add items to the favorites, one to remove them, and one to get the favorites list. We'll begin by adding favorites to `shared_preferences`, as follows:

1. In the `BooksHelper` class, add a new asynchronous method called `addToFavorites()`. This will take a `Book` object and return a `Future`. In the method, call an instance of `SharedPreferences` called `preferences`.

2. Next, we will check if the book already exists in the local storage: if it doesn't, call the setString() method of the preferences to add it to the store.

3. SharedPreferences only take simple data, so we need to transform the object into a string, and we can achieve this by calling the json.encode() method over the book, transformed in json format, as shown in the following code snippet:

```
Future addToFavorites(Book book) async {
    SharedPreferences preferences = await
SharedPreferences.getInstance();
    String id = preferences.getString(book.id);
    if (id != '') {
      await preferences.setString(book.id,
json.encode(book.toJson())));
    }
}
```

Next, we'll write the method to delete an existing book from the favorites list. This takes the book to be deleted, and the current BuildContext. This is to reload the FavoriteScreen so that it gets updated. It's probably not the most elegant solution, as we could use a different approach to keep the state of the app, but it's good enough for this example.

The method to remove data from SharedPreferences is called remove(), and only takes the key of the value to be deleted.

4. Add the following code to add the removeFromFavorites() method to the app:

```
Future removeFromFavorites(Book book, BuildContext context) async {
    SharedPreferences preferences = await
     SharedPreferences.getInstance();
    String id = preferences.getString(book.id);
    if (id != '') {
       await preferences.remove(book.id);
       Navigator.push(context, MaterialPageRoute(builder:
       (context)=> FavoriteScreen()));
    }
}
```

The last method we need to add in the BooksHelper class is the getFavorites() async method. This will return the list of books that we'll retrieve from SharedPreferences.

5. After creating an instance of `SharedPreferences` and creating the list that contains the books, use the `getKeys()` method to retrieve all the keys currently stored in `SharedPreferences`.

6. If the set of keys is not empty, for each key, retrieve the value at the current position, using the `get()` method of the instance of `SharedPreferences`. This will be a `String`, so after converting it to a `json`, create a `Book` from the `json`, and add it to the list of books.

7. Add the following code to complete the `getFavorites()` method:

```
Future<List<dynamic>> getFavorites() async {
// returns the favorite books or an empty list
    final SharedPreferences prefs = await
     SharedPreferences.getInstance();
    List<dynamic> favBooks = List<dynamic>();
    Set allKeys = prefs.getKeys();
    if (allKeys.isNotEmpty) {
       for(int i = 0; i < allKeys.length; i++) {
           String key = (allKeys.elementAt(i).toString());
           String value = prefs.get(key);
           dynamic json = jsonDecode(value);
           Book book = Book(json['id'], json['title'],
           json['authors'], json['description'],
           json['publisher']);
         favBooks.add(book);
       }
    }
    return favBooks;
}
```

Now that the methods to read and write data to the favorites in our app are ready, we need to call them from the UI. Let's do that in the next section.

Completing the UI of the app

On the home page of the app, we already have an `IconButton` that the user can press to add a book to their favorites. We only need to connect it to the `addFavorites()` method in the `BooksHelper` class to make it work. Let's look at the steps to do that here:

1. Get to the `ui.dart` file, and in the `BooksTable` class in the `build()` method, in the last `TableCell`, edit the `IconButton` so that in the `onPressed()` method, it can add (or remove) a book in the favorites list, as follows:

```
child: IconButton(
    color: (isFavorite) ? Colors.red : Colors.amber,
    tooltip: (isFavorite) ? 'Remove from favorites' :
    'Add to favorites',
    icon: Icon(Icons.star),
    onPressed: () {
        if (isFavorite) {
            helper.removeFromFavorites(book, context);
        } else {
            helper.addToFavorites(book);
        }
})))
```

2. We'll need to do the same in the `BookList` widget. In the trailing `IconButton` in the `build()` method, update the code so that it calls the `addToFavorites()` or `removeFromFavorites()` methods of the `BooksHelper` class, as follows:

```
trailing: IconButton(
    color: (isFavorite) ? Colors.red : Colors.amber,
    tooltip: (isFavorite) ? 'Remove from favorites' :
     'Add to favorites',
    icon: Icon(Icons.star),
    onPressed: () {
        if (isFavorite) {
        helper.removeFromFavorites(books[position], context);
        } else {
        helper.addToFavorites(books[position]);
} }),
```

The last step to complete the app is adding the second page of the app, the favorites screen, which can be done in the following way:

1. In the `lib` folder, add a new file called `favorite_screen.dart`.

2. At the top of the file, add the required imports, as follows:

```
import 'package:flutter/material.dart';
import 'ui.dart';
import 'data/books_helper.dart';
import 'main.dart';
```

3. Create a new stateful widget, called `FavoriteScreen`, like this:

```
class FavoriteScreen extends StatefulWidget {
@override
    _FavoriteScreenState createState() => _FavoriteScreenState();
}

class _FavoriteScreenState extends State<FavoriteScreen> {
@override
    Widget build(BuildContext context) {
        return Container();
}}
```

4. In the `_FavoriteScreenState` class, add a `BooksHelper` object and the properties that make the state—a list called `books` and an integer called `booksCount`, as follows:

```
BooksHelper helper;
List<dynamic> books = List<dynamic>();
int booksCount;
```

When this screen is called, it should load the favorite books currently stored in `SharedPreferences`.

5. Create a new asynchronous method called `initialize()` that will update the state of the screen, and, in particular, the `books` list and the `bookCount` property, as shown in the following code block:

```
Future initialize() async {
    books = await helper.getFavorites();
    setState(() {
        booksCount = books.length;
        books = books;
}); }
```

6. Override the `initState()` method, calling an instance of the `BooksHelper` class and calling the `initialize()` method that we've just created, like this:

```
@override
void initState() {
    helper = BooksHelper();
    initialize();
    super.initState();
}
```

The `build()` method will be very similar to the `build()` method in the `MyHomePage` class: it will share the same menu and will check whether the screen is small or large, and, depending on that, it will choose whether to show a `Table` or a `ListView` for the favorites. Note that the `isFavorite` parameter of the `BooksList` and `BooksTable` is set to `true` from now on.

7. The following snippet shows the code for the `build()` method of the Favorites screen. Add it to your project:

```
@override
Widget build(BuildContext context) {
    bool isSmall = false;
    if (MediaQuery.of(context).size.width < 600) {
      isSmall = true;
    }
    return Scaffold(
       appBar: AppBar(title: Text('Favorite Books'),
       actions: <Widget>[
          InkWell(
             child: Padding(
             padding: EdgeInsets.all(20.0),
             child: (isSmall) ? Icon(Icons.home) : Text('Home')),
             onTap: () {
                Navigator.push(context,
                MaterialPageRoute(builder: (context) =>
                MyHomePage())
          ); }, ),
          InkWell(
             child: Padding(
             padding: EdgeInsets.all(20.0),
             child:(isSmall) ? Icon(Icons.star) :
             Text('Favorites')),
       ) , ],),
         body: Column(children: <Widget>[
            Padding(
             padding: EdgeInsets.all(20),
             child: Text('My Favourite Books')
```

```
    ),
    Padding(
        padding: EdgeInsets.all(20),
        child: (isSmall) ? BooksList(books, true) :
        BooksTable(books, true)
    ),
],),
); }
```

From here, we can easily navigate to the HomePage, but we also need a way to get from the home page to the Favorites screen.

8. Get back to the main.dart file, and, in the InkWell that contains the star icon or the 'Favorites' text, add the code to navigate to the FavoriteScreen, as follows:

```
InkWell(
    child: Padding(
    padding: EdgeInsets.all(20.0),
    child: (isSmall) ? Icon(Icons.star) : Text('Favorites')),
    onTap: () {
        Navigator.push(context,
            MaterialPageRoute(builder: (context) =>
            FavoriteScreen()));
    },
),
```

Try the app in your browser, add favorites to your list, change the size of the window to see how the UI responds to the available space, and think of the (many) ways you could make this app better, including building a details page with the description of the book, which we retrieved from the API but never used.

Also, **congratulate yourself**, as this completes this app and the last project of this book!

Publishing a Flutter app to a web server

Now that our web app is complete, you might wonder how to publish it to a web server. At this time, browsers only support HTML, CSS, and JavaScript, so you cannot just publish your code to a web server and expect it to run on a browser as we did during the debug process.

Fortunately, the support for building web apps in Flutter includes a tool to transform your Flutter code into JavaScript. From the command-line interface on your development machine, just run the following command:

```
flutter build web
```

Running this command will create the \build\web folder in your app directory. If you open it, you should see an index.html file, which is the home page of your web app.

 When you build a web release version, the framework will minify and perform obfuscation on your files. For more information about the process, see https://flutter.dev/docs/deployment/web.

If you open the file, you should see a very simple HTML code, as shown here:

```html
<!DOCTYPE html>
<html>
<head>
 <meta charset="UTF-8">
 <title>web_app</title>
</head>
<body>
 <script src="main.dart.js" type="application/javascript"></script>
</body>
</html>
```

The body of the web page only contains a JavaScript file called main.dart.js. This is the actual translation of our Dart code into JavaScript. As this file is minified for performance reasons, if you open the main.dart.js file, you will not be able to see anything very interesting, but the key point here is that when you run the flutter build web command, the Flutter framework will translate your code into a fully compatible HTML, CSS, and JavaScript app that you'll be able to publish to any web server. After publishing, the app will be compatible with any browser, not only Chrome.

As the compiled web version is HTML, CSS, and JavaScript, you can use a **File Transfer Protocol (FTP)** client to publish to any web server. Linux and Windows servers will both work. The folder you'll need to copy is the \build\web directory of your project.

Summary

Flutter can now create apps for mobile, web, and desktop, and, while using the same code for several devices is a huge advantage for developers, the different form factors may be challenging when designing the UI of an app. A possible approach to deliver a great user experience to users is using responsive layouts. In the project in this chapter, you've used `MediaQuery.of(context).size.width` to choose different layouts based on the number of logical pixels available in the screen; a `Table` for larger screens; and a `ListView` for smaller screens.

Flutter for Web allows you to debug Flutter apps with a Chrome browser, but, once published, the apps will be compatible with any recent browser.

A challenge for apps that run on different systems is using their specific features. Saving data on iOS, Android, or a browser is radically different in each case. The Flutter approach involves creating wrappers around different platform-specific technologies. In the app you've built in this project, you've used the `shared_preferences` library to save data locally, avoiding writing custom code for each platform. There are several libraries that are already compatible with both mobile and web development, and the list is rapidly growing.

Browsers today only support HTML, CSS, and JavaScript. When you build a Flutter app for the web, the framework transforms your Flutter code into JavaScript, automatically performing minification and obfuscation. In order to build a Flutter app for the web, you need to use the `flutter build web` command from a Terminal window.

Thank you for being part of this journey of learning Flutter. I truly hope you found value in this book. Even if it may be challenging at times, *coding* is the only way to learn coding; so, again: congratulations on making it to the end. If you want to keep learning, the web is full of resources, as Flutter is getting more and more popular: who knows, maybe we'll make another part of this journey together in the future. Meanwhile, **keep coding**!

Questions

Please try to answer the following questions (when in doubt, have a look at the content in the chapter itself: you'll find all the answers there!):

1. What are the steps required to enable web development to your Flutter environment?
2. What's the difference between physical and logical pixels?
3. How can you know the width of your user's device?

4. When using a `Table` widget, how do you add rows and cells?
5. What's the meaning of responsive design?
6. What's the purpose of the `FlexColumnWidth` widget?
7. What's the purpose of `shared_preferences`?
8. Would you use `shared_preferences` to store passwords? Why?
9. How can a browser run a Flutter app?
10. How can you publish a Flutter app to a web server?

Further reading

The Google Books Library project is fascinating and ambitious. Imagine a service that allows anyone to search through millions of books, including rare and out-of-print books, for free. That's the Google Books Library project. As of October 2019, there are over 40 million books scanned and available on Google. For more information about the project, have a look at the following page: `https://support.google.com/books/partner/answer/3398488?hl=enref_topic=3396243`.

Many of the technologies we have used in this book are made by Google. These include Flutter itself, Dart, Android, and Firebase, just to name a few. However, there's a technology that is made by Microsoft: VS Code. I spend most of my time as a developer on that editor, not only for Flutter but for most client-side development. It's fast, reliable, and free. And it's not only me. Stack Overflow, in its 2019 Developer Survey, found that VS Code was the most popular developer tool, with over 50% of thousands of developers claiming to use it, just over 4 years after it was produced. Have a look at the official page for more info about this editor: `https://code.visualstudio.com/`.

This chapter focused on creating web apps with Flutter. Another great addition is **desktop** support for macOS, Windows, and Linux. It's still at its initial stages at this time, but it will be fascinating to see how this grows. For an updated view of desktop support, have a look at `https://flutter.dev/desktop`.

Appendix

Setting up your environment to build Flutter projects

In this section, we will be completing all the required installations you need to get started with Flutter. You'll see processes for Windows and Mac, but if you are using a Linux machine, you'll also be able to use Flutter. An updated, complete guide for setting up your devices to use Flutter is available at https://flutter.dev/docs/get-started/install.

The editors that we'll be covering and using throughout this chapter include Android Studio and **Visual Studio Code** (**VS Code**). For the remainder of the book, most of the screenshots will be taken from VS Code.

Installing Flutter on a Windows PC

In order to install Flutter on Windows, you will need Windows 7 **Service Pack 1** (**SP1**) (64-bit) or later.

The installation steps described in this section target a **Windows 10** machine, but they should work similarly for any other supported Windows system.

Flutter requires Windows PowerShell 5.0 or newer and Git for Windows. If you are using Windows 10, the correct version of PowerShell is already installed, so you'll only need to install Git.

Installing Git

Git is a **version control system** (**VCS**). It basically keeps track of any modifications in your source code. Among other things, it allows you to step back when you make a mistake, and it's invaluable when several developers work together and update different pieces of the source, which often creates potential conflicts that would be a nightmare to solve without a source control system.

You can download Git from `https://git-scm.com/downloads`. It's available for Windows, macOS, and Linux. The Git installation wizard is quite straightforward unless you have reasons to do the installation differently. You can just accept the default options in most screens, except the default editor, where I suggest you choose your favorite editor. My choice—and recommendation—is VS Code. The following screenshot shows how you would choose this as the default editor to be used by Git:

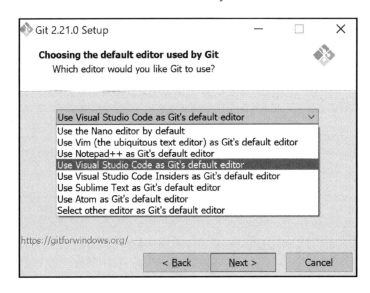

Then, just click **Next** until the end of the installation.

Installing the Flutter Software Development Kit (SDK)

You'll find many of the tools you need to set up your environment at `https://flutter.dev`. Perform the following steps to install the Flutter SDK:

1. Here, you can expect a very visible **Get Started** link or button on the page. Click this.
2. From there, you'll have to choose your operating system (Windows), and then download the Flutter SDK.
3. The Flutter SDK is a `.zip` file, and you will need to create a folder for the content of the file, such as `c:\FlutterSDK`.
4. Then, extract the content of the zipped file into the new folder. At the end of the process, you should have a folder containing the `flutter` folder, with its files.

5. Next, you'll need to update the PATH environment variable. In order to do so, from the Start search bar, type env. Then, click on the **Edit the system environment variables** icon and, from the **System Properties** window, in the **Advanced** tab, click on the **Environment Variables** button and add the bin folder of the FlutterSDK directory you have just created, as shown in the following screenshot:

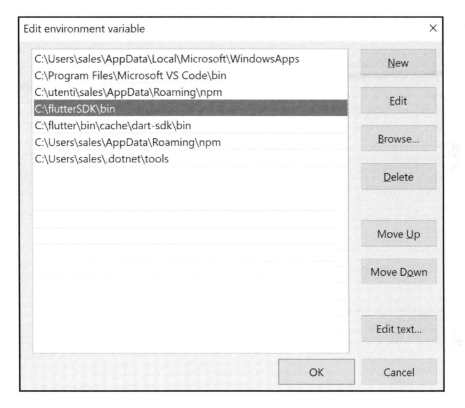

6. From the flutter folder, double-click on the flutter_console.bat file.
7. From the console that opens, type the following command:

```
flutter doctor
```

8. You will see a `Doctor summary`, as shown in the following screenshot:

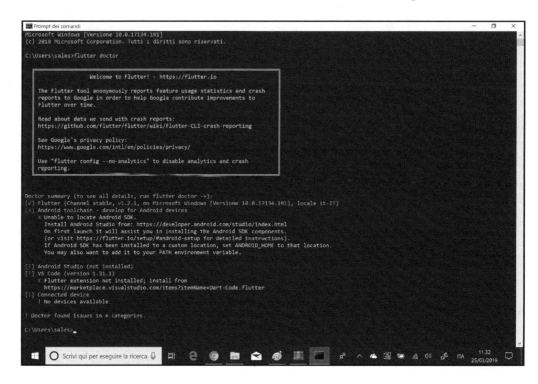

Don't worry if at this point the doctor is showing elements you need to fix, such as the Android toolchain: we haven't finished the installation yet. `flutter doctor` is an easy tool that you can use to solve issues for the Flutter installation on your system. We'll use it again later.

Installing Android Studio

Next, we'll install Android Studio. This is not necessarily the editor you'll be using to code, but it's the easiest way to install the Android SDK and emulators. Let's look at the installation steps, as follows:

1. Find Android Studio at the following link: `https://developer.android.com/studioD`.

2. On the **Download Android Studio** page, check the box at the bottom of the page and click on **Download Android Studio for Windows**. This is an installation wizard. On the first screen, make sure that **Android Virtual Device** is selected before clicking **Next**. You can leave the default options as-is.

3. The installation will be completed when you open Android Studio for the first time. The following screenshot shows how Android Studio will be displayed on your screen:

4. From the **Welcome to Android Studio** screen, click the **Configure** button and select the **AVD Manager** option.

5. Click on the **Create Virtual Device** option. In this book, you'll see screenshots from the Pixel Emulator, but feel free to choose another device for your system. For the system image, choose the most recent stable release. The examples in this book are tested on Android Pie (API level 28—Android 9.0), as shown in the following screenshot:

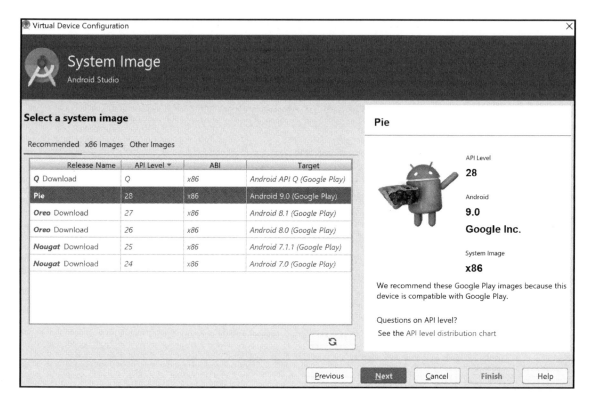

After installing the **Android Virtual Device** (**AVD**), you can test it by clicking on the **Launch** button from the action bar. If everything worked as expected, you will be able to see the emulator running on your system.

Connecting an Android physical device

You can also choose to run and test your apps on a physical device, and I'd especially recommend this option if you have an older PC, as an emulator takes its toll on system memory and resources.

Depending on your Android device, you may need to download a driver.

 For a list of the available third-party drivers, have a look at the following link: https://developer.android.com/studio/run/oem-usb.

If you have a Nexus device, you will need to install the Google USB Driver, available at https://developer.android.com/studio/run/win-usb.html.

Before debugging, you should enable the developers' options on your device. The process may depend on the version of Android that you are using, but if you have a recent version of Android, the process is as follows:

1. Open the Settings app.
2. Select **System**.
3. At the bottom of the screen, select **About Phone**.
4. At the bottom of the screen, tap seven times on the **Build Number**.
5. On the **Settings** screen, you'll find the **Developer options**. From there, make sure that **USB Debugging** is enabled.
6. In order to test whether the setup of your device worked as expected, from the Command Prompt, type `flutter devices`.

7. You will see your device listed on the screen, as shown in the following screenshot:

In case something didn't work as expected during this setup process, make sure to review the preceding steps, and have a look at the following page: `https://flutter.dev/docs/get-started/install/windows`.

The last step you need to complete before creating your first app is choosing your editor. The recommended choices are Android Studio, IntelliJ IDEA, or VS Code.

Configuring Android Studio

You should already have Android Studio if you followed the preceding instructions, so you only need to install the Flutter and Dart plugins. After starting Android Studio, execute the following steps:

1. Choose **File** | **Settings** | **Plugins**.
2. Select **Browse Repositories**, and search for **Flutter**.

3. Install the Flutter plugin. You'll receive a message that will inform you that Flutter depends on Dart. Accept this by clicking **Yes**.
4. Restart Android Studio.

You are now ready to start developing applications in Flutter with Android Studio.

Installing and configuring VS Code

Alternatively, or in addition, you can also use VS Code to develop with Flutter. You can download it from `https://code.visualstudio.com/download`.

Again, the setup is a wizard; you can leave the default options as-is and complete the installation. After installing VS Code, you'll need to install the Flutter and Dart plugins by executing the following steps:

1. From the **View** menu, select **Command Palette**.
2. Type `install` and choose **Extensions | Install Extensions**.
3. Type `flutter` and install the Flutter support and debugger for VS Code.
4. From the **View** menu, select **Command Palette**.
5. Type `doctor` and click on the **Flutter: Run Flutter Doctor** option.
6. You may have to accept some Android licenses. If needed, type the following command:

```
flutter doctor --android-licenses
```

7. Accept the required licenses.

Congratulations! Now, your PC should be ready to start developing with Flutter, both with Android Studio and VS Code.

Installing Flutter on a Mac

In order to install Flutter on a Mac, you need to have a 64-bit version of macOS. The installation steps and images highlighted here are for macOS Mojave.

At the time of writing, a Mac is the only system that allows you to test and run your apps on both Android and iOS.

Installing the Flutter SDK

You'll find many of the tools you need to set up your environment at `https://flutter.dev`. Execute the following steps:

1. Click on a very visible **Get Started** link or button on the page.
2. From there, you'll have to choose your operating system (in this case, macOS), and then download the Flutter SDK, which is a `.zip` file. Create a folder for the content of the file, such as `~/flutterdev`.
3. In order to create a new directory on the root of your Mac, open a Terminal window, and type the following command:

   ```
   mkdir ~/flutterdev
   ```

4. Next, extract the content of the zipped file into the new directory. From the Terminal, type the following code:

   ```
   cd ~/ flutterdev
   ```

   ```
   $ unzip ~/Downloads/flutter_macos_v1.2.1-stable.zip
   ```

5. You may need to change the Flutter SDK version, depending on the version available at the time you perform the installation.
6. At the end of the process, you should have a folder containing the `flutterdev` folder, with its files.
7. Next, you'll need to update your `PATH` variable. This will allow you to run Flutter commands in any Terminal session.
8. From a Terminal window, go to your root folder by typing `cd ~/`.
9. Then, if you haven't created a `.bash_profile` yet, type the following command:

   ```
   touch .bash_profile
   ```

10. Create your new file. Edit `.bash_profile` with your favorite editor, or type the following command:

```
open -e .bash_profile
```

11. In the file, type `export PATH=/home/flutterdev/bin:$PATH` and then, from the Terminal, run `source $HOME/.bash_profile`.

12. Check whether the `PATH` has been correctly updated by typing `$ echo $PATH`.

You will see the path you've set on the Terminal.

Installing Xcode

Xcode is Apple's official **integrated development environment (IDE)** for Mac and iOS. To develop apps for iOS with Flutter, you need Xcode 9.0 or newer. You can download it from the Mac App Store or from the web, at the following address: `https://developer.apple.com/xcode/`.

You can also get and install Xcode from the Mac App Store by following these steps:

1. Open the App Store from the launcher and type `Xcode` in the search box.
2. Press the **get** button to download and install the app.
3. Once it's installed, open it to accept all the required licenses.
4. Next, open a simulator from a Terminal window, by typing the following command:

```
Open -a Simulator
```

5. You can choose which device to use from the **Hardware | Devices Manage Devices** menu. Make sure you're using an iPhone 5s or later. The following screenshot shows an iPhone XR:

6. To make sure everything is working as expected, from the Terminal window type `flutter doctor`, and the result is shown in the following screenshot:

```
● ● ●                        🏠 simoales — -bash — 80×24
Last login: Tue Apr  2 08:59:45 on console
[Air-di-Simone:~ simoales$ open -a Simulator
[Air-di-Simone:~ simoales$ flutter doctor
Doctor summary (to see all details, run flutter doctor -v):
[✓] Flutter (Channel beta, v1.1.8, on Mac OS X 10.14.3 18D109, locale en-IT)
[✗] Android toolchain - develop for Android devices
    ✗ Unable to locate Android SDK.
      Install Android Studio from:
      https://developer.android.com/studio/index.html
      On first launch it will assist you in installing the Android SDK
      components.
      (or visit https://flutter.io/setup/#android-setup for detailed
      instructions).
      If Android SDK has been installed to a custom location, set ANDROID_HOME
      to that location.
      You may also want to add it to your PATH environment variable.

[✓] iOS toolchain - develop for iOS devices (Xcode 10.1)
[!] Android Studio (not installed)
[✓] VS Code (version 1.32.1)
[✓] Connected device (1 available)

! Doctor found issues in 2 categories.
Air-di-Simone:~ simoales$ █
```

The iOS toolchain should now be correctly installed!

 If you want to test your apps on a physical device (iPhone/iPad), you'll need to have an Apple account and to do some configuration, which is subject to change with an incoming update of `libusbmuxd`. Please have a look at the following link for an updated installation guide: `https://flutter.dev/docs/get-started/install/macos#deploy-to-ios-devices`.

You can also use a Mac to deploy to Android. In order to do that, just follow the instructions in the *Installing Android Studio* section. If you want to also use VS Code to develop your apps, also have a look at the *Installing and configuring VS Code* section.

Assessment

Assessment

You'll find the answers to the questions at the end of each chapter here.

Chapter 1

1. **What is a widget?**
   A widget is a description of the user interface. This description gets "inflated" into an actual view when objects are built.

2. **What is the starting point of a Dart and Flutter app?**
   The `main()` function is the starting point of every Dart and Flutter application.

3. **How many named constructors can you have in a Dart/Flutter class?**
   In a Dart/Flutter class, you can have any number of named constructors, but only one unnamed constructor.

4. **Can you name three `EdgeInsets` constructors?**
   In this chapter, we used `EdgeInsets.all`, `EdgeInsets.only`, and `EdgeInsets.symmetric`.

5. **How can you style the text in a `Text` widget?**
   The Text widget has a `style` property. There you can use `TextStyle()` to set the font size, its weight, color, and several other properties.

6. **What is the purpose of the `flutter doctor` command?**
   It is a CLI tool that you can use to check the Flutter installation on your system.

7. **What widget would you use to contain several other widgets, one below the other?**
   The `Column` widget contains a `children` property that places widgets one below the other.

8. **What is the "arrow syntax"?**
   The arrow syntax is a concise way to return values in a function. An example of arrow syntax is as follows:

   ```
   bool convertToBool(int value) => (value == 0) ? false : true;
   ```

9. **Which widget can you use to create space between widgets?**
   Several widgets can be used for that. A `Padding` widget can be used to create space between its child and all other widgets on the screen.

10. **How can you show an image to the user?**
    You can show images using the `Image` widget. Image has a `network` constructor, which automatically downloads an image from a URL with a single line of code.

Chapter 2

1. **When should you use Stateful widgets in your apps?**
   In your apps, you use Stateful widgets when your widgets need to keep a State, which is information that can change during the lifecycle of the user interface.

2. **Which method updates the State of your class?**
   The `setState()` method updates the State.

3. **Which widget would you use to allow your user to select an option from a dropdown list?**
   The `DropdownButton` widget allows you to create a list of `DropdownMenuItem` widgets that can be selected by the user.

4. **Which widget would you use to allow your user to type some text?**
   A `TextField` is a widget that allows the user to type some text.

5. **Which event can you use when you want to react to some user input?**
   The `onChanged` event allows you to respond to changes in the content of `TextField`.

6. **What happens when your widgets take more space than what's available on the screen? How do you solve this issue?**
   You can enclose your widgets into a scrolling widget, like the `SingleChildScrollView` widget.

7. **How can you get the width of the screen?**
   You can use the `MediaQuery.of(context).size.width` instruction to get the width of the screen.

8. **What is** `Map` **in Flutter?**
   In Flutter, `Map` widgets allow you to insert key-value pairs, where the first element is the key, and the second is the value.

9. **How can you style your text?**
   You can create a `TextStyle` widget, and you can use it to apply the same text style to several widgets.

10. **How can you separate the logic of your apps from the UI?**
    There are several approaches to separate the logic from the UI in Flutter. The most basic one, that you've seen in this chapter, is creating classes that contain the logic of your app, and use them from the user interface when appropriate.

Chapter 3

1. **Which is the cross-axis for a GridView scrolling vertically?**
   If the main axis is vertical, the cross axis is horizontal.

2. **How do you retrieve a value from SharedPreferences?**
   After creating an instance of SharedPreferences, you can call one of its methods, like `getInt` or `getString`, passing the key. This will retrieve its value. An example is shown in the following code block:

   ```
   prefs = await SharedPreferences.getInstance();
   int workTime = prefs.getInt(WORKTIME);
   ```

3. **Which instruction would you use to retrieve the width of the screen?**
   You can use the `MediaQuery.of(context).size.width` instruction to get the width of the screen.

4. **How do you open another screen on your app?**
You can call the push() method of the Navigator to add a route to the navigation stack. For example:

```
Navigator.push(
    context, MaterialPageRoute(builder: (context)
=>SettingsScreen()));
}
```

5. **Which file contains all the dependencies of your app?**
The pubspec.yaml file contains the dependencies of your app.

6. **What's the difference between a** Stream **and a** Future**?**
A Stream is a sequence of results: any number of events can be returned in a Stream, whereas a Future only returns once.

7. **How do you change the value of a** TextField**?**
You can use a TextEditingController to change the values inside a TextField.

8. **How do you create a new** Duration **object?**
Duration is a Dart class used to contain a span of time. In order to create a Duration you call its constructor specifying the length of the duration, like in this example:

```
Duration(seconds: 1)
```

9. **How can you add a menu button to your apps?**
You can use a PopupMenuButton widget, adding it to the AppBar in the Scaffold, like this:

```
appBar: AppBar(
    title: Text('My Work Timer'),
        actions: [
            PopupMenuButton<String>(
                itemBuilder: (BuildContext context) {
                    return menuItems.toList(); },
```

10. **What are the steps to install an external library into your app?**
You add the dependency in the pubspec.yaml file, then you import the library at the top of the file that will use it, and finally, you can use it in your code.

Chapter 4

1. **Which child widget can you use inside a Stack to decide exactly its position relative to the borders of the Stack?**
   The `Positioned` widget controls where a child of a stack is positioned.

2. **What's the difference between the `initState()` and `build()` methods?**
   The `initState()` method is called once for each State object when the State is built. This is where you generally put the initial values that you might need when you build your classes. The `build()` method is called after `initState` and every time the state changes.

3. **How can you set the duration of an animation?**
   You can set the `duration` property of an `AnimationController`, and there you can use a `Duration` object like shown in the following example:

   ```
   AnimationController(
       duration: const Duration(seconds: 3)
   );
   ```

4. **How can you use a `Mixin` class in your own classes?**
   A `Mixin` is a class that contains methods that can be used by other classes without having to be the parent class of those other classes. In Flutter you use the `with` clause to use a Mixin in your classes like shown in the following code block:

   ```
   class _PongState extends State<Pong> with
   SingleTickerProviderStateMixin {}
   ```

5. **What is a Ticker?**
   A Ticker is a class that sends a signal at an almost regular interval, which, in Flutter, is about 60 times per second, or once every 16 milliseconds, if your device allows this frame rate.

6. **What's the difference between an `Animation` and an `AnimationController`?**
   An `AnimationController` controls one or more `Animation` objects.

7. **How do you stop a running animation? And how do you free its resources?**
   You can use the `stop()` method in `AnimationController` to stop a running animation and the `dispose()` method to free the resources.

8. **How can you generate a random number between 0 and 10?**

   You can generate a random number between 0 and 10 using the `Random` class, and calling the `nextInt()` method. The `nextInt()` method takes a max value. The random number starts from 0 and the max value is exclusive, so for a number between 0 and 10 you could write:

   ```
   Random random = new Random();
   int randomNumber = random.nextInt(11);
   ```

9. **If you wanted to respond to a tap of the user over one of your widgets, for example, a container, which widget could you use?**
   A `GestureDetector` is a widget that detects gestures, including tap. So you could enclose a `Container` into a `GestureDetector` in order to respond to the tap of your users.

10. **How do you show an** `AlertDialog` **in an app?**
    `AlertDialog` is a widget that you use to give feedback or to ask for some information from your user. Showing an `AlertDialog` widget requires the following steps:

    1. Calling the `showDialog()` method
    2. Setting the context
    3. Setting the builder
    4. Returning the `AlertDialog` property
    5. Setting the `AlertDialog` properties

    In the following code block you can find an example of a method showing an `AlertDialog`:

    ```
    void contactUs(BuildContext context) {
       showDialog(
          context: context,
          builder: (BuildContext context) {
             return AlertDialog(
                title: Text('Contact Us'),
                content: Text('Mail us at hello@world.com'),
                actions: <Widget>[
                   FlatButton(
                      child: Text('Close'),
                      onPressed: () => Navigator.of(context).pop(),
    ) ],); },); }
    ```

Chapter 5

1. **Is this code correct?**

   ```
   String data = http.get(url);
   ```

   If not, why?

   The code is not correct, as the **get ()** method of http is asynchronous, and therefore returns a Future and not a String.

2. **What are the JSON and XML formats used for?**
   JSON and XML are text formats that represent data. They can be returned by web services and then used in client apps.

3. **What is a thread?**
   A thread is a single line of execution.

4. **Can you name a few common asynchronous scenarios?**
   Some scenarios where you need to use asynchronous programming include http requests, database writes, and in general all long-running tasks.

5. **When should you use the async/await keywords?**
   Asynchronous operations return **Future** objects (futures), which is something to be completed at a later time. To suspend execution until a Future completes, we use await in an async function.

6. **What's the difference between** ListView **and** ListTile**?**
   A ListTile is a material widget that can contain one to three lines of text with optional icons at the beginning and end. A ListView is a scrolling widget that displays its children one after another either horizontally or vertically. You can include ListTile widgets into a ListView.

7. **How can you use the map method to parse data and create a list?**
   The map() method transforms each element in a list and returns the result of the transformation in a new list. For example, you can transform some JSON data into an object, as shown in the following code block:

   ```
   final moviesMap = jsonResponse['results'];
   List movies = moviesMap.map((i) => Movie.fromJson(i)).toList();
   ```

8. **How do you pass data from one screen to another?**
   You need to pass the data in the builder when you create the new route as shown in the following example:

   ```
   MaterialPageRoute route = MaterialPageRoute(builder: (_) =>
   YourScreen(yourData));
   Navigator.push(context, route);
   ```

9. **When should you use the** json.decode() **method over the body of a Response object?**
   You use the json.decode() method to convert the Response into a list of data that is usable in your app, like custom objects or Strings.

10. **What is a** CircleAvatar?
    CircleAvatar is a widget that draws a circle that can contain an image or some text.

Chapter 6

1. **What happens when you call the** openDatabase() **method?**
   The sqflite library has an openDatabase() method, that opens and returns an existing database. The method takes the path of the database to be opened and the version of the database. The optional onCreate parameter will be called if the database does not exist. There you can specify the instruction to create the database.

2. **What's the difference between the** rawQuery() **and** query() **methods of a database object?**
   Both are methods to retrieve data from a database. The rawQuery() method takes a SQL instruction, the query() method is a helper where you specify the table, a where filter, and a whereArgs parameter. An example of the two methods is shown in the following code block:

   ```
   List places = await db.rawQuery('select * from items where idList =
   1');
   List places = await db.query('items', where: 'idList = ?',
   whereArgs: [1]);
   ```

3. **How do you use a factory constructor? When should you use it?**

   A factory constructor overrides the default behavior of the constructor of a class, instead of creating a new instance, the factory constructor only returns a single instance of the class. The syntax to create a factory constructor is as follows:

   ```
   static final DbHelper _dbHelper = DbHelper._internal();
   DbHelper._internal();
   factory DbHelper() {
       return _dbHelper;
   }
   ```

4. **What's the purpose of a** Dismissible **widget?**

   A Dismissible is a widget that detects the left and right swipe gestures of the user and shows an animation that removes an object. Using Dismissible is ideal when you want to delete an item.

5. **How do we use the** where **and** whereArgs **parameters of a** query() **method?**

   You use where and whereArgs when you want to filter the data retrieved from the query() method. The where parameter takes field names and the comparison operators and whereArgs takes the values. An example is shown in the following code block:

   ```
   List places = await db.query('items', where: 'idList = ?',
   whereArgs: [1]);
   ```

6. **When should you use model classes in an app?**

   Model classes create objects that mirror the structure of the tables in a database: this makes the code more reliable, easier to read, and helps prevent data inconsistencies.

7. **When would you use a** SnackBar**?**

   A SnackBar is a widget that shows messages at the bottom of your app. Generally, you use a SnackBar to inform your users that an action has been performed.

8. **What's the syntax of an** `insert()` **method on an SQLite database?**

   The `insert()` asynchronous method allows you to specify the name of the table where we want to insert data, a `Map` of the data that you want to insert, and optionally a `conflictAlgorithm` that specifies the behavior that should be followed when you try to insert a record with the same ID twice. It will return the ID of the new record that was inserted. Take a look at the following example:

   ```
   int id = await this.db.insert( 'lists',list.toMap(),
   conflictAlgorithm: ConflictAlgorithm.replace, );
   ```

9. **What is the purpose of the** `key` **in a** `Dismissible` **widget?**

   The `key` in a `Dismissible` widget is used to uniquely identify the item that will be deleted.

10. **When would you use a FAB?**

    The FAB, or Floating Action Button, is a circular button that you can use for the main action on the screen. If you have a list of items, the main action could be adding a new item.

Chapter 7

1. **In a Cloud Firestore database, what's the difference between a document and a collection? And can a document contain a collection?**

   A Collection is a container for a set of documents, where a document is the data itself, expressed in key-value pairs. A document can contain a collection.

2. **Can you name three of the main differences between a SQL and a NoSQL database?**

   SQL Databases use the SQL language to perform queries, use of JOINS to express relations between tables, and have a fixed schema. NOSQL stores contain self-describing data, do not require a schema and do not allow using the SQL language to perform queries.

3. **Consider the following code:**

   ```
   docs = await db.collection('favorites') .where('userId', isEqualTo:
   uid) .getDocuments();
   ```

What does this query perform? And which data type is the docs variable?

The `getDocuments()` asynchronous method retrieves data from the specified collection (in this case favorites), where the `userId` is equal to the value of the variable `uid`. `docs` will contain a `QuerySnapshot` object.

4. **In a Cloud Firestore database, is it possible to allow data access only to authenticated users? If so, how can you achieve that?**
   In a Cloud Firestore database, it is possible to allow data access only to authenticated users by setting a rule. An example is shown here:

   ```
   application
   service cloud.firestore {
   match /databases/{database}/documents { match /{document=**} {
   allow read, write: if request.auth.uid != null; } }}
   ```

5. **How can you create an instance of a `FirebaseAuth` class?**
   `FirebaseAuth` is the object that enables the use of Firebase Authentication's methods and properties. You can create an instance of a `FirebaseAuth` class with the instruction:

   ```
   final FirebaseAuth _firebaseAuth = FirebaseAuth.instance;
   ```

6. **Consider the following code:**
   ```
   var result = db.collection('favorites').add(fav.toMap()
   .then((value) => print(value.documentID)) .catchError((error)=>
   print (error));
   ```

   Can you explain what these instructions perform?

   A new document is added to the favorites collection. If the task succeeds, the code will print the `documentId` of the new document in the Debug Console. In case of error, the error itself will be printed.

7. **When would you create a getter method for a property in a class? And how do you write the code to create it?**
A getter method returns a property value of an instance of the class, In this way, you can check or transform values before reading them in your classes. You specify getters by adding the get keyword before the field name. The getter returns a value of the type that you specify: an example is shown here:

```
int get price {
    return _price * 1.2;
}
```

8. **When do you need a** Map **object to interact with a Cloud Firestore database?**
When interacting with a Cloud Firestore database, you can pass a Map object to write data to a collection. You can also parse the results of queries into Map objects when retrieving data.

9. **How do you delete a document from a Cloud Firestore database?**
You use the delete() method on a document, as shown in the following code block:

```
await db.collection('favourites').document(favId).delete();
```

10. **How do you pass data from one screen to another?**
You need to pass the data in the builder when you create the new route like shown in the following example:

```
MaterialPageRoute route = MaterialPageRoute(builder: (_) =>
YourScreen(yourData));
Navigator.push(context, route);
```

Chapter 8

1. **What is the purpose of adding the** path **and** path_provider **libraries into your app?**
The path package provides common operations for manipulating paths: joining, splitting, and normalizing. You can use path_provider to retrieve commonly used locations on the Android and iOS file systems, like the data folder.'

2. **In which files do you add the API key for Google Maps in your project for Android and/or iOS?**
   For Android, you need to add the information into the `android/app/src/main/AndroidManifest.xml` application manifest. For iOS, you need to update the `AppDelegate` file at `ios/Runner/AppDelegate.swift`.

3. **When you pass the** `initialCameraPosition` **to a** `GoogleMap` **widget, which type of widget do you need to pass?**
   When you pass the `initialCameraPosition` to a `GoogleMap` widget, you pass a `CameraPosition`, which in turn takes a `LatLng` object. An example is shown here:

   ```
   CameraPosition( target: LatLng(41.9028, 12.4964),
       zoom: 12,
   );
   ```

4. **How can you get the current position of a device?**
   You can use the `Geolocator` package: from a `Geolocator` instance, you can call the `getCurrentPosition()` method, that returns a `Position` object like shown in the following example:

   ```
   pos = await Geolocator().getCurrentPosition(desiredAccuracy:
   LocationAccuracy.best);
   ```

5. **What is a Marker and when do you use it?**
   A `Marker` identifies a location on a `Map`. You can use markers to show your user their current position, or any relevant position in the context of your app.

6. **When do you need to use a** `LatLng` **widget in a Marker?**
   A Marker takes a `LatLng` in its position property, to identify its position on a map.

   ```
   final marker = Marker(
   position: LatLng(pos.latitude, pos.longitude)),
   ```

7. **Which is the method that returns a List of the available cameras on a device?**
   The `availableCameras()` method of the `camera` package returns a List of the available cameras on a device.

8. **How can you show the camera preview to your users?**
The camera package contains a `CameraController`. Passing a `CameraController`, you can create an instance of a `CameraPreview`, that you can then show in your app. An example of using a `CameraPreview` is as follows:

```
cameraPreview = Center(child: CameraPreview(_controller));
```

9. **What's the purpose of a** `CameraController`, **and how do you create one?**
A `CameraController`, part of the camera package, establishes a connection to the device's camera, and you can use it to actually take the pictures. An example of creation is shown in the following code block:

```
_controller = CameraController(camera,
ResolutionPreset.medium,
);
```

10. **How do you take a picture in Flutter?**
In order to take a picture you need to retrieve a `CameraController`, and over that call the `takePicture()` method passing the path where you want to save the file like shown in the following example:

```
await _controller.takePicture(path);
```

Chapter 9

1. **In the** `pubspec.yaml` **file, where should you place the** `.flr` **file you have exported from Flare?**
In the `pubspec.yaml` file, you have to place your `.flr` animation in the assets section, like this:

```
assets:
  - assets/dice.flr
```

2. **In Flare, what is the difference between the Design and Animate modes?**
Flare has two modes of operations: Design and Animate. In Design mode, you create graphic objects, and in Animate mode, you animate the objects that you have designed. Flare's interface and tools will change based on the mode in which you are working.

3. **How many Artboards are required in a Flare project?**
An Artboard is the top-level node of a Flare hierarchy, and this is where you place all your objects and animations. Each Flare project requires at least one Artboard, but you can create as many as you like.

4. **What is the purpose of the timeline in Flare?**
A timeline is where you control the progression of your animation. In Flare, you can also specify the duration of the animation and the number of **Frames Per Second (FPS)**.

5. **What is a hierarchy in Flare?**
The Hierarchy is a tree view that shows the parent/child relationships between the items on the stage.

6. **When using a Flare asset in a Flutter project, when and why do you use the animation name?**
A `FlareActor` widget allows you to specify the asset you wish to use, the animation you wish to show, and how the animation should fit into the screen: it's there that you specify the animation name like shown here:

```
FlareActor( animation: currentAnimation, [...] )
```

7. **Which widget can you use to show a Flare animation in Flutter?**
You use a `FlareActor` to show a Flare animation in Flutter.

8. **How do you generate a random number between 1 and 6 in a Flutter app?**
You can use the `Random` library, and call the `nextInt()` method passing the max limit and adding 1 as the first value is 0: the code is shown here:

```
var random = Random();
int num = random.nextInt(5) + 1;
```

9. **When would you use a Flare animation in an app, instead of built-in animations?**
Flare is a vector design and animation tool that exports directly to Flutter and allows you to work on the same assets that will be used in your Flutter app. The animations you create with Flare can be changed from your Flutter code at runtime, making it great for apps that need user interaction.

You use it whenever you need a designer's tool to create assets and animate them, and then enclose the final results of your design work into Flutter.

10. **In the following code, what would you put as the first parameter?**

```
FlareActor([YOUR ANSWER HERE], fit: BoxFit.contain, animation:
_animation1,)
```

The first parameter requires the file name of your `.flr` animation file.

Chapter 10

1. **When would you prefer to use sembast over SQLite in an app?**
When your data is not structured, or it's so simple that you don't need an SQL database, the simple embedded application store database (sembast) is an ideal solution.

2. **How can you retrieve all the documents from a store in a sembast database?**
The `find()` method allows you to retrieve documents from a store in a sembast database. If you want to retrieve all documents from a store, you don't specify any filter when calling the `find()` method. An example is shown in the following code block:

```
final todosSnapshot = await store.find(_database, finder: finder);
```

3. **How can you delete all the documents from a store in a sembast database?**
You can call the `delete()` method without any filter over a store to delete all the documents in the store as shown here:

```
await store.delete(_database);
```

4. **How would you complete the following method to update an existing object in a sembast database?**

```
Future updateTodo(Todo todo) async {
//add your code here
}
```

You can call the `update()` method over the store, passing the document that can be found by using a filter, as shown here:

```
final finder = Finder(filter: Filter.byKey(todo.id));
await store.update(_database, todo.toMap(), finder: finder);
```

5. **What are the main differences between Futures and Streams?**
A `Stream` is a sequence of results: any number of events can be returned in a `Stream`, whereas a `Future` only returns once.

6. **When would you use the BLoC pattern in an app?**
The BLoC pattern is a state management system for Flutter recommended by Google developers. BLoC helps in managing the state and accessing data from a shared class in your project, and you can use it when you want to manage the state of your app centrally, in a class separated from the other components of your app.

7. **In a `StreamController`, what are the purposes of stream and sink?**
In a `StreamController`, the way into the `Stream` is the `sink` property, the way out is the `stream`.

8. **Which is the object that allows you to listen to the events from the Stream and rebuild all its descendants?**
A `StreamBuilder` rebuilds its children after any change in the `Stream`.

9. **How do you listen to changes in a Stream?**
The `StreamBuilder` widget listens to the events from the `Stream` and rebuilds all its descendants, using the latest data in the `Stream`. You can connect it to the Streams through the `stream` property and a builder that contains the UI that needs to be updated.

10. **Why would you use a stateful widget when dealing with BLoCs, even though you never called the `setState()` method?**Stateful widgets override the `dispose()` method, which is useful to free the resources used in implementing the BLoC pattern.

Chapter 11

1. **What are the steps required to enable web development to your Flutter environment?**
   As of Flutter version 1.14, web development for Flutter is available in the beta channel, and you need to set up the environment to explicitly enable web support. In your Terminal/command prompt you need to type the following command to enable the beta channel and web development:

   ```
   flutter channel beta flutter config --enable-web
   ```

2. **What's the difference between physical and logical pixels?**
   Physical pixels are the actual number of pixels that a device has. In Flutter, when we speak of pixels, we are actually speaking of logical pixels, and not physical pixels. Each device has a multiplier so that when you use logical pixels, you don't have to worry too much about the resolution of a screen.

3. **How can you know the width of your user's device?**
   You can use the `MediaQuery.of(context).size.width` instruction to get the width of your user's device.

4. **When using a `Table` widget, how do you add rows and cells?**
   In the `children` property of a `Table`, you return as many `TableRow` widgets as are required. The `TableRow` widget contains `TableCell` widgets, which in turn contain the data that will be shown in the `Table`.

5. **What's the meaning of responsive design?**
   It's a design that responds to the user's device. In this chapter, we chose different layouts based on the number of logical pixels available on the screen.

6. **What's the purpose of the `FlexColumnWidth` widget?**
   A `FlexColumnWidth` widget makes each column take a relative space in the `Table`. For example, if you create a `Table` with two columns, one with a width of `FlexColumnWidth(1)` and the second with a width of `FlexColumnWidth(2)`, the second column will take twice the space of the first one.

7. **What's the purpose of** `shared_preferences`**?**
   `shared_preferences` is an easy way to persist key-value data on disk. You can only store primitive data: int, double, bool, String, and stringList. `shared_preferences` data is saved within the app and is not designed to store a lot of data.

8. **Would you use** `shared_preferences` **to store passwords? Why?**
   It's not recommended to use `shared_preferences` to store passwords: data stored there is not encrypted, and writes are not always guaranteed.

9. **How can a browser run a Flutter app?**
   Browsers today support HTML, JavaScript, and CSS. With Flutter Web, your code gets compiled in those languages, and therefore you don't need any browser plugin, nor any specific web server.

10. **How can you publish a Flutter app to a web server?**
    From the console of your developing machine, you can run the command:

    ```
    flutter build web
    ```

    This will create the `\build\web` folder in your app directory, that contains the web version of your app. The `index.html` file is the home page of the web app.

Other Books You May Enjoy

If you enjoyed this book, you may be interested in these other books by Packt:

iOS 13 Programming for Beginners - Fourth Edition
Ahmad Sahar, Craig Clayton

ISBN: 978-1-83882-190-6

- Get to grips with the fundamentals of Xcode 11 and Swift 5, the building blocks of iOS development
- Understand how to prototype an app using storyboards
- Discover the Model-View-Controller design pattern, and how to implement the desired functionality within the app
- Implement the latest iOS features such as Dark Mode and Sign In with Apple
- Understand how to convert an existing iPad app into a Mac app
- Design, deploy, and test your iOS applications with industry patterns and practices

Mastering Xamarin.Forms - Third Edition
Ed Snider

ISBN: 978-1-83921-338-0

- Find out how, when, and why to use architecture patterns and best practices with Xamarin.Forms
- Implement the Model-View-ViewModel (MVVM) pattern and data binding in Xamarin.Forms mobile apps
- Incorporate client-side validation in Xamarin.Forms mobile apps
- Extend the Xamarin.Forms navigation API with a custom ViewModel-centric navigation service
- Leverage the inversion of control and dependency injection patterns in Xamarin.Forms mobile apps
- Work with online and offline data in Xamarin.Forms mobile apps
- Use platform-specific APIs to build rich custom user interfaces in Xamarin.Forms mobile apps
- Explore how to monitor mobile app quality using Visual Studio App Center

Leave a review - let other readers know what you think

Please share your thoughts on this book with others by leaving a review on the site that you bought it from. If you purchased the book from Amazon, please leave us an honest review on this book's Amazon page. This is vital so that other potential readers can see and use your unbiased opinion to make purchasing decisions, we can understand what our customers think about our products, and our authors can see your feedback on the title that they have worked with Packt to create. It will only take a few minutes of your time, but is valuable to other potential customers, our authors, and Packt. Thank you!

Index

Printed in Great Britain
by Amazon

57950568R00278